R. B. BENNETT

A BIOGRAPHY

R. B. Bennett

A Biography

BY

ERNEST WATKINS

TORONTO

Kingswood House

First Published in Canada 1963 by
Kingswood House
1068 Broadview Avenue,
Toronto 6

PRINTED IN ENGLAND

"There is an image in Pasternak's great novel, *Doctor Zhivago*, which has moved me very much—of a candle, which has melted a little patch in the icy crust on a windowpane, through which the candle's light is seen by Yura from the dark street below. 'Its light seemed to fall into the street as deliberately as a glance, as if the flame were keeping a watch on the passing carriages and waiting for someone.' Perhaps that is the most that a biographer can ever hope to do: to clear, in the icy crust of each man's incomprehension of other men, a little patch, through which a faint intermittent light can shine. But at the best, it will always be a very little patch of light, in a great sea of darkness. . . . All that needs to be said about this was said by Sir William Temple in his essay on poetry, in a single perfect sentence: 'Human life is, at the greatest and the best, but like a froward child, that must be played with and humoured a little to keep it quiet till it falls asleep—and then the care is over.' "

Iris Origo,
"Biography, True and False,"
The Atlantic, February, 1959.

CONTENTS

ACKNOWLEDGEMENTS

My greatest debt of gratitude is due to Lord Beaverbrook who, in his capacity as Chancellor of the University of New Brunswick, gave me permission to read and use the collection of Bennett papers which he has given to the University and housed at Fredericton. Second only to that is my debt to the many individuals who have, in so many ways, helped me to form some impression of Bennett as he was and as they knew him, in Calgary and in Ottawa.

Amongst those whom I would like to mention in particular are Miss Alice Millar, of Vancouver, who was his secretary and confidante for so long, the late W. Kent Power, Q.C., of Calgary, who gave me my first glimpse of what I came to believe was the true emotional drive in Bennett's life, and Hon. H. H. Stevens, P.C., of Vancouver, for his full account of the events of 1934 and 1935.

I am also indebted to the authors, agents and publishers of the books from which I have been permitted to quote in the pages that follow for their permission so to do, and to the Marchese Origo for her permission to use the quotation with which the book opens.

And, of course, I am as always deeply indebted to my wife, not only for her forbearance but also for her work as a typist over this book.

As I feel this book can at best be regarded as a sketch, not a formal biography, I have avoided footnotes. The letters quoted in the text are, unless otherwise indicated, from the Bennett papers at Fredericton.

INTRODUCTION

To attempt to write the life of someone who was in part contemporary, but whom one had never met, is bold, possibly reckless. When the subject of the account belongs to the country that is the writer's by adoption, not birth, some would say that the attempt is sheer impertinence. It is useless to say in defence that this is a sketch of a man, not his biography; that may well make the crime worse. None the less, the attempt will be made.

Bennett was thirty-two when I was born. When he died I knew very few Canadians and had never seen Canada. One of my uncles had spent most of his life in Canada until he came back in the '30s, to die in his native city, Liverpool, but when he returned I had so little interest in the country from which he had come that I never thought to ask him where he had lived or what he had done. Canada had been called the land of promise, so Somerset Maugham said, satirically, and I think my uncle would have agreed with him, mildly. He was a very gentle man.

And yet I lived for a time in a countryside that must have been not unlike Hopewell Cape in the '70s, the island of Anglesey in the years before the First World War. It had the same dirt roads, and their straggling, entrancing hedges, such as the road I walked from Rhosgoch to William Jones's farm at Llanol and on to his cousin's farm with a name that still sounds like a blessing, Llys y Gwint, the place of the winds, and the roads over which we drove in the trap, south to market at Llanerchymedd and north to the port of Amlwch. Richard Bennett must have known the same muffled sound of the hooves as the pony walked, the smell of her sweat, the patina of the leather reins, the cracked patent leather piping of the dirty cushions, the peeling varnish that I industriously destroyed still further with my finger-nails.

That countryside must have had the same fields, too, and the scents the summer sun drew from them, and the same silence that came when one first lay in the grass, until gradually the silence was a multitude of small sounds from the myriad of living creatures all around. And the same horizon of low, rounded hills, green or yellow or dark brown, and in one direction or another the thin blue line of the sea wherever they dipped.

And the same people? Not so very different, surely, for they were all farmers or fishermen or the occasional storekeeper. As a child he must have had the same fears, the same concerns, the same adults to watch and listen to, to know but not to understand. And from them, and from all his surroundings, he would have had time to imagine what the rest of the world was like and what he could do there when he had broken into it.

Now I have lived eight years in Western Canada, in Calgary, as Bennett did; of course, not the same Calgary, and yet not a totally different Calgary. The Bow River is still there, and the Rockies on the western horizon, the sweep of the foothills from Cochrane, or Turner Valley, or Highwood, and above all the sun and the sky. To live in Western Alberta marks a man for life. And I am a lawyer in the same courts and have fought elections in the same city, and sat in the Alberta Legislature, in opposition, as a Conservative, as Bennett did, and thought in moments of depression, as he may well have done, that in a provincial legislature the party in power can make trumps of any suit it leads, the rules being silent on that point.

I, too, became an immigrant late in life, as he did, changing citizenship, if not nationality; that parallel is far from complete, for Bennett knew Britain long before he settled there. But he knew it as a visitor, as a welcomed guest, either as a Canadian K.C. appearing before the Privy Council, or as a lifelong friend of Lord Beaverbrook (or Sir Max Aitken, M.P., as he was when Bennett first intruded on the British political scene), or as a member of Sir Robert Borden's mission to Britain in the First War, or as a Prime Minister of the oldest dominion. Yet to visit is only to visit; there is a remarkable finality about the uprooting involved in the decision to emigrate. One slams and locks the door behind one, and since I am sure for him, as for me, the compelling motive was distaste for what one was leaving, rather than an attraction to what was new, the impulse of pride alone compels one to throw away the key.

This is not to say that I imagine that I resemble Richard

Bedford Bennett in any way, save one. As a figure in time, he has the fascination that flows from all great men on the stage of events. He has the fascination that comes from the spectacle of great success and great failure in the one man. He has the fascination excited by what might have been, of history re-written by choosing, from hindsight, the alternative that those who made the decision rejected. But for me—and this is our one resemblance—he has the fascination of the familiar, the knowledge that he, too, had his personality shaped more by his mother than by any other circumstance.

PART ONE

Chapter One

MOTHERS AND SONS

B ENNETT had two loyalties, deep seated and changing very little, and I do not think that his life can be understood save in those terms. One was political, to the British Empire, a conception of empire that was in part romantic, in part practical, and never fully realizable. The other was emotional, to his mother. Bennett's conception of the Empire should wait for its explanation in a more appropriate place, but the other loyalty is so important to his understanding that I believe it must be considered at the start. His relationship with his mother, his relationships with others because of his mother, moulded him from birth.

Bennett's mother, Henrietta, was the daughter of David Stiles, and the Stiles, like the Bennetts, were true Maritimers, men whose ancestors had fought the French at Louisburg and Quebec, who had settled in Nova Scotia or New Brunswick when settlement really began in the eighteenth century. But David Stiles was a sea captain, and sea captains in the middle of the last century were remarkable men. My mother's father was one, too; she was born in his ship in the Mediterranean, off the coast of Sicily, and he died of yellow fever in Bombay at a comparatively early age. Consider, first, their inevitable characteristics.

They were men of immense experience, both in seamanship and in commerce; they did not come to command a ship, still less to own one, unless they excelled in both. They were men of command and decision. Those who lacked these qualities had little hope of reaching such a position, and no hope of retaining it for long if they did. The winds are without mercy to any sailing ship whose crew is ill-trained or whose master is indecisive.

They were solitary men. A man who must expect instant and complete obedience from his crew, even at the risk of death, dare not allow himself to become too friendly with anyone on board, officers included, lest discipline thereby suffer. And they tended to be proud and puritanical men. They lived in a world of contrast. At sea their life was one of austerity, action, command and the satisfaction that comes from their exercise. On shore, they either stepped into the security of a familiar home or into the vice and squalor of a foreign port.

Wives could find them satisfactory husbands; they lived with them, and the wife who cannot understand the husband she lives with is incapable of understanding anything. But consider their effect upon daughters, particularly on a daughter naturally possessed of a capacity for idealism and a strong sense of duty.

A daughter's first standards for men are set by her father. Imagine the picture she will form of men in general if her first impressions of any man are of a mysterious being who appears at infrequent intervals, who is always welcomed when he does, both because his arrival will end a period of uncertainty and because he will surely clinch the welcome with a gift from foreign parts. Her father is a man who when home has time to spend with his family and the urge to pour out love and affection when he does so, who has courage and determination to a degree that is immediately recognizable, whose experience of women, elsewhere, either direct or observed, is purely commercial and who will in consequence place his own on some pedestal in his mind.

Imagine again the daughter who sees such a man, her father, against a background of Victorian certainty and the frugality of the Maritimes of that day. Bear in mind that she herself will live on the shores of the Bay of Fundy and will know at first hand in some degree the dangers and the glories of a life at sea.

Given all that, it is likely that she will emerge from childhood into maturity either as a total rebel against all she has so far encountered or as a woman with the belief that moral perfection is not only desirable. She may be quite certain that any man can attain it if he strives hard enough. It will be extremely difficult for such a girl to make a happy marriage, unless she in her turn is fortunate enough to meet another man with the qualities needed to command a foreign-going sailing ship.

It is obvious that Bennett's mother had the intensity and strength of character one would expect from such an upbringing, and it is equally likely that she found the marriage she did make not entirely satisfactory.

Richard Bennett's father, Henry, was a very different personality, and a more commonplace man. He was easy-going, cheerful, and inclined to drink, and of alcohol she strongly disapproved. He had no strong religious convictions; although he came from a family of strict Baptists, he married Henrietta Stiles in a Methodist church, and raised no objection when she decided to bring Richard up in that religion. He must have had pride and skill in his craft; one Bennett ship, the *Emma*, launched in 1855, became one of the famous seven clippers that sailed from Liverpool under the White Star flag with the Australian mails. He had inherited the Bennett yard at Hopewell Cape and was in relatively comfortable circumstances at the time of his marriage, and when Richard was born, but when the whole Maritime shipbuilding industry began to decay he failed to set to work and re-establish the family fortunes by tackling something else.

As a result, Richard Bennett grew into a world in which every cent had come to count. The effect on Henrietta of her husband's inertia can be imagined. Disappointed in him, probably blaming herself more than him for the resulting sense of failure, she became the devoted mother to her five children, the three boys, Richard, George and Ronald, and the two girls, Evelyn and Mildred. And she poured all her frustrated ambitions, for her husband and perhaps less consciously for herself, into her eldest child, Richard.

The silver cord is a recognized theme, but I still doubt if sufficient sympathetic understanding is given to the son who is made, from birth, the receptacle of both a mother's passionate devotion and her frustrated ambition. As a child he returns the devotion without much understanding, and so creates within himself in her image a censor whom he must always strive to obey and who generates sensations of guilt whenever he does not. It is very difficult for him to make a satisfactory marriage;

Bennett never attempted it. He is filled with a sense of mission,
yet the mission may have an induced, rather than a natural,
goal, and the search may soon transmute itself into no more
than a greed for success or recognition. Failure can never be
tolerated, not even failure to be first when the place actually
won would in itself be a triumph. In short, he starts out as a
neurotic.

I am convinced Bennett was such a neurotic. That alone can
explain his furious energy, his driving ambition, his resentment
of competition, his moods of despair, his inability to work
with others on terms of equality, his outbursts of temper, his
apparent arrogance and insensitivity to those around him. His
brother George was a neurotic, too, but George, after service
overseas in the First War, drank himself to death, relatively
quietly, on a pension provided by Richard, for the most part
in the North West Territories. Richard Bennett's early surroundings could account for any failings he possessed.

But Bennett was not a failure and his upbringing certainly
does not account for his success. The whole moral of his story,
the true measure of his greatness as a man, lies in what he
achieved despite it all. A neurosis of this kind—and probably
a severe one, at that—is one of the handicaps imposed by Fate
or Providence on one individual and not on another. To my
mind, it is exactly parallel with some physical handicap—
blindness, a deformed back, an impediment in the speech.
What matters, what has always mattered, is the response the
individual so afflicted makes to the challenge his affliction
presents. He may fold up completely under its burden and be
useless to himself and his fellow-men. He may find the handicap
so crippling that he must walk quietly and obscurely all his
days. Or he may fight it, and fight with it. He may tame it and
twist it and in the end make a climbing stick from what others
would treat as a cross to be borne.

Bennett had many natural gifts: a remarkable memory, a
clear mind, the gift of speech, and an ability to win love and
respect as well as dislike and scorn. He was an exceptional man
in many ways, but most of all in his triumph over his emotional
handicaps. Despite these, he fought to the end for his beliefs, his
principles and his country. He had tenacity and courage. His

personal defeats were never final, his despairs were never bottomless. He was in consequence, the greater man in the end.

Those are the considerations that attracted me to the story of Richard Bedford Bennett.

Chapter Two

HOPEWELL TO CALGARY

FOR me, the first fifteen years of Bennett's life exist primarily in the imagination. I came to Canada too late—and then to the wrong part of the country—to hope to be able to meet anyone who had known him then as a boy, living in his first surroundings, the countryside of the Province of New Brunswick at the head of the Bay of Fundy.

Hopewell Cape, as a place, does not present the same difficulty. A journalist visiting it in 1927, in search of the native land of the new Conservative leader, wrote this:

"Frame houses on either side of a mile-long stretch of road on the shores of the Petitcodiac River form the major part of Hopewell Cape. They are comfortable wooden houses, many of them large, most of them trim and painted white— all are embowered in orchards and in maple trees. A double row of glorious maples over-arches the roadway. Between it and the river bank lie cultivated pasture lots and dyked-in fields of marsh hay a hundred feet in depth. Sage grass grows where the land is low, and when the Bay of Fundy's forty-five-foot tide is out, mud flats stretch far into the river. At high tide the river is three miles in width. Always it is beautiful. Its mudstained water is in turn pearl grey, gold, blue or amethyst in hue, reflecting all the shades of sun and sky.

"A creek tumbles down from the uplands toward a high dark wharf. Below the bridge where it crosses the road big ships and barquentines were launched.

"There is little evidence of industry outside of garden produce and small fields of oats or hay, but nearly every householder has some backwood lots. Lumber from these is being taken off. A portable mill has deals and scantlings, boards and laths piled by the roadway. There is a courthouse, a public hall, a Baptist church, a schoolhouse, a hotel and one general store. Several stores closed when shipbuilding ceased in Hopewell Cape. Good houses and outbuildings stood vacant. They were offered for sale at three or four hundred dollars. Population has dwindled from nearly five hundred to around two hundred, but there is no suggestion of down-at-heelness or helplessness about the place. Hopewell Cape has the peaceful look of a life well spent and beautiful with happy memories."

That could describe, with not too many changes, parts of England or Wales that I know well enough.

But the boy himself?

By all accounts he was tall, and freckled. He was healthy and active, but not thought of as particularly robust. He belonged to a small village at a time when all villages were relatively remote and therefore self-contained, and there he would be known and accepted. He had around him relatives and friends who would give him some diversity in the beginnings of his contacts with others. He was never very interested in games or sport, but in any event a great deal of his spare time was bound to be swallowed up by the chores of house and yard and garden.

He worked hard at school, when schools were small enough and schoolmasters dedicated enough for a child to be taught as an individual amongst other individuals. He formed habits of reading, of work and application, which he never afterwards lost. But he was not fundamentally of a scholastic mind. School learning for him must have been something to be used for some other purpose. It was not an end in itself.

Despite that, he was almost certainly shy and introspective. He was a mother's boy. He was never in actual want, but he must always have known that there would never be anything approaching luxury in his home, unless he provided it. Today, the experts in child psychology would undoubtedly tag him as 'insecure'.

An older word for that is 'ambitious', and that he undoubtedly

was. As I see him, from the start he was a child under
pressure, and whether one thinks of his life afterwards as an
escape from the past or a search for fulfilment in the future, the
force that drove him onwards was built up in those first fifteen
years.

A boy leaving New Brunswick might go anywhere. His
native province had a strong personality and sense of corporate
life, but in those days it still held a tinge of bitterness and frus-
tration. Its people had been talked into Confederation but they
were not yet conscious of being Canadians, or indeed that there
was such a country as 'Canada'. There were Upper Canada
and Lower Canada, but they were very different things.
The people of New Brunswick were not be to classed as colonists.
Their province had been settled for over a century and those
who constituted its backbone had come not from Britain but
from the parts of New England that later became the United
States. Bennett was never a United Empire Loyalist. Nine
generations of Bennetts had lived in New Brunswick. They
traced their family back to Zadok Bennett, who came from
Lyme, in Connecticut, in 1761, and settled in Norton County
in Nova Scotia, and it was his son, Benjamin, who had first
come to Albert County, New Brunswick. Bennett's forebears, in
whom he had immense pride, and he himself were citizens of
the Crown living in a part of North America which had
always been loyal to the Crown. They belonged wherever the
Union Jack flew.

Over the last century, many young men and girls have left
New Brunswick to settle in other parts of Canada—and sometimes, as in the case of Max Aitken and Bonar Law, to cross the
Atlantic as well—and one does not have to fall back on pyscho-
logical maladjustments to explain this exodus. Plain economic
considerations drove them out in search of better or more
secure living. But I don't feel satisfied that it was economics
alone that sent Bennett off on his journeyings. I think he felt
compelled to leave home, but I think that if Fredericton or
Chatham had offered him the same chances of realizing his
ambitions as Calgary later seemed to do, he would have
stayed in the province where he was born. It is significant
that he never really became a westerner.

Any child enmeshed in the kind of emotional relationship that existed between Bennett's parents, and between Bennett and his mother, is certain sooner or later to be possessed by a desire to escape. Unfortunately for him, if he succeeds in doing so he will also be plagued by feelings of guilt for years to come. As he grows from child to young man, the direct and powerful relationship between his mother and himself is increasingly coloured by the obvious presence of the father. Without resorting to all the Freudian complications, the father becomes a more deeply resented person simply because the son has more varied and stronger motives for resenting him. The father should not exist, the son believes; since he does exist, he should go away, and if he does the silver cord may then become indestructible.

But if he stays, another reaction follows. Mother continues to be adored for what she is to the son, but now she is resented as well for what she is to the father, and what the father is to her. Since that state of emotional conflict is both bewildering and agonizing, the son himself is driven to be off, to escape. As a rationalization, he may add the fiction that he goes to build a place of refuge for the mother as well, but on the whole the son is fortunate if his mother will not, or cannot, follow him. Then at least he has some chance of achieving ultimate freedom for himself.

Bennett escaped, and it does not matter very much if one says he fled because he was ambitious or because he felt insecure at home. But, once away, whilst he dutifully spent every Christmas with his mother whenever it was possible for him to do so, he never made a home for her away from Hopewell Cape. It was not until he went to England at the age of sixty-nine that he even made a real home for himself.

But he could never escape from a great many of the things his mother had embedded in him during those first fifteen years. He was to succeed, of course. That was his right and his obligation. But he was also to live by the strict tenets of the Methodist Church and to be fearless in doing what he saw to be his duty. He was not to drink alcohol or smoke tobacco. He was to avoid the temptations of the flesh. He was to be rigorous in his attendances at church and if possible to teach in Sunday school. And he was to control his temper and bridle his tongue. In short, he was to be a Stiles and to fight the temptation to be too much a Bennett. It is remarkable how closely he hewed to the line she had pointed out.

Bennett's first move away from Hopewell Cape was in the direction of teaching, the quickest and least expensive route towards whatever summit lay beyond his immediate horizon. He completed Grade 8 in 1882, at the age of twelve, and qualified to go on to the Normal School of the Province, at Fredericton, the provincial capital. At Normal School he was considered quick-witted and ready of speech; the couplet his fellow pupils composed on him ran:

"First there came Bennett, conceited and young,
Who never knew quite when to hold his quick tongue."

His first teaching post, when only sixteen, was at Irishtown, near Moncton, New Brunswick, and his salary $160 a year, but as the holder of a first-class teaching licence from Normal School at eighteen he was offered the post of Principal at Douglastown, close to Chatham in the northern part of the province, with four schools, four teachers and some 140 pupils under him, and a salary of $500 a year. Half of this he saved, and to add to his savings he enlisted in the Militia, in which he inevitably gravitated to the battalion pay office.

He was a good schoolmaster, strict and a disciplinarian, but conscientious and thorough. He took the greatest pains with his class, set them stiff examination papers and marked them without leniency. He insisted that his pupils should spell correctly and write well; one form of punishment he used was to stand the pupil before a window and require him or her to write a composition on what he or she saw from that position. Those pupils who won his respect won his friendship. He went to great trouble to make sure that all those in Grade 8 who wanted to go to Normal School were well enough taught to be able to do so, and with many of them he corresponded for years afterwards. But, as his mother knew, his temper was short. He could flare up into an immediate outburst of anger and when doing so use words of a harshness that stung and were remembered.

His sense of duty was equally engaged in his relations with the School Board Trustees. A report of his whilst at Douglastown contains this:

"It is incumbent upon me to submit my annual and final report on the schools under my supervision.

"The remarks made at the close of last term are applicable with equal force to the work of this term.

"During a stay of nearly two years in this place, I have come to the conclusion that the material is not lacking here to produce pupils of more than ordinary ability but while I feel that such is the case I cannot but remark that unless the parents are aroused and awakened from the apathy with which they now view all matters connected with the school work, the fine abilities of their children will never be shown.

"I would remark that the school officers are sadly deficient in their duties. During my stay here I have not been favoured by a visit from one of the trustees.

"(*Signed*) RICHARD B. BENNETT."

The appointment to Douglastown took him decisively away from home; he was now over ninety miles away from Hopewell Cape, and with very indifferent communications southward. By good fortune, it also provided other opportunities of the greatest importance. First, it enabled him to become a lawyer. In Chatham, he made the acquaintance of Lemuel Tweedie, Q.C., then a prominent Conservative lawyer in the town, a man who became in turn Premier of the Province and its Lieutenant-Governor, and Tweedie saw in him a young man who deserved to be helped.

He began by giving him part-time employment in his office, in the evenings and in vacations, and, when he showed his abilities, he promised him a junior partnership if he could qualify for admission to the Bar. In 1890, at the age of twenty, Bennett felt he could risk taking that step. He had now saved enough to make the three years of studentship at Dalhousie University a reasonable gamble. He had no real difficulty in graduating, and discreet help from Professor R. C. Weldon, Dean of the Faculty (who secured him the appointment of Librarian in the Law Library), enabled him to make his savings last the three years. He graduated in 1893 and returned to Chatham to become the junior partner in the firm of Tweedie and Bennett.

His second stroke of fortune came when he struck up a friendship with Max Aitken, later to become Lord Beaverbrook. Aitken's father held the manse at Newcastle, up the River Miramichi from Chatham, and Bennett and he met by chance on a wharf when Aitken was coming ashore. Despite the difference in their ages—Aitken was nine years the younger —their friendship deepened into a bond that lasted as long as Bennett lived. It was Aitken who passed on to Bennett in 1939 the Juniper Hill estate at Mickleham, Surrey, Aitken having agreed to buy it simply because it marched with his own. It was Aitken who ran Bennett's first election campaign, in 1896, for the City Council at Chatham.

It was an exciting contest, for this was to be Chatham's first City Council after incorporation into that status. Bennett thought that he had become sufficiently well known in the city to stand some chance of success, but Aitken was already convinced that, to be effective, organization and publicity must go hand in hand. He was friendly with J. L. Stewart, publisher of the *Chatham World*, and, according to the account of Albert McLennan, foreman of the printing establishment's foundry, Bennett's real campaign began with the appearance of Aitken in the foundry:

" 'What's on your mind today, Max?' McLennan asked.

" 'I'm going to get my pal Dick nominated for alderman,' Aitken replied.

" 'Dick who?'

" 'Dick Bennett'.

" 'He can't qualify. He needs $500 either personal or real estate. What's he got to qualify on?'

" 'A couple of law books.'

" 'What else?'

" 'A second-hand bicycle.'

" 'Is that all?'

" 'Oh, no. He has last year's *Bailey's Almanac*.' "

Bennett had the necessary $500, but the bicycle may have been of equal use for, when Aitken had composed and printed his own campaign sheet for Bennett, he used the bicycle to deliver a copy to virtually every house in the town.

McLennan's account concludes:

"By this day's work and by his great service on election day, Max Aitken succeeded in getting Dick Bennett elected as one of the first aldermen of the town of Chatham. This brought Dick for the first time into public life, and it was the boy of seventeen who did it."

Bennett's third gift from fortune at Chatham was his meeting and subsequent friendship with a girl named Jennie Shirreff, daughter of an established local family, and her brother Harry. Jennie Shirreff intended to be a nurse (she, too, left the Province) and after she qualified she became nurse to E. B. Eddy, proprietor of the E. B. Eddy Company of Hull, Quebec, the leading match-manufacturer in Canada. In 1894 she married him. Eddy did not live long, and on his death, with her brother Harry, she inherited a majority holding of the share capital in that company. That story belongs to a later period in Bennett's life; it was not until fifteen years later, in Ottawa, that their friendship was renewed, but from that friendship in Chatham was to come his inheritance of the ownership of that most profitable business, and his second fortune.

By the middle of the 1890's, at the age of twenty-six, Bennett was established as a rising young lawyer, practising in the fourth town of importance in his native province. He had grown to be tall, with a good carriage, and a high forehead (although his carefully brushed hair already hinted at the baldness that was to come later). He thought a great deal about his appearance and dressed well. He had overcome the first and most difficult obstacle in his path. He had won his way through university by his own efforts, and he had acquired a profession. Had he made no other changes in his life, he would almost certainly have risen to membership of the Provincial Legislature in his Province, associated as he was with Tweedie, leader of the Conservative Party. He might well have gone on to Ottawa as a member of the House of Commons.

He had not overcome all his failings, by any means. Beaverbrook says of him at that time:

"He was over-polite, yet again and again he would burst out in angry indignation against slights and injustice, fancied or real, using tough and tiresome language. His face would turn pale and his eyes would change colour. The storm would not pass quickly. But when his good humour was restored he would tell how his mother had warned him that he would never amount to much unless he controlled his temper."

But, in that year 1896, a third person was to come decisively into his life, the man who was, as lawyers would say, the true *sine qua non* of his final development. That was Senator James A. Lougheed, from the other side of the continent, a man practising law, amongst other activities, in the City of Calgary in the North West Territories, some 2,200 miles away to the west.

Lougheed's practice in this new settlement on the prairies was expanding. In the fall of 1896 he asked Dean Weldon, at Dalhousie, to suggest the name of some young lawyer whom he could ask to join him in partnership in Calgary; his list of requirements for the candidate was formidable. Weldon remembered Bennett and knew of his excellent start at Chatham. He suggested Bennett's name, and Lougheed journeyed to New Brunswick to meet him. Nothing was settled at that interview and the negotiations continued by letter. The terms Lougheed finally offered were certainly not ungenerous. For the first year, 1897, Bennett was to receive 20 per cent of the net earnings of the new partnership, up to $3,750, and 30 per cent of the excess beyond that figure. In the second year, each figure was to be increased by 5 per cent, and the arrangement was to be reconsidered afresh for the year 1899. Bennett accepted, and so the 'Lougheed and Bennett' partnership came into being.

Lougheed may have believed that he was acquiring a young man who would be content to sit at his desk in Calgary and devote himself to the development of the practice, leaving him the more free for politics. If he did, he was mistaken. Bennett was as interested in political activity as he was, and at Chatham he had already taken the first plunge. He also intended to be

Prime Minister of Canada. There was nothing unusual in that. Every young man who throws his cap into the political ring must, if only in his daydreams, cherish the hope that Chance will smile on his talents and that luck and hard work together will carry him to the top. Bennett was one of the minute minority who succeeded.

Two stories authenticate his possession of this dream. One is told by Mary Kearney, who taught school at Douglastown when Bennett was Principal there:

"On one occasion in the winter we were walking down to Douglastown together and were given a drive by a Mr. Brown, who had just come from a grist mill with a sled loaded with fresh buckwheat meal. I sat on a sack of meal while Richard Bennett stood up with the driver. Before long the two men were engaged in a spirited argument about religion.

"The argument waned and as Mr. Brown stopped the team to give the horses a drink at an old watering-place, Mr. Bennett recited Anthony's funeral speech from Shakespeare's *Julius Caesar*. I said he should be in public life, and his reply was: 'Some day I'm going to be Prime Minister of Canada.' "

Another is recorded by Mr. R. St. G. Stubbs in his essay on Bennett in his volume, *Prairie Portraits*:

"As a student at Dalhousie Law School, Bennett used to declare—and to himself the declaration was not so much a boast as the plain statement of an inevitable fact—that some day he would be Canada's First Minister. Mr. Justice W. H. Trueman, late of the Manitoba Court of Appeal, was one year his senior at Dalhousie. One day Bennett proposed to Trueman that they should attend together a political meeting to be addressed by Sir John A. Macdonald.

"Trueman accepted his invitation and they drove several miles by horse and buggy to the meeting. On the return journey, Bennett was full of the speech they had heard. His mood was serious as he turned over Sir John's words, and he was silent with his thoughts, until he said suddenly, 'I'm going to be Premier of Canada.' At the time his companion treated this remark as one would expect such a remark to be treated.

"In 1930, just after Bennett had been elected Prime Minister, when he was passing through Winnipeg on his way to Ottawa, Trueman called to see him at his hotel, and, as they were chatting over old times, Trueman asked, 'Do you remember the night we heard Sir John A. Macdonald speak, the night you told me you would be Prime Minister? Well, you made it all right.' 'I said I would, didn't I?' replied Bennett, and his tone implied that he was disappointed that he had not been taken at his word forty years before."

Confidence or boastfulness? Certainty or whistling in the dark? In his early twenties, Bennett probably alternated between the two. None the less, how can one escape, even if one would, from a feeling of profound pity for the same boy at fifteen when he left the protection of his home at Hopewell Cape for Normal School at Fredericton? True, he was to live in the provincial capital, a beautiful city on the banks of the St. John River, comfortable and secure, well ordered, living quietly under the trees lining its streets. He was moving into a much larger world, but he was so ill-equipped for any easy adjustment to it.

He needed love and understanding. Where was he to find it? He could talk fluently, but he found it difficult to communicate anything of himself; reciting Shakespeare to a girl on a sled is not communication. He must justify himself in his mother's eyes, but supposing he failed? He must fight his way alone, and the habit of loneliness persisted all his life.

Three years later, at Georgetown, the clouds were beginning to break. He found someone to lodge with who could give him some of the feeling of a mother and a home. He had very little money. His diaries for 1890 and 1891 have survived and they record his spendings. His receipts for the first six months of 1890 were $262.70, his expenditures $229.40; apart from the cost of his board and lodging, it was spent mostly on church collections, newspapers, apples and postage stamps. But he was supporting himself.

By the time he reached Dalhousie, he had overcome more of his handicaps, although in doing so he may have created new difficulties of another kind. In one sense, he had jumped ahead of his contemporaries. He had not only taught school; he had been in charge of schools, and he was that much more experienced than they. He was certainly more fluent than the average man around him. He enjoyed the debates and the legal moots. They gave him a chance to stand out, but at the same time that fact was a barrier between him and his fellow students. He made friendships, but already they contained some element of reserve on his part. He was, in his own mind, a man set apart, a man who would go further than the rest.

At Chatham, as a partner in the firm of Tweedie and Bennett, he had begun to settle down. He had greater confidence, for now he could measure his work, and its results, against what others in his own profession were doing. He could begin to turn his vague dreams of glory and renown into concrete ambitions for this year and the next. He could haggle with a Senator, Lougheed, over the terms on which he would exchange the certainties of New Brunswick for the gamble of life in a frontier town in the quite unknown west. But some of the scars he had from those ten years remained.

He left for Calgary by C.P.R. train towards the end of January, 1897, and arrived there just before the end of the month. He was still five months short of his twenty-seventh birthday. His life in the Maritimes was over.

Chapter Three

THE FOOTHILLS

B Y twenty-seven, for the majority of men and women the basic character is set, and for Bennett that was more true than for most, but environment, chance, the challenges and responses that events will still provoke, continue to play their parts in shaping the man or woman who ultimately emerges. By leaving New Brunswick, Bennett shifted himself into another world, and at onc equite different influences began their work upon him.

When he came to the city in 1897 (it had then been officially a city for three years) Calgary was a place of some 4,000 people. Its lifespan was twenty-three years, dating back to the day when a patrol of the North West Mounted Police, *en route* from Fort Edmonton southwards to Fort Macleod, forded the Bow River just above its confluence with the Elbow and pitched its tents close to the only other habitation in sight, a tepee containing a sick Indian and an Oblate priest. That river junction became the site of Fort Calgary, named for a remote village on the Isle of Arran, and the man who opened the first store in a tent outside the gates of the wooden fort and who became Calgary's first postmaster did not die until 1943.

The fact that the city by 1897 contained 4,000 people and already had come to consider itself the metropolis of that section of the western prairies was due entirely to the C.P.R. The new transcontinental line had kept as close as it decently could to the United States border as it ran westwards towards the Pacific, but at Medicine Hat it was compelled to turn north-westwards in order to use the most southerly of the feasible routes through the Rockies, up the valley of the Bow to the Great Divide and down the Kicking Horse Pass on the further side. Calgary became a divisional point, and the activities the railway brought were added to the small settlement around the fort.

Once founded, it grew fast. The Eau Claire Lumber Company began to clear the timber up the valleys of the Bow and the Ghost rivers, and was to provide the city with its first electric light. To the south, along the foothills, ranchers carved out their miles of pastures, and to the north and east were the new homesteads and settlements, to be peopled from Ontario, Quebec, the Middle Western States, and from every European country as far east as the Ukraine. Each family arrived intent on taking up its allotment of virgin land, on breaking it, on adding its share of effort to a country that was soon to be known as the bread-basket of Europe. The area now within the Province of Alberta, some 225,285 square miles, contained, in 1891, 25,277 people. By 1901 the number, at 75,022 had virtually tripled. Once the railway had replaced the river transportation system further north used by the fur-traders, Calgary was the natural centre of this growing land. Through it the grain and cattle were shipped out, and the needs of the settlers came in.

I myself first saw Calgary on an April afternoon in 1953. It was raining, and when I saw a bus with the destination sign 'Manchester' I wondered if I might not be back in my native county of Lancashire. But eighteen months later I arrived there again, at the end of a January, as Bennett had, by C.P.R. train, and, like him, I was settling in the west as a lawyer hitherto belonging to quite a different scene. And I still do not believe that there is any sight more exhilarating than the first glimpse of the Rockies just after sunrise, from the higher ground to the east of Calgary, their grandeur a miniature frieze along the whole length of the western horizon, the sun shining square on their snowfields and on their dark bands of bare rock.

The city is 3,500 feet above sea level. In winter, particularly in January, it may be cold—zero or even 20° below. But any day may bring a chinook arch to the western sky, a long bank of cloud over the crest of the Rockies, its lower edge a straight, clear-cut line above a band of tranquil blue sky; then the wind will have an unexpected warmth, as though spring had suddenly come. Always the air is crisp and dry, the sunshine vivid and unbefogged, and the sky an immense expanse of colour or, by night, a depth of star-filled darkness. That has not changed.

When Bennett arrived in Calgary, he had been in practice as

a lawyer for no more than three years, and these he had spent under the tutelage of a partner who was also, in a sense, his patron. Now he was expected to manage the business of Lougheed and Bennett, if necessary without very much supervision. Nor was the professional competition he would encounter to be considered negligible. The pond might be small, but he was not the only fish in it. The barristers practising in the west, centred on Calgary and Edmonton, were all from elsewhere, the majority from Ontario and the Maritimes, although the famous P. G. ('Paddy') Nolan had been called first to the Irish Bar. But the firm of Lougheed and Bennett had one advantage over the other lawyers in the city. It held a retainer from the C.P.R. for its legal work in that part of the Territories, and that produced a steady flow of work and gave the firm a considerable local prestige.

The country itself was different enough from New Brunswick. It was a bare and empty land, treeless save for the cottonwoods along the river banks, open but sweeping in vast waves like a solidified sea. The roads were dirt tracks over the open prairie, following either the old Indian trails, the Edmonton Trail northwards, the Macleod Trail southwards and the Blackfoot Trail itself south-eastwards along the line of the Bow River. Or they used the road allowances left between the 'sections' as the land was surveyed in a vast gridiron pattern, tracks that existed only on a map until men and horses and wagons had scoured a recognizable line across the country. Rail was the only form of relatively fast travel, and the telegraph the only form of fast communication.

Calgary itself lay just west of the junction of the Elbow and the Bow rivers, below the terraces that had marked the banks of the far wider streams that had flowed there when the icefields were melting and shrinking back northwards and westwards. It had been surveyed and laid out by the C.P.R. on the same gridiron pattern. Its axes were, east and west, Stephen Avenue, now 8th Avenue, two blocks north of the C.P.R. main line, and Centre Street, running north from the C.P.R. station. The barracks of the North West Mounted Police closed the eastern end of 8th Avenue; its western end now finishes at the Mewata Armoury.

A few of the buildings were of yellow sandstone, quarried a mile or so west of the city, none (save the Old Court House, now demolished) of any architectural merit. The majority were frame structures, opening on to wooden sidewalks, lined with hitching posts and rails, and unpaved roads muddy in spring, dusty in summer and ice-hard in winter. The hub of the city lay on Stephen Avenue between 1st Street East and 1st Street West, and at its centre, on the south-eastern corner of Stephen Avenue and 1st Street West, was the Alberta Hotel, built of the local sandstone and containing, so it boasted, the longest bar between Vancouver and Winnipeg. It is now a rather faded office block, peopled by dentists, chiropractors and real estate men. That was Bennett's Calgary.

Unfamiliar as the country was to anyone from New Brunswick, the people in it were stranger still. The foothills had been settled by relatively wealthy men from the United States and later, predominantly, from Britain, and by the cowpokes who came with them. The first cattle destined to replace the buffalo on the prairies had been bought in Montana and driven northwards to the Porcupine Hills, north of the eastern entrance to the Crow's Nest Pass, and on along the eastern slope of the Rockies to Cochrane west of Calgary, to pasture on the lands the buffalo had used. They could only be bought and raised on any paying scale by men with capital behind them. Service and secondary industries had followed them and settled in Calgary, on the railway; I. B. Baker's Store, Pat Burns packing plant, the Eau Claire Company, the grain merchants, the saddlery and implement dealers, and the host of smaller tradesmen and the smattering of professional men who tended this need and that. All had one characteristic; they were adventurers, in the old sense of that word. For whatever reason, and the reasons were as diverse as their personalities, they had all torn up roots to come.

While it was a free country, it was not a lawless one; the North West Mounted Police saw to that. They had come west to police the new border and suppress the illicit whisky traffic from Montana through Fort Whoop-up to the Indians. Treaty No. 7 was signed with Chief Crowfoot of the Blackfoot Indians in 1877, and after that not even Sitting Bull, the victor over General Custer's force, nor the second Riel Rebellion in 1885 disturbed the peace in this south-westerly segment of the Territories.

Against such a background, Bennett stood out like a sore thumb. He was a bachelor, a Methodist, a Sunday-school teacher, and a teetotaller; few of those around him were the last. He was elaborately polite in his manner and fastidious in his dress; for some years he continued to buy his clothes from his tailor in the Maritimes, and would write indignant letters if his instructions were not carried out in the last detail. He had little practical interest in either ranching or farming, although professionally he was bound to acquire a good working knowledge of their methods and phraseology, nor had he much interest in the sports that are naturally associated with those activities. He looked as though he would be more at home at a ladies' tea party than at the bar in the Alberta Hotel, and indeed he was. But he was not in Calgary to attempt to become rancher or farmer. He was a lawyer, and his interest was politics.

The photographs of him taken over this period are revealing. That taken at twenty-one, when he was still a schoolteacher, shows a certain wistfulness, a hint of a continuing search for understanding and support. At twenty-eight, after he had settled in Calgary, the wistfulness has gone and a rather brash self-confidence has taken its place. He has become a young man prepared to challenge people, and the law, driven to make his bid for success. By the time he has reached thirty-five, the confidence is assured. He has become accustomed to impressing those around him.

But, while Bennett did not conform to the outward pattern of the men around him in Western Canada, he was not so very different from them in kind. They were not intellectuals or aesthetes, nor was he. He was a practical man of affairs, courageous and commanding, and a man of strong emotions, but he was never given to any deep explorations into or over-much curiosity concerning the working of other men's minds. There can be no greater contrast than that between the course of his life at this point and that lived by his contemporaries in England, the men whom he would later meet in the conduct of affairs, as they made their way through university into politics and the professions.

And to them, when they met him, he would be a different kind of Canadian. Laurier and Borden had been 'colonials', Laurier a man of great culture and charm, Borden rougher and less outgoing, but both aware of a colonial past, even though they were insistent on greater independence for Canada in the future. In Mackenzie King they would encounter a more concealed, suspicious and tortuous mind, but all three of these Canadian Prime Ministers were men from eastern Canada, impregnated with its history. Bennett alone had developed in the west, in a land that was a frontier, with a future but without a past.

In Calgary he lived in a society that can be described as classless. Each man coming there wrote his own name at the head of a clean sheet in his ledger, and his neighbours were not disposed either to turn the pages back or allow him to do so. It was a society of second sons, some wastrels, some with more capacities than their elder brothers, but all men who had lived somewhere else and had chosen this place for themselves. In consequence, the years Bennett spent in Calgary from 1897 onwards had a great influence on his development. They countered his solid and inflexible upbringing, diluted his innate respect for form and ceremony, and added a wider Canadianism to his belief in Empire.

For the fifteen years that followed his move Bennett sought three linked but separate ends. His first obligation, to himself as well as to Lougheed, was to establish himself as a lawyer, and in that he succeeded. Some of the qualities of the greatest value in that profession were in him remarkably well developed. He had an exceptional memory, of the visual kind, which enabled him to carry in his mind, ready to use, a photographic impression of a great deal that he had read. This was a quality he cultivated, sometimes to the point of ostentation, but whatever the motive behind its use it remained an implement of great service in the practice of law. He had an immense capacity for work and a great concern for detail in the facts of each case he had to fight; all who knew him remember that. He had, too, a fighting spirit, a determination to win if he could, not so much springing from pure aggressiveness as from his need to prove himself over and over again. In argument his

weapon was the mace, not the rapier, and his use of that in
Court, guided by his memory for facts, could be a formidable
weapon. He was a man to be reckoned with.

He soon found that he could attract clients and win cases for
them. He gave them the feeling that they had a champion
among advocates, and it was well founded. He did tend to
make his client's cause his own, emotionally as well as professionally.

But with these qualities went others, often counterparts, that
made enemies as well as friends, particularly amongst colleagues
in the profession. Once emotionally involved, the lawyer on
the other side could become his personal, if temporary, enemy,
and some of his worst quarrels sprang from that approach, and
the reaction it naturally aroused. He could be quite insensitive
to the feelings of others, and assume that if he intended no
injury none would result. His compulsion to win could drive
him to lengths that anyone with a more natural assurance
would not have employed. He could carry attack, in debate as
well as in Court, to the point at which it became bullying, and
his facility of speech was equally at the service of vituperation
as argument. And, since his personality was very positive, those
he offended remembered him as clearly and for as long as
those he impressed.

He drove one infuriated counsel to make a physical attack on
him in Court; since the man was one of the smallest barristers
at the Territorial Bar, Bennett suffered a double humiliation.
He drove another, A. L. Smith, K.C., to call him a "God-
damned liar" in Court, with unfortunate after-effects on Smith's
own political career as a Conservative. Bennett did not forgive
easily.

His skin remained thin. Leonard Brockington, Q.C., then
a lawyer in Calgary (he articled in Bennett's office and later
became City Solicitor) remembers Bennett's reaction after a
local entertainer mimicked him at a public dinner. Bennett
came out fuming, and Brockington sought some means of
soothing him.

"There's one thing about being mimicked," he said. "It
shows you are somebody."

Bennett grunted suspiciously.

"You know the story of O'Toole and his imitation of Sir Beerbohm Tree in one of his most famous parts?" Brockington asked, and Bennett said he did not.

"After it was over, O'Toole, very pleased with himself, said to Tree: 'What did you think of it?' To which Tree replied:

" 'All I can say, my dear boy, is that one of us must have been bloody awful.' "

Calm was thereby restored.

Another picture of him in practice comes from Richard Tribe, who became his shorthand typist in April, 1903, at the age of eighteen and who was still living when I came to Calgary in 1955. By then, Bennett, had a room in a house on 4th Avenue kept by two old ladies, but took all his meals at the Alberta Hotel (at a cost of $50 a month, as Tribe remembers). His office was on the right at the top of the stairs in the Clarence Block, comfortably furnished, and adorned with a large portrait of Sir John A. Macdonald. Bennett drove his staff hard, but himself even harder. By then he was in demand as a lawyer, and as a speaker, and, again as Tribe remembers, his main themes were temperance and the British Empire and its future, as portrayed by Joseph Chamberlain and Cecil Rhodes:

> "He was very proud of his memory", Tribe said, "and used to boast of it. I remember, not long after I came, one evening he dictated two letters at the one time, one paragraph of one to Miss Ross, his other typist, and then a paragraph of the other to me. When he lost a case, he was very depressed, and bad-tempered, and then the assistant lawyer with the firm, Mr. Allison, caught it, but when he won one he would talk for hours, about himself and his ambitions. He told me he intended to be Prime Minister one day, and get a title. He talked a great deal of his mother, but never of his father. He was devoted to her."

> "He was a good employer. He bought me a new typewriter when I came, saying I shouldn't start with a worn-out machine. He expected you to stay late if he did—and there was no overtime—but he never forgot you were a human being. One night the block next to ours, the Norman Block, also owned by Senator Lougheed, caught fire. I heard of it

and went down to our block to see if it was in danger. It looked as though it might be—they were both frame buildings—so I set to work to get our books and files and papers out into the street, just in case. I'd got most of them out when the fire chief said he thought we'd be all right, so I sat down on the side walk—the smoke had made me a little groggy.

"I was still sitting there when Bennett and Senator Lougheed came up. Lougheed expected me to start and carry all the stuff back inside again but Bennett said no, 'He's done enough for tonight.'

"Bennett was making about $4,000 to $5,000 a year then from his own clients. He had to share that with Lougheed, and I don't think he altogether liked it."

Bennett could no longer be considered the object of pity he had been fifteen years before, the boy of fifteen leaving home for the first time. His success was mounting and he had no reason to doubt its continuance. It came to him with increasing ease, and each year his savings and investments grew. He was far from being a lawyer of academic brilliance, but he was an excellent man of business. Yet he remained moody and unstable. With no real interests outside his own work—and his own success—there was only one channel along which his vast energy might flow. In essence he had not changed.

He was still solitary and insecure. On the one hand, he knew that he could dominate the society in which he lived, on the other he was always aware of the deficiencies in his own education and background. He could master facts easily and thoroughly, but he had no urge to read literature for its own sake. Assured of success, he could be gracious and kind, truly a part of his essential nature, but threatened by failure, made conscious of a deficiency, he would resort to violence of word or gesture to fend off awareness of defeat. William McLaws, a lawyer in his office and later an enemy, but a shrewd and intelligent man, once said of him: "For all his bluster, R.B. never really faces an issue." It was true enough of him at this time.

Equally he was still a battlefield between the Bennetts and the Stiles, between the ease of material acceptance and the rigidity of self-denial and self-discipline. Max Aitken gives this account of one of his early commercial ventures and of Bennett's reaction to it (Aitken, too, was in Calgary at this time, having deserted law when Bennett left Chatham and followed him west):

"In the morning he would say, 'If only your character equalled your ability.' The afternoon judgment was, 'If only your industry equalled your energy.'

"It did not surprise him when I found another outlet for that energy though not for that ability.

"Across the street from Bennett's office a bowling alley was being built in leased premises. The builder was willing to sell the property for $250.

"The Union Bank of Canada had recently set up a branch in Calgary under the management of a man named Christie, and he was seeking clients.

"Here was opportunity. A boy named Jack McLean and I joined in a promissory note for $250, payable in three months, which the bank discounted. The bowling alley passed to us. . . .

". . . Bennett had washed his hands of me altogether. He was so angry about the bowling alley that we were not even on speaking terms."

Another contrast in his nature was that he remained divided between the man who could not tolerate opposition and the man who would go to very great lengths to give help to others. He could be brutal and generous, almost to the same man at the same time. These two threads, to be seen again in his constant urge to do good for others here and now, almost by force if necessary, and his patience and willingness to plan and to wait for the pieces to fall into place before taking the next step, run through all his life. Nothing illustrates it better than his relations with Bob Edwards.

Bob Edwards may be described, brutally, as a drunken Scottish journalist, of good family, who emigrated with his brother to the New World and who ended up in Calgary writing and publishing a rather scurrilous rag named *The Eye-opener*, something akin to its English contemporary, *Ally Sloper*, but with an occasional touch as from a Bob Hope script-writer. Edwards was in fact the grandson of Chambers, the Edinburgh publisher, and related to the Lehmanns, but he had grown up in the theatrical Kendal family. A conflict with Bennett was inevitable, and at the start Edwards was the more successful, as may be gathered from this quotation from his paper:

> " 'What,' thundered R. B. Bennett during the recent temperance address at Red Deer, 'could be more terrible than to feel the wild desire for strong drink surging through every vein?'
>
> "(The knowledge that you haven't got the price.)"

As a man in the public eye, Bennett was fair game, and, knowing where he was most vulnerable, Edwards concentrated his attack there. Bennett, equally in character, at first sought to kill this gadfly with the equivalent of a club. But there was more to Edwards than a mere desire to wound. He had a journalist's conscience, and an urge to use his talents in the public good as well as in the public entertainment. His real target was more the C.P.R. than Bennett.

In the first years of this century, the C.P.R. made an excellent whipping-boy for all the troubles that beset the west. It held a tight monopoly over the transportation of men, animals, grain and merchandise. It owned the section of land on which Calgary was being built. All over the west it was engaged in turning its original land grants into cash, and, a major crime in the eyes of Calgary's citizens, it had left the two crossings over its tracks in the centre of the city, at what are now 1st Street East and 1st Street West, totally unprotected. Constantly, it seemed, men were being injured and valuable animals destroyed by the combination of C.P.R. parsimony in management and negligence in operation.

This giant drew Edwards like a magnet. He began to print, if possible with illustrations, all the news he could collect of every accident on any of the C.P.R. tracks across the Province. When there was an accident, the accident itself was given the headlines. When there was no accident to report, he could treat that as news in itself. 'Calgary luck still in the ascendant,' he wrote in one issue in 1906. 'No tragedy at the crossings. This is fool's luck.' In the same issue he ran three pictures of recent

C.P.R. calamities on the front page and a pen-and-ink sketch of Bennett—and a very good one, too—on an inside page. Under this he wrote the caption: 'Another C.P.R. wreck.' Bennett was, after all, the C.P.R. solicitor in Calgary.

Bennett's first countermove was ponderous. He advised the Company to prohibit the sale of *The Eye-opener* on Company premises, and refuse Edwards, as its Editor, the customary pass over C.P.R. lines given to all newspapermen. Edwards was considerably annoyed, and hurt, by the boycott, and he now turned his attacks on Bennett the politician, with success. When Bennett failed to win election to the new Alberta Provincial Legislature in 1905 by a mere twenty-nine votes, he was compelled to take Edwards' opposition to him more seriously and in his turn look for ways in which the feud could be ended. His frontal attacks were always impetuous, but when it was clear they had failed and that he had to replan the assault, his sapping and mining were calculated and complex.

By now Bennett was an established figure in Calgary. He normally lunched at the Alberta Hotel, in the dining-room at a table known as the 'Bennett table', usually with half a dozen or so more men of business in the city. One of the regular attenders at the Bennett table was 'Paddy' Nolan, K.C., and Nolan's range of friendships included Edwards as well as Bennett, as Bennett well knew. Bennett also knew that Nolan, also a Conservative, would be glad to see peace restored between the two men and *The Eye-opener* brought in as an ally.

Bennett's plan was, in military terms, an encircling movement. His part in it was to make contact with Edwards (he did so by attending Sunday-morning service at the Salvation Army citadel and cornering Edwards before he could escape) and lure him towards membership of the Bennett table. Nolan's part was to reassure Edwards that a response to these advances could do no harm and might do good. Throughout Bennett remained patient, good-humoured, considerate and convivial. The operation was successful, and once drawn to Bennett's side Edwards never left it. The story of the pursuit and capture of Bob Edwards is told more fully in Grant MacEwan's account of his life, *The Eye-opener*, and these paragraphs from it should be quoted in full:

"Bennett's new wish to cultivate Edwards was quite obvious, and as the guests were called to take place at the banquet table, Mr. Bennett, as host and master of ceremonies, called upon Bob Edwards to say grace. There was an awkward moment of silence—one that seemed more like an hour—and then Bob spoke: 'If you don't mind, Mr. Chairman, I'd prefer that the good Lord didn't know I was here.' "

"On the first visit to the Bennett table, Bob was quiet and everybody except Paddy seemed uneasy. Gradually, however, the evidence of reserve disappeared and an entirely new mood pervaded the table's company. There was more laughter, more good-natured banter, and even Bennett found new enjoyment. He forgot his usual and dignified formality as he laughed at the trouble which George Peet, sitting opposite to him, was having with City officials. Bachelor Peet believed in cleanliness and had a big metal bath-tub in the centre of his one-room quarters over Hall's Hardware. There came an inspector to complain that a city by-law forbade bathrooms in bedrooms. George Peet, his anger aroused, replied loudly: 'Well, there's no by-law that says I can't have a bed in my bathroom. Now, get out, you fool.'

"For the first time, Bennett was displaying unreserved pleasure in relating stories about Paddy. Bob would come to the table enquiring if there were any choice bits for the pages of the 'Great Moral Weekly'. Bennett might reply; 'Can't think of anything breezy enough for that, but did you ever tell your readers the one about Paddy Nolan and Shorty McLaughin of High River? The C.P.R. train hit five of Shorty's cayuses and killed them. He wanted Paddy to act for him in suing for damages. Paddy listened to Shorty's account of the horses straying and getting in the way of the Calgary-Fort Macleod train. Paddy asked again if the C.P.R. train actually ran these horses down, and when Shorty confirmed that it did, Paddy said, 'Well, I'm sorry, Shorty, but I can't take that case. Any horses that can't outrun a C.P.R. train are better dead. You're lucky to be rid of them.'

"Bob was pleasantly surprised; Bennett was not only in a joking mood, but he was finding enjoyment in a story that

touched lightly upon the proud railroad company for which
he was solicitor. Bob found himself admiring the man. . . ."

The admiration deepened. When the 1911 election came,
Edwards was campaigning for Bennett, and later still Bennett
was one of the executors of Edwards' will.

Their reconciliation provided a small sequel, involving the
sketch of the C.P.R. wreck. Edwards, a little tentatively,
offered the original of the sketch to Bennett, not altogether sure
what the response would be. Bennett accepted it with glee.
Years afterwards, when he finally left Calgary and closed the
suite in the Palliser Hotel in which he had lived for so long, he
packed this sketch with a few personal papers he took with him.
It was, he said, one of his most prized possessions.

Bennett never became wholly a man of the west. He understood its problems and its people, because he had lived with
them, but he was never absorbed by them. He was not by
nature a man to put down the kind of roots that anchor a man
to a place. But for his country that was an advantage. To live on
the prairies forces a man to look towards horizons that are so
distant, and to think of what may lie beyond them. He is never
confined, as in a field or a valley. The world he sees every day
is very wide.

Chapter Four

THE CREATION OF ALBERTA

B ENNETT'S second objective was political, and it ranked second only because he felt he must establish himself in his profession before he could afford to venture into politics. At the start, he seemed to make headway comparable to his rapid emergence as a lawyer.

At the end of the nineteenth century, the North West Territories, the vast area between a much smaller Manitoba and the Great Divide, were governed from Regina by a Lieutenant-Governor, appointed from Ottawa, and a Territorial Assembly elected by a popular vote, and the two were then engaged in what is usually the last phase of the struggle by a colony to win independence, the fight for a fully representative government. In the Territories the struggle took the form of a demand by the Premier, as head of the Executive Council, that he should consider himself responsible to the elected Assembly and not to the Lieutenant-Governor who had appointed him, and who represented the Crown, or external government. In 1897, colonial rule in the Territories was very nearly at an end. The demand was for autonomy, or full provincial status within the Canadian federation.

For Bennett there could be no question over the party to which he belonged. He was a Conservative, and an Imperial Conservative at that. Almost on his arrival he had been taken to a political meeting in Calgary to be addressed by Frank Oliver, the Federal Liberal M.P. from Edmonton, founder and owner of the Edmonton *Bulletin*, and the major power in Liberal politics in the western Territories. Bennett could not refrain from heckling Oliver when he spoke—he would see no reason to refrain—and his interruptions were so pointed that there was a call from the audience that he should be allowed to speak after Oliver had finished. That he did, and his speech was so effective that his political reputation as a Conservative in Calgary was made that night.

This, however, did not remove all obstacles from his path, even within his own party. He might be accepted by Calgary, but in the area to the south he was still thought of primarily as a protégé of Lougheed, and therefore tainted with what some thought was Lougheed's over-powerful position in the party. None the less, and despite some complaints that the nominating convention had been too carefully planned with this end in view, he won nomination as the Conservative candidate for the Calgary provincial riding in the Territorial election in November, 1898, and in the election itself he was returned with a majority of 100 over his nearest rival, the Liberal. He had become a Member of the Territorial Assembly in less than two years of his arrival in Calgary. Shortly after, he made an ambitious attempt in the federal field, challenging Frank Oliver in the 1900 general election, but he lost by 4,029 votes to 5,203.

Long afterwards, in 1941, on the day his peerage was announced, he sat down to write to Beaverbrook a letter expressing his deep gratitude for their lifetime friendship. In it he said:

"In the foothills city of Calgary I was a candidate for the Territorial Legislature supported by John Donohoe and his friends. . . . But the youth of nineteen who 'looked after' the half-breed in the Hotel of 'Irish' at the Elbow Bridge was the Max of Chatham days. So in my second venture in public life you were my supporter. I recall you at the Alberta Hotel telegraph office and Miss Cameron at the key as we waited for the result from Olds, while George Tempest scurried about in the distance.

"We had practically tied with Muir in Calgary and you made a bet regarding Olds, for I did feel confident in the result there with George Cloakey working so hard. Soon the word came I had 93 and my nearest opponent but 18. We had won."

The Government of Canada had power under the British North America Act to create fresh provinces within the Dominion. When Bennett entered the Territorial Legislature, that Government was securely Liberal, under Sir Wilfrid Laurier, and Laurier was far too shrewd a politician to wish to loosen the grip he held in the west without doing his best to ensure that any power transferred fell into Liberal hands. In the west, the outstanding Liberal figures were Frank Oliver, Bulyea, Minister of Public Works in the Territorial Administration, and Arthur Sifton, brother of the Clifford Sifton who was Minister of the Interior in the Laurier Government, a lawyer like his brother, perhaps less politically ambitious, but as determined and as hard when engaged in battle. On the Conservative side, Senator Lougheed was the recognized pivot on the federal level, but the party could not claim the strength the Liberals had in the west. For one thing, it had no federal patronage to dispense.

Lougheed was a factor in Bennett's life for almost thirty years. He was sixteen years the elder, born in Ontario and called to the Bar of Upper Canada in 1882. The following year he moved west to Medicine Hat, then the end of steel, and, pitching a couple of tents, he had opened a law office in one and slept in the other alongside. It is said that he cut his stay in Medicine Hat short because, coming into his sleeping tent late one night, he had first intended to undress and drop into bed without bothering to light his lamp, but suddenly some protective instinct had driven him to follow his normal routine. When he had his lamp alight, he saw by its light the coiled body of a rattlesnake asleep on his bed. At least Calgary was free from snakes.

Lougheed was a man of quite different temperament from Bennett. He was more of a gambler and speculator, more interested in the west for the unpredictable chances to make money that it might bring. A year after he came to Calgary he married the eldest daughter of William Hardisty, Chief Factor of the Hudson's Bay Company, and in 1889, at the early age of thirty-five, he was sufficiently prominent in western affairs to be appointed to the Senate by Sir John A. Macdonald, one of the last appointments from the west that he made. For Lougheed, politics, like law, was a secondary pursuit. He had won power and prestige, and a position in the Senate suited him very well. He had no strong wish to shoulder any great measure of public work and responsibility.

The outstanding Conservative in Territorial affairs in the west was F. W. G. Haultain, who had been Premier of the Territorial Administration since 1892. Haultain was a lawyer practising in Regina, a man of great ability and repute, but a man who held to the view that party politics should not be introduced into Territorial affairs. In 1897 the Territories were still some way short of the full independence enjoyed by a Canadian province under the British North America Act. The administration had no power to borrow money, it could not grant charters for railways, and, above all, control of Crown lands and natural resources was still vested in the Government at Ottawa; and virtually all land was still Crown land.

Against that, the administration had to meet all the costs consequent on the rapid growth of the population in the Territories, with very few sources from which it could raise its own revenue. The grants it received from the Federal Government were neither certain nor, in its view, adequate. It needed more money. It resented the fact that Ottawa alone could decide who would receive a railway charter or a grant of land, and it was suspicious of the patronage that accompanied the exercises of those rights.

Haultain never slackened his pressure on Ottawa for the creation of a single new province in the west, but, as he said in the Territorial Assembly during the course of the 1903 session, while he subscribed to both Conservative principles and policy in the larger field, "the policy of that party and those principles have nothing whatsoever to do with my position in this House or with the business of this House".

Bennett did not share these views at all. He came from a province in which party politics, the continuing conflict between Conservative and Liberal, had always been a part of the warp and woof of public life. He was in no position to challenge Haultain on this issue directly, but neither was he content to allow those views to go without some challenge. All he could do was to campaign within the party, and to press for the calling of a party convention at which the issue could be debated and settled by the party members themselves.

Bennett's conservatism at this time was a mixture of a number of strands. Like many Canadians, he was a Conservative because his family was, but that was a very minor ingredient. Practically, his connection with the C.P.R. virtually dictated at least a formal adherence to the Party; the C.P.R. had been created by a Conservative Government, and, whether true or not, its rivals believed that it lived within the orbit of Conservative politics. Bennett was never a political servant of the C.P.R.; as a Member of the Assembly, he was prepared to vote to shear away some of its privileges when occasion so required. But it is true that he saw railway matters from the standpoint of the first and most important railway in that part of Canada, and he was suspicious of its rivals, of their motives and of their methods. In fact, in the long run, it was his connection with the C.P.R. that, more than anything else, was to label him a Conservative of a certain kind, the railway corporation lawyer.

If those had been the only reasons for Bennett's Conservatism, at that stage he would have had no reason to challenge Haultain's dictum that party politics had no place in the Territorial Assembly. With no formal party organization there, there was also far less party discipline. The members were more free to be independent, in both thought and speech, and at this period Bennett was extremely reluctant to suffer any curbs on his freedom of expression. Members could speak for the interests of their ridings, which were certainly diverse enough to need explanation to the Administration, and the public. But Bennett's Conservatism, then as ever, was not a matter of simple loyalty to the party machine. It was basically emotional, a personal loyalty to the British Crown and the British connection.

It is worth while, I think, pausing for a moment at this point to recall, as best one can, the climate of feeling at that time, the turn of the century, with both the Diamond Jubilee and the South African War just over and the radicalism of Lloyd George and the pacifism of Ramsay MacDonald yet to come, for it was in this time that the key to an understanding of Bennett as a politician was forged. He was not a traditional Conservative, a disciple of the Salisburys or the Cecils. He was an emotional Conservative, and his heroes of that day were Cecil Rhodes, Joseph Chamberlain and Rudyard Kipling, and he lived in a country in which the influences that later discredited and destroyed the conceptions of Joseph Chamberlain

were far weaker than they were in Britain. I do not think the
Bennett of the next fifteen years can be fully understood unless
one keeps this in mind.

But, while Bennett drew his political colour from this remoter
world, he did not shut his eyes to the fact that parties can only
grow upwards from roots. If he was to succeed, his party must
be active, and if he wished to make his party more active it
must have some practicable objective to fight for, and some
practice in fighting for it. The Liberals knew that; they had no
intention of leaving the Territorial field deserted. Bennett's
first success in this endeavour was the promotion of a party
convention for members within the Territories. His first public
demand for this was made in a speech in Yorkton in January,
1903, and two weeks later Robert Borden, as leader of the
national party, summoned such a convention, to meet at Moose
Jaw in the following March. Two hundred attended it.

The convention passed a number of sound Conservative
resolutions. It called for an ending of land grants to railway
companies, for the construction of a railway to Hudson Bay
to provide the prairies with their own port, for larger grants
to the Territorial Administration from Ottawa and for provincial autonomy, and it concluded with a general resolution
in support of protection for Canadian industry and the creation
of a protective tariff within the Empire. But a main battle
was on the issue of the party's attitude to Territorial and, later,
Provincial affairs. Bennett led the argument for participation
as a party, and, although opposed by Haultain, the convention
carried a resolution to campaign in the next Territorial election
as a party. Bennett had reversed the decision of his nominal
leader. But he had not persuaded him. In the Assembly the
following June Haultain repeated his own repudiation of party
action in Territorial affairs.

The next federal election came in the following year, 1904,
and once again the Liberals under Laurier were returned to
power. But during the campaign Laurier had made a definite
commitment to give provincial status to the western prairie
lands, and with the election over Haultain and Bulyea returned to Ottawa to continue the negotiations. The Ministers
they met were Laurier himself, Scott, the Secretary of State,

Charles Fitzpatrick, Minister of Justice, and Sir William
Muloch, Postmaster-General. Clifford Sifton, who as the
Minister mainly responsible should have taken a major part in
the discussions, was not in Ottawa at the time.

Judging by the Bill produced the following February, the
Ministers from the west had had little success in persuading the
Federal Government to accept their point of view. Two
provinces, Alberta and Saskatchewan, were to be created, not
one, as Haultain had urged. Control of Crown land and
natural resources was to remain with Ottawa, not be transferred
to the new provincial governments. Only over finance could
anyone say that the new provisions were more generous than
those in existence. But the toughest controversial question
to be settled was that of education, an issue which resolved
itself into the question of separate schools for Roman Catholics,
and this was another issue in which Bennett was liable to find
his emotions taking charge.

The clause in the Alberta Bill that dealt with education,
Clause 16, may have been intended, certainly by Laurier, to
follow the pattern of what was known as the 'eastern compromise', but it was open to criticism, by Protestants, on
two grounds. It was dangerously—some said deliberately—
vague in its language, and it was by no means easy to
square it with the provisions for control over education by
provinces contained in the British North America Act. In
consequence, many felt that it would leave the way open to
real changes being made in a régime that had been in existence
in the Territories for the previous thirteen years. In form it
provided that a religious minority should have the right to
establish its own schools, and to have access to public funds for
their construction. It was silent on the question of the limitations on those rights imposed by Ordinance of the Territorial
Assembly and therefore already existing within the Territories.

At first, Bennett's attitude was one of cautious suspicion. On
his customary visit to his mother for the Christmas of 1904 he had
given a statement to the Saint John *Star* in New Brunswick. He said:

"The opinion prevails that the neglect of the Federal
Government to deal with the repeated demands of the

Legislature for autonomy has been owing to the difficulties that surround a solution of the educational problem. Whether Separate Schools shall exist by law or whether they shall be prohibited, is the first question calling for decision, and shall the new Province or Provinces be given full power to deal with the matter without any limitations whatever? At the present time Separate Schools exist, but the teachers must possess the same qualifications as those in the public schools. The same text-books are used and a system of uniform inspection prevails."

After February, when the Autonomy Bills were introduced into the Federal Parliament and their terms were public property, his political temperature began rapidly to rise. In his view, Clause 16 had an ugly look. The vague language in which it was cast was, in his view, indefensible, and he felt that if the Act passed with that section left in the same form as the original clause, the Roman Catholic Church would be free to claim both a greater control over the education of Roman Catholic children and greater contribution towards the cost of their separate schools than they were enjoying under the Territorial Ordinance. Again, had the provision in the British North America Act declaring that education was solely a provincial responsibility no application to any new province created after 1867?

But Clause 16 produced reactions within the Laurier Government itself. The first shock was the resignation of Clifford Sifton on February 28th. He had not seen the original draft of the clause because of his absence from Ottawa, but when he did learn of its details he returned at once, saw Laurier, and, still unsatisfied, made his decision to resign. It was not a decision motivated solely by his dislike of this clause. Personal disagreements with Fitzpatrick entered into it, too, but the clause, Fitzpatrick's own draft, seems to have been the last straw. Another Minister had been in Europe during the Cabinet discussions on the Bill, W. S. Fielding, and on his return he, too, expressed his disagreement and hinted at resignation. Outside Parliament protests gathered force, particularly amongst Protestants in Ontario.

Laurier was never insensitive to trends in public sentiment; although himself a believer in religious teaching in schools, he was prepared for compromise. The original Clause 16 was withdrawn and a fresh draft introduced when the Bill was read a second time in May, and the effect of the new clause was to retain in the new provinces the régime as it had existed in the Territories. By doing so, Laurier saved his government from further embarrassment and won back Sifton, not to office, but to support for the Bill. The Second Reading of the Bill was carried by 140 votes to 59, and thirteen Conservatives—ten from Quebec—voted for it.

It would be unwise, perhaps, to suggest that the issue of religious education and separate schools in Canada is dead today, but there is little point in describing the 1905 controversy in detail. For Bennett its significance was that for the first time he moved into debate outside his own province. He was invited to take part, on the Conservative side, in two by-elections fought in Ontario whilst the Bill was before the House and in which this Clause was a major issue, and he did so with all his vigour. When the fights were over (without too much success to the Conservative side), his name had at least been spread across Canada as one of the younger Conservative politicians.

The Alberta Act received Royal Assent on July 20th, 1905, and came into operation on September 1st in the same year. To the Liberals in the Territories the separate schools issue had been a storm centre through which they were bound to pass if they were to consolidate their political power in western Canada, as they intended to do. For one of them, Frank Oliver, the clash had had a most satisfactory outcome in the resignation of Clifford Sifton. Oliver cherished aspirations to Cabinet rank, and now a vacancy had opened up before his eyes. Until then he had left it uncertain whether he sought appointment as Premier of the new Province of Alberta or not. On April 8th Laurier announced that he had been appointed to the post Sifton had previously held. The Liberal choice for leader in Alberta was A. C. Rutherford, an Edmonton lawyer and Member of the Territorial Assembly for Strathcona. He was not brilliant, but he looked and sounded reliable. He could, it was hoped, create the impression of solid competence.

By September 1st, when the Province of Alberta came officially into being, the Liberal plans were complete. Bulyea had been made the first Lieutenant-Governor of the Province, and on September 2nd he announced that he had called on Rutherford to form the new provincial government. Writs for the first provincial election were issued six weeks later, and polling day was set for November 9th. When the votes were counted, the Liberals had carried every seat in the province save two, those at High River and Rosebud. Bennett, again contesting Calgary, was among the defeated, by the small but decisive majority of twenty-nine votes.

Bennett's record in politics over the first seven years of his activities in the west was indecisive. He had made a very rapid start, but to some extent it had been a false one. His victory in 1898 projected him too suddenly and too violently against a man, Haultain, whose firmly-held views on the conduct of affairs were quite contrary to his own. In any new and rapidly expanding society there is bound to be a conflict between the old-timer and the newcomer; certainly there has been one in western Canada since the time when such a distinction could first be made. The old-timer remembers things as they were, and often misjudges the speed of change. The newcomer has usually been drawn in by the changes already apparent and by the anticipation that they will continue at least as fast. He may be impatient with the old-timer; it is even more likely that the old-timer will be suspicious of him. And Bennett, of course, had all the characteristics of an aggressive newcomer well developed when he first arrived in Calgary.

He would have liked to have made the Conservative Party in the west a fighting unit on all levels at once. Haultain disagreed, and his view prevailed, as it was bound to do, given his vast experience in the government of the Territories and the respect with which he was held in the west. Politically, Haultain lost by his stand. The Liberals had no intention of sharing his self-denying ordinance, and in the end they captured the governments of the two new provinces without very much of a fight. It is possible that if Bennett had then been solely concerned with political affairs in the Territories he could have done more than he did to change that situation. One man can work wonders if he has enthusiasm and a determination to work, for even those lukewarm to his efforts are unlikely to oppose them.

But Bennett was not dedicated to the task of becoming the Conservative Premier of Alberta as soon as the Province was formed. He had wider ambitions and thirty years ahead of him in which to fulfil them. As he saw it, in 1905 the surest foundation for his future would be a substantial bank balance, not an immediate Alberta victory. He led the provincial party in that election, but he did not give the impression that here was a man who believed that he should and must win. In the sight of the electors, without an aura of that kind around him, he was certain to lose, as he did.

Not that he can have intended to lose his own seat in Calgary. That was a shock, and a useful one. It showed him that no vote is ever unimportant, that men like Bob Edwards can never be offended or ignored with safety. It made him think of organization as well as speechifying, and it left him a little humiliated. This was the year in which he had first established his name as a Conservative politician outside the area in which he lived, but it finished with him as a defeated provincial leader and without a seat in any Assembly.

He was then thirty-five.

Chapter Five

THE FIRST RAILWAY SCANDAL

THROUGHOUT his life, Bennett's political career, provincial and federal, held to a curious double pattern. At each first attempt he won a measure of success, as though in rehearsal, but this ended sharply in defeat and was succeeded by an interval of political quiescence, almost indifference. Then followed a second period of activity, bringing greater success, but ending again in defeat, this time total, at the hands of some shrewd Liberal tactician.

He had won his first seat in the Territorial Assembly almost on his arrival in Calgary and he remained a Member until 1905, when the new Provinces of Alberta and Saskatchewan were carved out of the Territories and the Territorial Assembly ceased to exist. He narrowly failed to secure election to the first Alberta Legislature and spent the next five years almost out of politics. At the end of 1909 he was returned a Member for Calgary and immediately plunged into a major battle with the Liberal Administration, centred on the Alberta and Great Waterways Railway project. In that he was outmanoeuvred and held off by Arthur Sifton, the Liberal Premier, and in 1911 he resigned his seat at Edmonton and left provincial politics for good.

His first period at Ottawa began the same year and was one of relative unsuccess, ending in 1917 with his decision not to run in the war-time election of that year. From 1917 to 1925 he was out of federal politics, occupied mainly as a lawyer and a man of business; it was during this period that the Lougheed-Bennett partnership was dissolved, with far-reaching consequences, and that he inherited the Eddy-Shirreff fortune. He returned to the Commons in 1925, succeeded to leadership of the Conservative Party in 1927, led the party to victory in the

1930 election and was beaten by the Liberals, under Mackenzie King, five years later. For him the defeat proved to be decisive. He resigned his leadership of the Party in 1938 and made his final break with Canada, and with his parliamentary seat at Calgary West, in the January of 1939.

So did this cycle repeat itself, but few cycles of human experience are exact repetitions. Bennett's were not, for the man himself changed in, and was changed by, the process itself. For him, while the first cycle may have been the more gruelling, the second must have been the more bitter.

Bennett entered the Alberta Legislature in the provincial general election of 1909 as the junior Member for what had become the two-member constituency of Calgary. The senior Member was a Liberal, W. H. Cushing, a Minister in the Rutherford Government. The polling in Calgary was:

Hon. W. H. Cushing (Lib.)	.	2,579
R. B. Bennett (Con.) .	.	2,423
Dr. Egbert (Lib.) .	.	1,933
Dr. Blow (Con.) .	.	1,907
George Howell (Socialist) .	.	747

It was not a successful election for the Conservatives; once again they emerged with only two party members elected, Bennett in Calgary and George Hoadley in the adjoining riding to the south, Okotoks. A third Conservative, Edward Mitchener, had been successful at Red Deer, but he had run as an Independent Conservative, not as a full party member. Apart from the solitary Socialist returned, C. M. O'Brien, from the coal-mining riding of Rocky Mountain, the new Assembly was Liberal.

Bennett's interest in politics in the years intervening between 1905 and 1909 had not been pronounced. He held no office in the provincial association. He had not sought the Conservative candidacy in Calgary at the federal election of 1908. 1909 had been the year of the federal debates on the proposed naval programme: should Canada contribute money towards the expansion of an Imperial Navy, or should she begin the rather slower process of building one of her own? In his customary statement to the Press in New Brunswick during his Christmas visit to his mother, Bennett claimed that Canada could, and should, do both—contribute to the cost of the Royal Navy, and start on the construction of what would become the R.C.N.

In Alberta, 1909 had opened with a provincial election as an immediate prospect, and provincially the Conservative organization was in poor shape. Bennett was pressed to accept the formal position of leader, but refused. He did accept nomination for the Calgary seat, with Dr. T. H. Blow as his running mate. The Liberals, on the other hand, had a substantial record of achievement as a Government to offer. The Rutherford Government had built up an efficient system of popular education, made progress in providing bridges and roads, fostered agriculture and the dairy and cheese-making industries, regulated and encouraged coal-mining, and given the miner an eight-hour day and a Workmen's Compensation Act for his protection. Above all, it had kept the new province free from debt, save for the cost of establishing a provincially-owned telephone system.

Bennett opened the Conservative campaign at Strathmore on March 15th, and from the line he followed it is clear that he had no real belief that his party could carry the province this time. His appeal was basically a call for more opposition representation, particularly from the south. The Liberals, he said, had favoured Edmonton in all they had done, economically, educationally, and in matters of public works. The most positive thing he could say concerned Rutherford's railway programme; when giving provincial guarantees for the bonds issued by the new undertakings that had sprung up, it had, he claimed, thrown away a very good chance to take power to control the rates these railways would charge. It was a relatively modest criticism.

The newly elected Legislature did not meet until February, 1910, and almost immediately it ran headlong into the opening phases of a major crisis involving the projected Alberta and Great Waterways Railway Company.

The Alberta and Great Waterways Railway was only one of a number of railway-construction scandals that have plagued Canadian politics, and it was less sordid than many. It came at a time when railway building was the rage, when the Canadian Pacific was criticized for not building more feeder lines along its route in Southern Alberta, when complaints of its inability to haul away the mounting wheat harvests were a staple criticism by those who wanted to build competing lines. Two new trans-continental lines were establishing themselves in northern Alberta, the Grand Trunk Pacific and the Canadian Northern, the latter the creation of the Mackenzie and Mann partnership, and local enterprise was desperately anxious to fill up the interstices across the province.

The Conservative opposition in the first Legislature had been strongly in favour of government ownership and operation of these lines. Rutherford, as Premier, had rejected this as impracticable; he had his own plans, and part of them had been embodied in the Act incorporating the Alberta and Great Waterways Railway Company, hastily passed in the last session before the 1909 election. They were to come into full flower in the years from 1910 onwards—as flowers they had a certain magnificence.

It is hardly necessary, after this length of time, to follow the ramifications of the Alberta and Great Waterways enterprise in all its details. It began in the usual way, with a promoter having some political influence with the Provincial Government (he was the Liberal Member for Peace River) obtaining a Dominion Charter from the Laurier Government for a railway in Northern Alberta. Then followed the formation of a syndicate to breathe life into the charter, and the passing of ownership of that syndicate to a citizen of the State of Kansas, one Clarke. Clarke then carried through the next phase, the preparation of the usual specifications for the construction of the road, and the usual inflations in the estimates of cost per mile before the plans were presented to the Government for financial backing. The Rutherford Government finally swallowed the whole glittering lure with one quick snap.

One of the more surprising things about the special Act that incorporated the Alberta and Great Waterways Railway as an Alberta company was the relief it gave that company from some of the more onerous provisions imposed on other specially incorporated railways. Instead of being permitted to commence business only when 25 per cent of the capital had been subscribed and 10 per cent of that deposited in cash, the new company, with a capital of $7,000,000, was allowed to start as soon as no more than $50,000 had been subscribed and paid. Even that requirement was neatly side-stepped by Clarke. He arranged an overdraft with a bank for $50,000, used the money so obtained to subscribe for shares, and banked that as the company's $50,000 initial subscription. The money was then immediately paid out to Clarke, in payment of fees and expenses he claimed to have incurred earlier, and with that he repaid his own overdraft. As a result, everyone was satisfied. The one bright note in the whole story was a comment by one of the promoters on the attitude of Cushing, a Minister engaged in the negotiations on the government side: "He won't stand for watered stock."

The statute that contained the Government guarantee provided that the proceeds of the sales of any bonds subject to the guarantee should be paid into such bank as the Provincial Government might nominate "to the credit of a special account in the name of the Treasurer of the Province". The chosen instrument for the disposal of the bonds was the J. P. Morgan organization of London, Paris, and New York. The chosen bank (possibly, in view of the subsequent litigation, to its regret) was the Royal Bank of Canada. By February, 1910, the credits from bond sales in that bank had risen to $6,042,083. The financial transactions ran smoothly; they were about the only features of the railway that did.

When Bennett took his seat for the first time in the Provincial Legislature in February, 1910, the surface of affairs was unruffled. The first gust of a disturbing wind came from the Liberal benches, from John W. Boyle, Member for Sturgeon, an Edmonton lawyer, who, it was said, had once coveted the position of solicitor to the Alberta and Great Waterways Railway Company. He opened his attack with a series of innocent-seeming but probing questions into the Company's affairs directed to the Premier. Before the questions were answered by Rutherford another rumour swept Edmonton. Cushing, minister of Public Works, had resigned his office. The rumour proved to be true.

The acute phase of the resulting crisis lasted from the opening of the session in February, 1910, to May 26th, when the Lieutenant-Governor, Bulyea, wearing a tweed suit, entered the chamber to announce that he had that morning accepted the resignation of Rutherford as Premier of the Province and called on Arthur Sifton, who had become Chief Justice of the Province in 1907, to form a government in his stead; having done that, he at once prorogued the Assembly. Its main features were a revolt by a section of the Liberal Party, led by Boyle, which on one occasion went so far as to reduce the Government's majority in the Assembly to three, a long series of charges and counter-charges exchanged between Ministers and members, which on occasions involved Deputy Ministers as well, the appointment of a Royal Commission, consisting of three justices of the Alberta Supreme Court, to investigate the whole episode, and a speech by Bennett in the Assembly on March 2nd that even his opponents recognized as outstanding.

When Bennett spoke in the debate the effective resolutions before the House were two. The first condemned the agreement with the Alberta and Great Waterways Railway Company root and branch, the other, rather milder, did no more than empower the Government to cancel the old contract and write a more satisfactory one with the Company. Bennett knew this was an occasion. He arrived in Edmonton from Calgary by special train, and at once plunged into the debate. His speech lasted five hours, and it closed with a personal attack on one Hopkins, who, so Bennett alleged, had sought a contribution of $12,000 to Liberal Party Funds from some of the business community in Calgary as the price for Government agreement to pay the cost of manning the automatic telephone switchboard then about to be installed in the city, an attack which, so the Press said, left Hopkins white and shaken.

From one aspect, Bennett's task was not too difficult. He was attacking a transaction and a series of agreements that had clearly turned out badly for the province. In a position to use that hindsight, it was comparatively easy for him, with his professional experience, to put his finger on the original weaknesses and mistakes. His success, so those who heard the speech thought, lay in his immense capacity to digest the material and to present such a complicated story in a way that laid it clear and naked before his audience, the jurors at the inquest on the Alberta and Great Waterways Railway. As a reporter for the *Calgary Daily Herald* wrote in the issue of the following day:

> "When Bennett finished his wonderful speech, he had torn the contract and agreement to shreds. . . . The spectacle of the Premier sitting absolutely dumb when a single word from him would have brought to the House the assurance of a better position regarding the contract was one that had the effect of cementing the determination of the doubtful members to vote for Riley's motion."

Yet Bennett's attack failed. It failed to defeat the Government, either then or later. In the vote the following day on the more damaging motion, the Riley motion, the Government had twenty-three votes, its opponents only fifteen. The Government survived a later division by an even narrower margin, but it survived.

This escape was due in part to the tactical skill of the succeeding provincial Premier, Arthur Sifton, who was an adroit politician. But it was also due in part to Bennett.

For one thing, in politics, Bennett had the defects of his qualities. In reviewing the debate and Bennett's speech a little later, the *Calgary Daily Herald* reporter wrote:

> "Bennett had a handicap, which is granted to few men in debate. His ability is recognized to such an extent that even when he lays a problem bare, talking in language that any man can understand, the rank and file of the remaining Government supporters, though they can see the picture of what he painted as clearly as if it stood before them, refused to be influenced by him because they feared his cleverness was simply twisting things to appear his way."

Bennett was always in danger of losing touch with his audience, and with the common man, for those reasons. It was not that he was too good to be true. It was that he sometimes seemed too clever to be right.

For another, he had by then obviously lost some interest in provincial affairs. It is not often that governments are overthrown by or during a single debate, especially a debate that

c

opens a crisis, not one that marks its climax. Normally public
opinion needs time in which to recover from its first shock of
dismay and mobilize itself with sufficient strength to defeat the
established party. Bennett failed to follow through, to carry the
debate on into the province for the two years that were left
before the Assembly's five-year term of life expired and an
election must be held.

The decision to leave Albertan affairs for Ottawa was his,
and he was entitled to make it, but it is a pity that he left
behind him this unfinished business at Edmonton. No one can
predict whether he would have defeated the Liberal Administration in the province when the next election came if he had
stayed to fight out the scandal to its bitter end, but his life
would have been very different if he had. Perhaps the history
of Canada would have been, too.

Rutherford's misfortunes within his Cabinet and in the
Assembly alarmed the Liberal command. Their problem was to
find the right replacement, and it took two weeks for Talbot,
the Liberal Senator, and Bulyea to settle in their minds that
the 'only permanent solution', to use Bulyea's own words, was
Arthur Sifton. It took a little longer for the two of them to
persuade Sifton himself to accept the office. Sifton was then
fifty-one. He had refused political office in 1905, on the formation of the first provincial government. Clifford, his brother,
had resigned from the Laurier Government earlier in that year,
and it is doubtful if Arthur Sifton felt any strong sense of personal loyalty to Sir Wilfrid Laurier. But there was a considerable difference between accepting office under Rutherford and
replacing Rutherford as Premier of the Province. Bennett was
convinced that there was a cash consideration as well, something of the order of $100,000 paid to Sifton by the Party. Be
that as it may, Sifton turned out to be a first-class fighting
Liberal politician; perhaps his period as Chief Justice of the
Province should be regarded as a deviation from his true
pattern.

Bennett, however, had not finished with the Alberta and
Great Waterways affair. Once the Assembly had been prorogued by the obedient Bulyea, Sifton had the rest of the
summer in which to make his plans for the future of the railway,

if it was to have one, and of the $7,400,000 lying in the banks. His solution had a certain ruthless simplicity. Since the principal and interest due on the bonds had now become a direct provincial debt, he considered that he was free to treat the cash subscribed for the bonds and now lying in the banks as a general asset of the Province, and to use it for such other purposes as his Executive Council should decide.

Accordingly, as soon as the Assembly reassembled in the November for its second session of 1910, he introduced a Government Bill to provide for the future of the railway funds. It declared that the moneys in the Provincial Treasurer's special account at the three chartered banks were part of the general Revenue Fund of the Province of Alberta "free and clear of any claim by the Alberta and Great Waterways Railway Company, their successors or Assigns", and required the banks to pay over the moneys in these accounts to the Provincial Treasurer "without any set-off, counterclaim or other deductions whatsoever".

Bennett, still a member, had no need to feign indignation at this proposal. It drove headlong against two of his deepest convictions, the sanctity of contract, and the sanctity of private property. This was confiscation, in his view; and he had the strongest objection to any government in any part of the Crown's realms attempting to legalize confiscation by statute. But once again, there were no more than fourteen votes against the twenty-five the Government could muster, and the Bill passed. Sifton wasted no time once it had received Royal Assent.

On the day the Act was passed a body of six men, including a notary public, descended on the Edmonton Manager of the Royal Bank (as well as on the other two banks involved) and presented to him a cheque in the sum of $6,042,083 drawn on the special account, signed by Arthur L. Sifton as Provincial Treasurer and payable to the Government's main bankers, the Imperial Bank of Canada. The manager replied that he had instructions not to pay the cheque, whereupon the notary protested it. Since this response had been anticipated, a Statement of Claim was ready and was filed the same day in the Supreme Court of Alberta, with the King and the Provincial

Treasurer as plaintiffs, and the Royal Bank of Canada as a defendant. The claim was for the amount of the dishonoured cheque. Bennett's second battle over the Alberta and Great Waterways Railway had begun.

In the subsequent litigation he appeared as counsel for the Bank at the trial of the action, which took place in the following October before Mr. Justice Stuart, and in the subsequent appeals. At the trial, there was little dispute over the facts. The plaintiffs did no more than prove the nature of the default, the amount in the special account at the Bank, and the dishonouring of the cheque drawn on it. With that, they let their case stand. Bennett's defence for the Bank went into a little more detail, mainly to put into evidence all the documents involved. From his point of view, the substantial points at issue were two: Had the original payment by Morgan's actually reached Alberta as 'property' in the legal sense or had it, technically, remained at the head office of the Bank of Montreal, outside the province? His second was the submission that the Provincial Act transferring the money at the Royal Bank to the General Revenue Fund of the Province was *ultra vires* the Provincial Legislature because it attempted to legislate in the field of banking, the prerogative of the Dominion Parliament.

From the point of view of the public, sated as it might have been from the evidence already called before the Royal Commission, the trial still provided some surprises. Both Rutherford and Sifton were called as witnesses, and were cross-examined. Since it was a part of the case for the railway company (joined as a defendant at its request) that it had not been in default in the performance of its contract, its counsel asked Rutherford if it were not true that the company had lodged the plans and profile for the line with his office in the February of the previous year, and that the plans had been mislaid, being found in the following December, six months after Rutherford's resignation, behind a desk in the Speaker's Room in the Legislature Building? Rutherford was rather taken aback. He was unaware, he replied, that the plans had ever been lost.

Mr. Justice Stuart handed down his judgment on November

4th, 1911 (reported at 1 W.W.R., p. 1). It was short. He began
by saying that he thought he should deliver a prompt decision
rather than delay it for research, and he concluded by finding
for the plaintiffs—in effect, for the Provincial Government. He
rejected Bennett's argument that the funds in dispute were not
legally within the province; in his judgment they were at the
Edmonton Branch of the Bank, and so subject to the authority
of the Provincial Legislature. He was even more definite in
tossing to one side Bennett's second argument, that the Provincial Act transferring the money to the general revenues of
the province was an invasion of the federal jurisdiction over
banking. So to state, he said, appeared to him to be 'utterly
unreasonable, a proposition for which no authority cited to me
furnishes, so far as I can up to the present time discern, the
slightest foundation'. He gave judgment for the plaintiffs for
$6,042,083·26, plus the interest that had accrued in the special
accounts since the moneys had been paid in.

Bennett at once advised an appeal to the Appellate Division
of the Court and in the appeal raised a third point, that the
Provincial Act was *ultra vires* the Provincial Legislature because
it was basically confiscatory in nature. The appeal came before
three judges sitting *en banc*, and they delivered judgment on
13th April, 1912 (1 W.W.R., p. 1,159). They were unanimous
in dismissing the appeals. There still remained a further right
of appeal to the Privy Council and Bennett strongly advised
the Bank to take advantage of it. It accepted his advice and an
appeal was entered in London.

The appeal is an interesting one. For the first time, the case
was argued in an atmosphere far removed from the political
passions it had engendered in Alberta, and before judges who
had never been party politicians in Canada. Haldane was
Lord Chancellor; he presided and delivered the judgment of
the Court on January 31st, 1913 (1912 A.C. 283). The problem
was one that appealed to his mind, and his enjoyment of the
opportunity is clear enough in the words of his judgment.
'Their Lordships', he said, 'are not concerned with the merits
of the political controversy which gave rise to the validity of
the Statute, the validity of which is impeached [the 1910 Act].
. . . Elaborately as the case was argued in the judgments of the

learned judges in the Courts below, their Lordships were not satisfied that what appears to them to be the fundamental question at issue has been adequately considered.' He then proceeded to consider it, and to dispose of it in remarkably few words. This Court was approaching the dispute from the point of view of the lenders who had supplied the $6,000,000 involved in the case. "When the action of the Government in 1910 altered the conditions (the conditions of the bonds), the lenders in London were entitled to claim from the Bank at its head office in Montreal the money which they had advanced solely for a purpose which had ceased to exist. Their right was a civil right outside the province and the Legislature of the province could not legislate validly in derogation of that right." Their Lordships humbly advised His Majesty to allow the appeal and to dismiss the action, with costs against the respondents throughout. Bennett's confidence in the final outcome had been vindicated.

Rex v. *Royal Bank*, as it came to be called, was one of the most illustrative cases in Bennett's career. It is doubtful if the Bank itself would have carried the appeal to the Privy Council if Bennett had not urged them to do so. The fact that the Alberta Court had ordered it to pay the moneys in the Special Accounts over to the Province would have been an answer to any bondholder who might subsequently have sued in the province. Yet Bennett would have carried the appeal to the Privy Council, so long as he felt there was the remotest chance of success, simply as a matter of pride, and with indifference to fees. This was a case which touched his deepest beliefs, both as a politician and as a man. He did believe that no British government anywhere should, or could, disregard the basic conceptions of the society it existed to defend, and he considered the Government of Alberta was doing exactly that.

Fundamentally, it was an even simpler proposition than that on which Haldane decided the appeal. Haldane was conditioned to think as a lawyer of the United Kingdom. His fellow citizens had lent money overseas on one kind of bond, and now the Government that had guaranteed that bond was trying to rewrite its terms after the money had been paid over. It wasn't quite proper, and as Lord Chancellor he could stop it.

To Bennett it was not so much a matter of rewriting a contract, although he considered contracts sacred once made. It was a question of whether Alberta had the right to confiscate money lent to build a railway and use it for any other purpose that happened to suit its convenience.

The Privy Council appeal had one consequence that gave Bennett very great personal satisfaction. For him the Judicial Committee of the Privy Council was the highest legal authority in the hierarchy he served, and it was a matter of pride to him that a lawyer from the Province of New Brunswick, as from anywhere else in the Empire, could appear before it if he had talent enough. During the course of the argument before the Committee, he received this note from one of the members, Lord Macnaghten:

> Dear Mr. Bennett,—May I take the liberty of congratulating you on your appearance before the P.C. this afternoon. I thought you argued your point extremely well—and I may add we all thought so.
>
> Yours very truly,
> Macnaghten.

It was a letter he cherished all his life.

For Bennett, the Alberta and Great Waterways Railway scandal had its ambivalent aspects. It brought him political failure and legal success, but the success did not seem to counterbalance the failure. It came when he was beginning to accumulate a substantial private fortune from activities that had no direct connection with either law or politics, yet this affair seemed to usher in what were to be the most frustrating ten years of his life. The one positive thing about it was that it deepened his dislike for and distrust of the Siftons, and that meant only one thing. Arthur Sifton had outmanœuvred him in Alberta, and what Arthur Sifton had done once all the Siftons would be prepared to do again any time the occasion offered.

Being the man he was, Bennett would probably have failed in any attempt to use Rutherford's mishandling of the Alberta and Great Waterways Railway as a means of defeating the Liberal Party in Alberta, either in 1911 or 1913, even if that had been his single political purpose. But it was not. At that time he had no single political purpose, certainly none held with intensity and certainty. He had not whole-heartedly committed himself to political life in Alberta, or indeed in Canada itself. Another ten years were to pass before he collected all his energies and set off in the pursuit of a single end, and even then perhaps it might be said that he had his mind made up for him by someone else.

Chapter Six

OTTAWA AND MEIGHEN

IN 1911, at forty-one, Bennett remained as complex a character as ever, his contradictions still unresolved. He had bought one of the first motor cars to be seen in Calgary, and on his first drive down town a cyclist crossed his path and caused him to swerve. The car hit a pole and was damaged. Unhurt, Bennett stepped from the car, extremely angry, and declared that he would never himself drive again. He never did.

His home—if that word may be used in a limited sense—was a suite of rooms in the Palliser Hotel, the C.P.R. hotel in Calgary, still preserved by the management as he left it. There he was well looked after and lived in style and comfort. He was fond of good food and his tastes were increasingly running towards sweets. There he could entertain and be entertained. He could be an excellent host; although he still did not drink wines or spirits, he was prepared to serve them to others. But this was a home life without responsibilities—to family, even to staff. His concerns for others were generalized, and matters entirely of his choice.

He remained unmarried. He was attractive to women and attracted by women, but his liaisons lacked permanence and left him unchanged. He had at this time all the marks of a restless, unsatisfied and fundamentally lonely man.

Professionally he was busy. Calgary was growing, and legal business grew with it. He had taken silk in 1905 and could fairly be said to be one of the four leading counsel of that time in southern Alberta. The firm of Lougheed and Bennett was under his control, for all practical purposes. Between 1900 and 1905 Lougheed and he had shared its profits equally. After 1905 Bennett was no longer a member of any legislature, whilst Lougheed was increasingly busy at Ottawa and elsewhere in

the east. In consequence, the agreement was amended again.
Lougheed received a fixed payment of $3,000 a year from the
firm and the rest of the profits went to Bennett. By then others
were becoming associated with the partnership—H. A. Allison
in 1902, W. P. Taylor in 1905, and William H. McLaws in
1907—but Bennett did not regard them as partners; they were
assistants paid by a share in the profits.

Bennett's principal concern professionally was the work of
the C.P.R. He was their solicitor and counsel in the west and
a Vice-President of their subsidiary irrigation company, and
drew a retainer of $10,000 a year. He had a separate office in
the C.P.R. Natural Resources building, a block away from the
Lougheed and Bennett office in the Clarence Building, and the
two were connected by a direct telephone line. J. E. Brownlee,
Q.C., later to become provincial leader of the United Farmers
of Alberta and Premier of the province, came to Alberta about
this time as a young lawyer from Ontario, and spent a year
with the firm completing his articles. He was at the other end of
the direct line, and as he remembered it it was in constant use.

"I saw a good deal of Bennett that year," he later recalled.
"What impressed me from the start was his phenomenal
memory. His desk was usually piled a foot or so high with
papers. He would say: 'Halfway down that pile there's a
Statement of Claim in such and such a case, and it needs an
appearance entering now. Will you see to it?'

"He had a quick, explosive temper, yet he could be
extremely patient. I frequently came back to the office to
work in the evening, and so did he. He would glance at
whatever book I was reading and as often as not immediately
give me and my fellow student a lucid and comprehensive
lecture on that field of law. James Muir, whose firm I joined
the following year, was perhaps the best lawyer of his day—
certainly in consultation—and equally helpful. Muir would
discuss a subject as a tutor might, making you solve the
problem for yourself. Bennett was the lecturer, and again, in
lecturing, he would astonish me with his ability to remember
not only the names and facts of decided cases, but also the
judges who heard them, and the dates of the hearings."

Bennett was known and respected throughout Calgary, but it is hard to find that he was as generally liked. His closest, perhaps his one complete friend was George Robinson. Robinson was a real estate and insurance agent in Calgary, a man in complete contrast to Bennett. He was Bennett's political adviser and manager in Alberta. He knew the organizational side of politics instinctively and completely. He could fix anything that could be fixed. Equally instinctively, he knew how to handle Bennett himself. He never stood in awe of him, as so many did. When he went to see him, almost ostentatiously he kept his bowler hat on and continued to smoke his cigar, although he knew Bennett detested the smell of tobacco in his office. He could ignore Bennett's bursts of temper as though they had never happened, and Bennett knew it.

On one occasion he was travelling with Bennett on a speaking tour in the province and they arrived at nightfall in a small town with only one hotel. Robinson went to the desk to see about the room, and the proprietor, recognizing Bennett, thought it a suitable occasion to advance his asking price considerably.

"What?" roared Robinson when he heard the figure. "For that women must be included. Bring 'em out."

Bennett was not amused, but George was George.

There were plenty of men and women devoted to him: George Cloakey, a land agent, who had worked for him in his first election campaign, Bishop Pinkham, the Anglican Bishop, and his family. But friendship is a matter of reciprocation, and on that some felt they could never rely. Every meeting with Bennett seemed to be a fresh encounter. One could never assume that one could begin again where one had left off last time.

It was at this time that he began to make his first fortune. From the start his third objective had been to make money. At first the compulsion sprang from the circumstances of his childhood. He had grown up counting every cent, with no reserve of money or expectation of money to fall back upon. Money at first meant security, freedom from anxiety over what disaster and distress might follow an illness or chance accident. At no time, except in some individual years in his later political life, did he fail to save some portion of each year's income, however small that might be.

E. J. Chambers, Q.C., of Calgary, later to become the senior partner in what is still known in Western Canada as 'the Bennett firm', remembers Bennett taking him out of the office for a walk along 8th Avenue; it was in 1922, a few weeks after Chambers had arrived in Calgary from his native New Brunswick, and he assumed Bennett wanted to weigh him up.

"Young man," Bennett said, 'the first thing you must do in this city is establish your credit."

Chambers, who had not yet been admitted to the Alberta Bar, and who was then being paid the monthly sum of $50 and no more, had not hitherto applied his mind to the question of his credit status in Calgary. He had been brought up in a part of New Brunswick where one's reputation depended upon neither asking for nor expecting credit, but upon how promptly one paid cash for one's purchases. However, he did not feel that was the moment to attempt any explanation to Bennett. After all, Bennett knew New Brunswick very well.

"What you should do," Bennett went on, "is to get a $500 Government bond."

Again Chambers felt that the advice could hardly be directed to him. Presumably his salary would increase beyond $50 a month some day; until it did he saw no immediate means of acquiring a bond of any denomination.

Then Bennett began to put the pieces together.

"You'll have to live on a salary for some time, young man," he said, "and that salary is not going to take care of the un-expected expense—illness, accident, doctor—who knows? No salary ever does. But never forget this. Banks make their money by lending it, and somebody who has saved enough to buy a $500 bond is someone a bank manager is going to wel-come. When you ask for a loan and can offer them that kind of security, it's you who are doing the bank a favour. You are giving them your business."

Bennett was neither gambler nor speculator. The investments he preferred were the ordinary stocks of the Canadian chartered banks, and these investments served him and the trusts which he founded with an initial gift of bank stock very well indeed.

But he was able to make his first fortune because he had become a good customer of the bank, and the bank in turn was prepared to give him support when Max Aitken offered him a chance to participate in what did become a substantial financial venture. By then the original motive had expanded.

Money saved and invested was not only a hedge against misfortune. It could also buy freedom in the fields in which his ambitions still ran. He realized early on that, in Canadian politics of all places, the man who did not have to give up some time each year to earn that year's income had a very great advantage over the one that did. Bennett would always urge any man aspiring to a political life to make a fortune first. He broke that rule once himself, when he stood for a federal seat in 1900, but never again.

One of his ventures was a partnership venture. With Lougheed (and partly from political motives) he tried to buy majority control of the Calgary *Albertan* newspaper, but they found themselves in the end with no more than 46 per cent of the voting rights (forty-six ordinary shares, registered in Bennett's name) and W. M. Davidson, Editor and a Liberal, holding firmly both to the remaining 54 per cent of the capital and to his expressed policy of beating the Conservatives over the head with every editorial he wrote. Still, however little it was worth politically, almost half the *Albertan* belonged to Lougheed and Bennett.

(The *Albertan* investment never brought any luck for Bennett. He took over the forty-six shares on the final dissolution of the Lougheed-Bennett partnership, and thereafter as the minority shareholder had to wait the chance of a purchaser and in the meantime suffer the political attacks of his co-proprietor. "No dividend for me ever came out of '*The Albertan*', save curses," he said. A purchaser finally appeared, George Bell, and the transaction took the form of an exchange. Believing that the Conservatives needed more Press support in the western provinces, Bennett traded the *Albertan* holding for one that gave him control of the Regina *Star*, but the *Star* proved to be an even more irritating concern and financial drain, until the time when, in 1939, he disposed of his interest in it at a price below that which his accountants, the year before, had said was a poor one, even by depression standards. He estimated that he lost over $100,000 in that investment. The paper itself ended its independent life in 1940.)

His continued association with Max Aitken was much more happy. Aitken had not stayed long in Calgary. He had entered the world of commercial promotions and investment, first in Canada and later in the United Kindgom, with great success, and he had money to provide from Britain for suitable ventures in Canada. The first of these was an amalgamation that produced Canada Cement, which included the cement plant west of Calgary at Exshaw. Bennett handled the Canadian end of the negotiations, and was a member of the original syndicate. The second was an amalgamation of some ninety-four individually-owned country grain elevators, which emerged as Alberta Pacific Grain Elevators. In that new company Bennett had a sizeable holding, which in 1918 produced an income of $33,750. It was sold to Spillers, Ltd., in Great Britain, in 1923, and Bennett's capital gain, according to Aitken, was $1,350,000. The third was the formation of Calgary Power Ltd.

The nucleus of Calgary Power Ltd. was a small hydro-electric generating plant up the Bow Valley above Calgary, whose main customer was the Canada Cement plant, but from that grew a massive utility corporation, supplying most of Alberta with power. Bennett was President of the company for ten years. He also became personally interested in oil when it was first brought in in Turner Valley, south-west of Calgary, in 1913, and later became a director of Imperial Oil Ltd. All these activities produced a fortune which, by the war years, was giving him a substantial income of between $30,000 and $45,000 a year from dividends and bond interest. By North American standards, his first fortune was modest, but it gave him independence. He could use his time as he wished.

In 1911 he decided that the time was ripe for him to attempt federal politics again. He secured nomination as the Conservative candidate for the riding of Calgary West, and at the General Election on September 21st he was returned with a poll of 7,671 as against the 4,816 cast for his Liberal opponent. It was an exhilarating moment for him. At forty-one he was a member of the Federal House, and in politics at that age he was a young

man. He was a member of the party that had won a decisive
victory; across Canada it had 133 seats to the Liberals 88. His
prospects within the party looked bright, for he was the only
Conservative from his province. He was busy. He had the brief
for the Royal Bank in the Alberta and Great Waterways
Railway litigation, and the trial was due to open in Edmonton
in three weeks' time. Once again he had made a remarkably
good start in the opening phase of his new career.

His elation cannot have lasted long. Whatever hopes he may
have had of some Ministerial appointment were dashed
almost at once. He considered he had some claims to office.
He was able, industrious and experienced in the work of a
legislature. He was not unknown across Canada, and if geo-
graphical considerations were taken into account, as they always
had been, he was one of the only two party members from
Alberta and Saskatchewan. Borden thought otherwise, and to
rub salt into the wound Lougheed, his partner, was given the
position of Minister without Portfolio. Borden could argue that
Lougheed had equally valid claims and a longer record of
service in the party, and that it was quite impossible to include
in his Cabinet the two senior members of the same law firm in
Calgary.

But that would have been something of an excuse. Borden
had first met Bennett when on a speaking tour in the west some
eight years before, and while he had respect for Bennett's
abilities he had doubts over his usefulness to him at that time.
In addition, he had another able young lawyer from the west,
Arthur Meighen, who had served with him in the previous
Parliament as part of the opposition team he had led. In short,
Bennett had already encountered indirectly his most serious
rival in the federal field.

Nor was that the whole story. Although Bennett may have
been unaware of it, so far he had avoided much of the real
responsibility for the well-being of his party in Alberta. He
could win a seat in Calgary, and he worked hard to perfect his
grip on the riding, but when doing so he was far more Bennett
than the Conservative candidate. After 1905 he had declined
to continue as provincial leader, and he had not even served as
a party official in the province. He had thrown himself into

battle in the Provincial Legislature after his election in 1909 with gusto, but again it was Bennett speaking. He had failed to establish himself as leader of an alternative party with its own alternative party programme. Nor had he carried that particular political battle through. He had quit halfway.

It would not be true to say that things had come to him too easily. He had worked hard and used all his talent to the full in reaching the position he had won. But so far he had not really had to face failure; in fact, he had avoided it.

As I see Bennett at this stage in his career, he was still temperamentally in escape. He had not come to terms with his need for recognition and success, nor with all the urges implanted in him by his mother. His success to that point is not of itself really remarkable; by nature he had the gifts and the energy to climb as far as he had. What is more relevant is the use he had made of his talents, and what is noticeable there is his careful avoidance of any situation in which he might be forced to face failure—really to face it—as the ugly but transitory thing it is. True, he had been defeated politically, but the defeats, so far, could be explained away, or vented on someone else (as Tribe, his secretary, considered he did over his early reverses in Court), or they could be buried from sight under another series of successes in some other field of activity. But that process could not be continued indefinitely. He had now reached the field of his ultimate ambitions. Failure here could not be disguised or dodged, and yet it is significant that in his correspondence with Aitken over the next few years he returns more than once to the theme of quitting Canadian politics altogether and of launching himself afresh in Britain instead. He still needed some escape hatch.

Most certainly he knew that he was now ranged against a most formidable rival within his own party, Arthur Meighen. Meighen was four years his junior—he had been born in June, 1874—but within the federal party had the advantage of seniority. He had first been elected for Portage la Prairie, Manitoba, three years before, at his first attempt, and had been returned in the 1911 election with an increased majority.

Superficially there were many resemblances between the two men. Both had come from rural communities, Bennett in

New Brunswick, Meighen in Ontario, and both had won their education by their own exertions. Both had thought first of school-teaching (Meighen had changed course whilst at the university) and taken to law later. Both had gone to western Canada to make their careers, Bennett to Calgary, Meighen to Portage la Prairie. Both had wide-ranging minds and great lucidity in expression. Both were instinctive Conservatives and had never been otherwise. But there the resemblances end.

Bennett was in contact with Meighen all his political life, and their relationship underwent various modifications, but there is no doubt that Bennett at the start regarded, rightly, Meighen as his most dangerous competitor for advancement within the party. Borden was the established leader; no one would dream of challenging him in that position. But of the younger men anyone surveying the party after the 1911 victory would have named Meighen and Bennett as the two most likely to succeed.

In Canadian politics this century Meighen has remained unrivalled in debate, in his command of the English language and in his ability to use it as it should be used. He had great assurance and great ambition. Quiet, on the whole withdrawn, austere in his dress and personal habits, devoted to his wife and children; in these things he was the antithesis of Bennett. And, since his abilities were so easily apparent, he seemed destined, bar accidents, to lead Bennett throughout the whole of the race. In 1913 Meighen was given his first promotion, to the office of Solicitor-General. Bennett remained a backbencher.

Bennett began his life in Parliament despondent. In a letter to Max (now Sir Max) Aitken in London, written at the end of that year, 1911, he poured out his disillusionment:

"I am sick of it here (Ottawa). There is little or nothing to do and what there is to do is that of a party hack or departmental clerk or messenger. I will probably leave here. There must be more doing that counts than is at present apparent. I really cannot tell you what I think of the Government. I will do that later on when I have more adequately sized up the situation."

Then came his clashes with Meighen, and with Borden, over the Mackenzie and Mann railway enterprise. He was involved again in what he regarded as another railway scandal.

In *Life and Letters of Sir Wilfrid Laurier*, the late Dr. O. D. Skelton has this to say of the Canadian Northern Railway, in 1911 the most prominent of the Mackenzie and Mann undertakings:

"The Canadian Northern project was marked by the simplicity of all works of genius. It was merely to have the public build a trans-continental railway with all the usual steamship, express, hotel and land-company attachments, and yet to vest ownership wholly in two promoters who had put into it little but their ambition. Two Ontario boys who had gone from school-teaching and lumbering into railway contracting had discovered in the west their own capacities and the country's opportunities. William Mackenzie, master planner and financial wizard, Donald Mann, as forceful in rounding up a lobbyful of politicians as in driving a section gang, joined by Zebulon Lash, the subtlest framer of strictly legal clauses and financial expedients in Canada's annals, planned and worked for a score of years and saw a little hundred-mile Manitoba road, running from nowhere to nowhere, all but reach by 1914 to both oceans and ten thousand miles. . . . It was a project with more than the usual interweaving of good and evil in conception and execution. The planning was constructive, the strategy in the selection of routes in the early years admirable, the services rendered the prairie country of immense value. The financing was radically unsound in its lack of share capital to tide over a waiting time. The reliance upon the public Treasury for guarantees, subsidies, loans, brought into Canadian politics the most corrupting single factor since in Confederation times. . . . No little of the decline of the Liberal Party from its original ideals, no little of its overthrow in 1911, no little of the demoralization of the Borden Cabinet, no little of the Union movement in 1917, can be traced directly to the manœuvres and exigencies of Mackenzie and Mann or of those who saw gain in their profit or in their emergencies."

'Zebulon Lash': Surely no sane investor would trust a man with a name like that? Even Charles Dickens would have shrunk from pinning it on any character, however minor.

It was a fabulous period. My first recollection of even the name 'Canada' is from the promotional literature freely handed out by the Grand Trunk Company from its booth in a Liverpool Exhibition about the year 1910, as a result of which I immediately entered their competition to choose a name for the town which is now Prince Rupert. I forget what the prize was; probably a town-site at some undisclosed and inaccessible location in northern British Columbia. Today, with hindsight, we may well wish that Daimler and Diesel had been born before Trevithick and Stephenson.

But of all the promoters of railways, Mackenzie and Mann were outstanding in their particular field, the extraction of money, credit and land from governments. Fifty years afterwards it is possible, with the aid of the immense labours of Colonel G. R. Stevens, in his history of the Canadian National Railway, to piece together a coherent account of their activities. In 1911 it was considerably more difficult.

Bennett undertook it. It can hardly be described wholly as a labour of love. Although his formal retainer from the C.P.R. had ended when he entered Parliament, he had worked with and for that company for all his professional life in the west, and he naturally regarded the activities and methods of Mackenzie and Mann with suspicion. But added to that was the fact that Clifford Sifton had played some part in the earliest days of Mackenzie and Mann in Manitoba, and now Meighen, from the same province, had become their principal protagonist on the Government side. Suspicion was piled on suspicion.

He made his major attack in the 1914 Session. On May 13th Borden moved a lengthy financial resolution, drafted by Meighen, intended to approve the terms of the agreement made by the Government with the Canadian Northern, and he had been followed in the debate by Meighen. Bennett began to speak on the following afternoon. He was still speaking when the House adjourned at 6 p.m.; he resumed at 8 p.m. and he spoke for some four and a half hours in all. It was one of the major speeches of his public life to that point, to be compared with his speech four years before in the Alberta Assembly on the Alberta and Great Waterways Railway.

He began with an explanation of why he was opposing his own party leaders on the resolution. No one party could claim to be better than the other, he said, and he added, with a touch of sincerity that won some response:

> "I am not concerned about the argument of how much better we are doing than someone else did. The argument that I am holier than thou is getting rather played out, if I may use a common expression."

He then turned to the history of Mackenzie and Mann, which he knew as intimately as Meighen. Before 1907, he said, they had been a firm of railway contractors, operating in Manitoba in a small way, and their first bid had been for the proposed Hudson Bay Railway. But then there had been grants of land in the fertile areas of Saskatchewan:

> "That is the reason the Canadian Northern emerged from the position it then occupied, of a short road running from nowhere to nowhere . . . into a road stretching out, branching out, reaching out, extending, if you will, ultimately to Edmonton. . . ."

and from there he moved into his main attack:

> "I appeal to every man in this House and say that if he will take the time to read the history of the operations of Mackenzie and Mann from that time till now, he will find nothing but a long trail of parliamentary corruption, of lobbying, of degradation of parliamentary institutions, of the lowering of the morale of public life. . . . Both sides of the House have been to blame. Look to the statute books for the aid that has been given to this Company. Just a few days before a General Election, one party proposes and the other acquiesces. They are bound to ask a few questions in order that the contributions to party funds may be large enough. Let us look the business squarely in the face."

The C.P.R. and the Grand Trunk companies, he went on,

were public companies in which the public had made the investment. But:

"These two men conceived the ambition of having the people of Canada build a transcontinental system which they would control and own."

He then made his own apology for the past:

"Last year and the year before we were induced to grant extensive aid . . . to this Canadian Northern system. I voted for it on a statement of facts that, I am bound to say, I did not believe . . . which was presented to me as being true, which I did not believe to be true . . . I failed in my duty as a member of this House last year. . . . but I am not going to fail again."

Then Bennett settled down to display his immense capacity for the absorption of facts and for their orderly arrangement in presentation before a court. First he surveyed the Canadian Northern system as he knew it, with some deadly asides:

". . . last year I journeyed especially to look at certain parts of the line (in British Columbia) and I know that certain parts of it between Kamloops and Vancouver along the Fraser River that do not slip into the river in the spring manage to get there in the fall. It will require an enormous expenditure of money in the building of retaining walls to bring portions of that road to a proper state of efficiency."

He dealt with the extraordinary convolutions of the Mackenzie and Mann financial empire, and described how and why every separate form of property had a separate corporate structure. It made borrowing easier, it made financial manipulation easier. He instanced the creation of separate companies to own the new terminal in the centre of Montreal. He explained the operations of the Imperial Rolling Stock Company, and of the share transactions between the Canadian Northern and its affiliated land company, Canadian Northern Prairie Lands, both controlled by Mackenzie and Mann. Finally, he came to the substance of the resolution.

It was, he said, a proposal to relieve Mackenzie and Mann of the need to pay their own debts. They were the main contractors for the building of the roads. The Canadian Northern could no longer pay the bills presented by the Mackenzie and Mann construction organization. In those circumstances, rather than face any loss themselves, Mackenzie and Mann came to the people of Canada and asked them to give the railway company money to pay Mackenzie and Mann the contractors.

"Either there is a contract to build this road or there is not. If there is a contract, let us call upon the contractors to finish their work, and if they cannot finish their work let us take an assignment of their assets as security for the money we shall advance."

And later:

"My whole argument is that these men have assets, that they will not use their assets, and that they want us to pay their debts for them."

Bennett's speech was not directly aimed at Meighen, but it was intended to sting him, amongst others, and it did. Towards the end of his speech he asked that Meighen, in his capacity as Solicitor-General, should inquire into the whole affair, and he promised to accept the result. But he could not conceal his hostility towards Meighen the individual. His first response to an interruption by Meighen was comparatively mild:

"I am glad to see that the Solicitor-General has become the advocate of these two men. Before I finish he will regret that he has become their apologist."

But as the evening wore on, as he became more and more convinced that the main purpose of Meighen's interventions was to break his stride, his final reply was sharp:

"I will not be diverted from my argument by the impertinent interruptions of this young man."

Bennett's attack did not, of course, defeat the transaction. The Bill was duly passed by both Commons and Senate. The Canadian Northern sank still further into disaster, as did its rival, the Grand Trunk system, and during the lifetime of that same Parliament the Canadian Northern was to appear again

as a suppliant for relief, once in 1916, with a straight request
for a further loan, and again the following year, when it was
finally bought out by the State. But Bennett did not again
attack the Mackenzie and Mann System with the passion he
had displayed in 1914. In the 1916 debate, on May 15th, he said:

> "I have had my say as to that, and I am reminded of the
> words of a very great exponent of principle who said: 'Not
> Heaven itself can change the past. What has been, has been.'
> And he closed with these words: 'And I have had my day.'
> That may be true also."

A very revealing comment.

The Mackenzie and Mann debates are important to an
understanding of Bennett both in themselves and because of the
light they throw on his relations with those around him.

Bennett in Parliament at Ottawa is first a man in despondency.
Nothing goes as he thought it should. He is given little or no
recognition, and he is in no mood to fight back. When he is
made a member of the House Committee set up to study the
possibility of introducing closure rules into the Commons for
the first time, he leaves Meighen to do most of the work, and
earn the glory, or discredit, that came from it.

For the next two years he is uncertain and vacillating. In
1912 he visits Britain and speaks in Max Aitken's constituency.
Should he cross over to British politics and attach himself to
Aitken's political star? An oil boom in Calgary adds to his
commercial ventures. Perhaps his real place is in business and
finance? Again, Meighen is neither invulnerable nor immortal.
Should he find and adopt the proper humility of a back-bencher
and look to loyal industry to bring its due reward? He found no
complete satisfaction in any of these roles.

Then came his attack on the Canadian Northern in May,
1914, an attack not only on the promoters, but directly on
Borden, who had moved the resolution and who was bound to
accept full responsibility for it. His mood may have been
desperation, but his judgment in chosing the issue on which
to revolt shows through. Only two Conservative members
opposed the 1914 agreement with the Mackenzie and Mann
System; Bennett was one of them. Hindsight would say he was

right—that the sooner Canada got that system off its back the better.

The scene changed with the outbreak of war. Some of Bennett's energies were thrown into work with the Canadian Red Cross. The pressures on Borden led him to push more quickly to the back of his mind Bennett's maverick qualities where railways were concerned. In 1915 Borden asked Bennett to go with him on his mission to Britain (he obviously had Bennett's friendship with Aitken in mind), and the following year he made him head of the National Service Board that he set up as an alternative to conscription. It was a thankless task and, probably from the start, one known to be fruitless, but it was some political recognition. Certainly Bennett threw himself into the effort with all his energy.

But the railway debates also illustrate a vital difference between Meighen and Bennett. All his political life Meighen had a curious insensitivity to the effect of his actions on others. He was competent, forceful, and ambitious and he knew, rightly, that in the ruthless and realistic world of politics men are judged and used on the basis of their practical value to their Party and their political leaders. Yet it is remarkable how many dangerous and politically damaging missions the party found for Meighen during the years between 1911 and 1917, and how obediently he accepted them all.

He devised and carried through the closure rules that were introduced into the Canadian Commons for the first time in April, 1913. He did almost all the work in the Committee and plotted out the strategy by which the rules were carried in the House. After that, to Liberals, he was the man branded with that black mark. He carried the Canadian Northern agreement through the Commons the following year. As Solicitor-General it was not his departmental responsibility, but he shouldered the burden, and again he made political enemies as a result. In 1917 he introduced the Military Service Bill and the Wartime Elections Bill, and was one of their main defenders in the attacks made on them in the Commons; in Liberals' eyes, that was the deepest mark on his record. In all these things Meighen was doing his duty as he saw it, but the simple discharge of duty is not a guarantee of success in politics.

There was one sense that Meighen never acquired—a gift Lloyd George had in the highest degree—the ability to be at once aware of the reactions of others, of how best to make the constant readjustments in speech and action that are needed to achieve the results for which one is striving. Bennett shared some of Meighen's weakness in this respect, but I believe that had he been in Meighen's shoes in the years between 1912 and 1917 he would have been far more aware than Meighen was of the likely consequences of the tasks his zeal led him to accept.

As Meighen climbed, Bennett sank. Under Borden, Meighen moved from ministry to ministry until he succeeded Borden as Prime Minister in July, 1920. In 1916 Bennett said he had had his day, and he may well have believed it. He had no need to reproach himself for the stands he had taken. Exasperation may have sparked off his original attack on Mackenzie and Mann, but in his view the system was bent on extracting public money from the Treasury without justification, and that was wrong. Certainly his stand required political courage. Any back-bencher must think more than twice before he challenges directly in public a major proposal of his chief, the Prime Minister. He must be very sure of his motives and of his judgment.

Bennett did not choose to stand again as a candidate for Calgary West in the 1917 election that December. His work with the National Service Board ended in the September with the passing of the Conscription Act. The Siftons were moving in on Ottawa again, and that he found hard to stomach. Clifford had played a considerable part in the creation of the new Unionist Government and Arthur had been offered the Cabinet post of Minister of Customs if he surrendered the Premiership of Alberta; it was an offer he was quite prepared to accept. Furthermore, Bennett believed that he had been offered by Borden appointment to the Senate, and that he was pre-pared to accept.

This is still a very obscure episode in his career. On June 8th, 1917, Bennett wrote to Max Aitken:

"My present intention is to retire from the House of Commons at the next election and to be appointed to the

Senate. I desire after the war, to visit the Dominions Overseas and other sections of the British Empire. I do not
desire to be entirely dissociated with the public life of my
own country ... perhaps the Canadian Senate may offer me
a medium through which to express independent opinions
that would be denied me as a Party man in the House of
Commons."

(Aitken's reply was to advise him that it would be more
sensible to become the Lieutenant-Governor of Alberta or New
Brunswick, because it would be easier to retire from such an
office after a reasonable length of time than to quit the Senate.)
Aitken (by then Lord Beaverbrook), in his story of his relations
with Bennett, *Friends*, continues:

"He had asked for a Senatorship and he was convinced
that Borden had agreed. When the Prime Minister denied
he had given any promise, Bennett was outraged. He wrote
a minatory letter, setting forth the time and place when and
where the promise was made. But Borden persisted in his
refusal to send Bennett to the Senate.

"Borden's rejection was fortunate, for a place in the Upper
House would have damaged Bennett's political career.

"The episode is curious. Borden was truthful and upright.
Bennett was honest and sincere. The only explanation was
that there had been a misunderstanding. But Bennett would
not accept any such interpretation. For several years he
persisted in his complaint, and he never forgot his grievance
against Borden."

Alice Millar, who became Bennett's secretary about that time
and who stayed with him for the rest of his life, remembers the
letters that passed between Bennett and Borden very well, and
that he later lent them to someone and they were never returned.
As she recalls them, the occasion on which Bennett was convinced Borden had offered him a Senatorship had been during
the visit the two men had made to England and France in
1915.
It is fortunate that the appointment was never made.

Chapter Seven

THE END OF THE PARTNERSHIP

B Y early 1918, Bennett was back in Calgary, and for him the three years that followed were relatively stagnant. Financially, he had no real concern. Over the years 1919 to 1924 his gross annual income ranged between $60,000 and $75,000, and income tax, first introduced into Canada as a wartime measure, was still more an irritant than a burden. But he was out of the Commons by his own choice and he was out of the Senate by, so he believed, something close to a breach of faith on the part of the Prime Minister. Politically, he seemed at a dead end. He had come to Ottawa, he had not conquered, and now he was back in Calgary.

His personal affairs were equally out of joint. He suffered an attack of erysipelas, an exasperating matter for one so energetic. Of much more serious concern was the state of the Lougheed-Bennett partnership. Although his personal relations with Lougheed had long since been formal rather than intimate, they were still partners, and he was the partner with the major responsibility. He had had to leave the practice in the charge of others whilst he had been in Ottawa, and now on his return he found that they had done a number of things of which he strongly disapproved, particularly in the lending of partnership moneys without what he considered proper security. Things would have to be tightened up.

That would have been less of a burden if he had been sure what he wanted to do. He was almost fifty, an age when any decision was apt to determine what one would do with the rest of one's life. Was he to settle down again in Calgary, resolved to be the provincial lawyer and no more? Was he to make some fresh start, and if so at what? He deferred decision, but it was unsettling.

Some change began in 1920, at first remote. Borden resigned as Prime Minister, and Meighen succeeded him, and he was now on rather better terms with Meighen. In 1921, the barriers ahead seemed to be opening up, and there were lanes of open water to be seen. Jennie Shirreff (Jennie Eddy) died. Arthur Meighen pressed him to accept a Cabinet post in the Ministry he was reconstructing in anticipation of the forthcoming General Election.

Bennett's earlier friendship with Jennie Eddy had been renewed whilst he had been in Ottawa; it had never been entirely broken. It is unlikely that it had any romantic overtones; Beaverbrook, who had known all the parties concerned most of his life, denies that it had. She was ten years older than Bennett, a woman with an excellent head for business, a strong sense of duty, and deep and conventional religious convictions. After she inherited the controlling interest in the E. B. Eddy Company on her husband's death in 1906, she had kept a close eye on its activities as the largest match company in Canada, with an extensive production of wood pulp and paper as well. She had arranged for Bennett's election as a director of the company (one qualifying share only was needed for that, and one share was all she transferred to him). She had become a wealthy woman. In the last year of her life her income from her holding in the Eddy Company alone was $52,745. Bennett was interesting as a friend and valuable as a man of business. She was grateful for that.

Jennie Eddy died on August 9th, 1921. There was no market quotation for the 1507 common shares she held in the Company, and they were tentatively valued by her executors at $800 each, which gave her holding an estimated value of $1,205,600. From this holding she gave 1,007 shares to her brother, Joseph Thompson Shirreff, and the remaining 500 to Bennett. The rest of her estate consisted of cash and other securities of a total value of approximately $1,350,000. Succession duties in Quebec took some $775,000 and $185,000 was still due to Dalhousie University under an earlier covenant. She set up a trust fund to provide an income for her sister Edith and gave annuities to other relatives. Subject to those, the residue of her estate went to charity, $200,000 to McGill University and the rest mainly to various funds of the Presbyterian Church in Canada.

(The bulk of Bennett's interest in the E. B. Eddy Company came to him from the brother, Joseph Thompson Shirreff. He lived another five years, dying in May, 1926, and his holding of Eddy shares—1,007 from his sister, one a qualifying share— made up the bulk of his estate. He bequeathed the shares to Bennett and by then their estimated value had risen to $1,500 a share.)

This inheritance translated Bennett from the ranks of the relatively wealthy to those of the very rich. For the first five years after Jennie Eddy's death, he accepted from the executors an annual payment of $7,500, the estate retaining all dividends paid by the Company. The shares were only finally transferred to him after the death of Joseph, but by 1929, the year of his largest income, his dividend income from the company was $181,000. His total income rose from $76,000 in 1924 to $150,000 in 1928. In that year his earned income was $25,827, made up of $12,500 from the law practice of Bennett, Hannah and Sanford in Calgary (the successors to Lougheed and Bennett), his sessional indemnity as a Member of Parliament of $4,000, and $9, 327, his allowance as Leader of the Opposi- tion (he had resigned all his former directorships of public companies on becoming party leader), and his income from dividends and interest accounted for the rest. 1929 was excep- tional; his gross income totalling $269,985. From that year it fell, with the depression, to about half that figure, rising gradually to $201,578 in 1936. His gross income whilst Prime Minister was never less than $150,000 a year. It is argu- able that he would have been happier and more successful, cer- tainly as a politician, if he had not acquired this second fortune, but it certainly made a considerable change to his circumstances.

The sudden prospect of a return to active political life was another matter altogether. At first, Bennett professed a certain reluctance to accept office. He told Beaverbrook that Meighen had made him various offers, all of which he declined, and that the offer of the Ministry of Justice was the last, and couched in terms which compelled him to accept. Certainly he did accept, joining Meighen's reconstructed Ministry on September 21st, 1921, and it is hard to believe that he did not feel some exhilaration at the thought of taking office for the first time. After all, politics had been his first love. But, willing or reluctant, Fate had not finished with him; hardly had this cup been raised to his lips than it was drawn away. He had neglected his fences in Calgary West. When the election came in the December his hold on that seat proved to be so precarious as to be non-existent.

On the night of the election, and at the official count eight days later, he thought he had just scraped home. The returning officer gave these figures on December 14th, 1921:

Bennett (Con.)	.	.	. 7372
Shaw (Labour)	.	.	. 7366
Ryan (Liberal)	.	.	. 1354

But with such a close result it was inevitable that Shaw should apply to the District Court of the Province for a recount. On December 23rd District Court Judge Winter certified the result as:

Shaw .	.	.	. 7369
Bennett	.	.	. 7353
Ryan	.	.	. 1351

and his scrutiny brought to light some interesting variations from the standard procedure of "making a cross with a black lead pencil" laid down by the Dominion Elections Act:

23 ballots marked in ink, 18 for Bennett, 5 for Shaw.
9 ballots marked with a coloured pencil, 5 for Bennett and 4 for Shaw, and
29 ballots marked with the figure '1' instead of a cross, 20 for Bennett and 9 for Shaw.

In addition one lady, a Mrs. Laird, admitted that she had voted twice, for Shaw (Shaw readily conceded that additional vote). In short, had all the rejected ballots been admitted, Bennett would have made a net gain of twenty-five votes and his majority over Shaw (allowing for Mrs. Laird's duplicity) would have been ten votes, disappointing when viewed dispassionately, but, after the three weeks of dispute and debate in Calgary, a very welcome victory.

Bennett was no more disposed to accept Judge Winter's ruling than Shaw had been to accept the first count and he presented his petition to the Supreme Court of Alberta, where it was heard by Stuart and Ives, J.J. They refused to overrule Judge Winter, and held that Shaw had won the seat by a majority of sixteen votes. From there Bennett appealed to the Supreme Court of Canada. The appeal was heard in Ottawa the following June and the judgment of the Court was handed down on June 17th, 1922. The five judges sitting were unanimous. The appeal was dismissed, and Shaw was confirmed as member for Calgary West.

Worse was to follow. The following month, in London, on an appeal to the Privy Council, he received a series of cables from Lougheed, culminating with one that reached him on July 29th ending with the words ". . . no other alternative now remains than dissolution, of which this is notice". The repercussions that followed have remained vividly imprinted on the minds of all Calgary lawyers alive at the time.

Bennett had not placed too much hope in the success of his own appeal to the Supreme Court. He was too good a lawyer to overrate his chances, in the face of the explicit words of the statute and the unanimous decisions against him in the Alberta Courts. According to J. C. Brokovski, one of his partners (or associates) in the Lougheed, Bennett firm (as sworn by Brokovski later), in the May of that year Bennett had talked to him of ending his connection with the Lougheed, Bennett firm, and perhaps with both law and Canada as well, at the end of the year. It is easy to understand that reaction and to sympathize with it. With his defeat the previous year he seemed to have lost his last chance of making his mark in the political world; even the electors in his own city had rejected him. Politicians always tell themselves that they expect no thanks for all they do, but a defeat remains a bitter and humiliating experience for all that, especially one brought about by technicalities. At the same time, he knew that with the death of Jennie Eddy he had become a very wealthy man. Was there any real need to continue knocking on the door of indifferent Fortune?

Alice Millar, Bennett's lifelong and devoted secretary, believes that Bennett was not prepared to make a firm decision

at that time. He had promised to take an appeal to the Privy
Council for the widow of an old Calgary friend, Dr. W. J.
Chambers, who had been killed in a train wreck on the C.P.R.
in Western Ontario. It was an important appeal for the family
and in relation to the general principles of assessment of
damages in cases such as these. Chambers had been a very
successful ear, nose and throat specialist in Calgary, aged
forty-six when killed, and with an income, in the last year of his
life, of some $18,000. The trial judge had awarded his family
$80,000 damages, but the Appellate Division had cut the
damages down to $40,000 (the Privy Council finally made
the figures $57,000). The cause was in the list for hearing at the
end of June and he sailed for England immediately the Supreme
Court decision on his own election appeal was handed down.
But before he left Ottawa he had a general discussion with
Lougheed, on June 10th and 11th, over the future of their
partnership, and of the firm.

To Bennett it was theirs alone. The original 1897 partnership had been extended indefinitely from year to year. The
division of the annual income had varied, but the capital
assets of the partnership were, in his view, still held only by
them, in equal shares. They had talked about a dissolution of
partnership before, but had never formally severed their
relationship, and Bennett was reluctant to see any such final
step taken. As he understood his conversations with Lougheed
in Ottawa, they had agreed that any further talks—certainly
any decision—should be deferred until his return in the fall.
After the Privy Council appeal, Bennett planned to spend some
time in England and on the Continent. He did not intend to be
back in Calgary before October. Lougheed's cables to him,
therefore, were not only a complete surprise. They seemed like
a stab in the back.

In Calgary a good deal had been happening. The other men
(partners or associates) sharing in the profits of the firm were
Macleod Sinclair, K.C., second string as counsel in the firm,
J. C. Brokovski, Alexander Hannah, specialist in company
law, D. Lee Redman, P. L. Sanford and Orrin Might. In the
background was William H. McLaws, a lawyer who had been
with the firm as a student, who had remained after his admis-

sion in 1897 and who had left, under something of a cloud, in Bennett's view, in 1918. Since then McLaws had been in business, but there were indications that he was anxious to return to the practice of law. Brokovski and Hannah both went on vacation early in July—Hannah to visit his native Scotland.

Early in the July Lougheed returned to Calgary and Bennett's view of what followed had, naturally, a certain black-and-white clarity. It was McLaws, he believed, who had conceived the plan to break up the Lougheed-Bennett relationship, his intention being that he should then join Lougheed as a partner and that the new partnership should take with them some of the junior partners in the old firm (those they chose from amongst those who would be willing to leave Bennett) and such clients as would follow them. To persuade Lougheed to agree to this drastic step—and at a time when Bennett was out of the country—McLaws had, so Bennett came to believe, used these arguments: The first was that this would merely be an anticipation of something that was inevitable, in that all the signs were that Bennett intended to quit the law and probably leave Canada for good and settle in England. The second was that Lougheed's son, Edgar, had just graduated in law from Dalhousie University and that here was an excellent opportunity to establish his future in Calgary. The third was that, if Lougheed took action to dissolve the partnership now, he would escape compulsion to pay to Bennett the considerable sum for goodwill that Bennett's interest in an established practice of that size and repute would be worth. If the partnership were dissolved, and a sizeable section of its clients took their business to the new firm, then obviously the value of Bennett's interest in the goodwill of the old firm would be so much the less.

That was Bennett's reconstruction of events, made when he returned, and set forth in the pleading he delivered in the subsequent action. Certainly Lougheed was in Calgary in July. Certainly he did take time to call on certain of the more influential clients of the firm. The first to agree to dissolution may have been Sinclair, who immediately afterwards joined the new association between Lougheed and McLaws, but

D

Lougheed's own cable showed that he, too, was not only prepared to see the old partnership dissolved but was also prepared to take the first step himself. And certainly the partners in the new firm of Lougheed, McLaws, Sinclair and Redman were ready to open for business on August 1st, and had already decided whom among the juniors they wished to employ. The next step followed at once. On August 7th, 1922, Lougheed issued a statement of claim in a partnership action, with himself as sole plaintiff and naming all the others, including McLaws, as defendants and as partners in the former firm. In fact, he claimed that there were three partnerships in existence, Lougheed and Bennett, Lougheed, Bennett, McLaws and Company, and Lougheed, Bennett and Company. The statement of claim asked for a declaration that each of these partnerships was dissolved, and the fourth item in the prayer asked for the appointment of a receiver of the partnership assets. Before Bennett could be served with the statement of claim, Lougheed obtained an order *ex parte* appointing the Trusts and Guaranty Company (now the Crown Trust Company) receiver.

These proceedings left those who would (and later did) support Bennett leaderless. Sinclair and Redman were the only two who were, as events showed, anxious to join Lougheed and McLaws. The others in Calgary had perforce to stay where they were (or, if fired, find temporary employment elsewhere) until Bennett's return. But the new partners made one tactical mistake. Although they had obtained from the Court an order appointing a receiver of all the partnership assets, they themselves remained in possession of at least some of them, those which were of immediate use in continuing the business. They continued to occupy the offices in the Clarence Block, and to use the books, desks and equipment that were the property of the Lougheed and Bennett firm.

Bennett sailed for Canada on August 10th and arrived in Calgary on the 24th. If the dissidents had imagined that he would come storming up to the Clarence Block demanding immediate explanations, they were underrating their opponent. Bennett was too shrewd a tactician. He went to his suite in the Palliser and sent for his allies, Alice Millar, and his friend, George Robinson. Both had been exceedingly active on his behalf in the interval before his return. George Robinson had already secured new offices on the sixth floor of the Lancaster Building (in which the Bennett firm was to remain until 1959) and, since his own office was on the same floor of the Clarence Block as the former firm, at that proximity he had heard every story and every rumour several times over. Having been informed of the local tactics and situation, Bennett sent for Horace Howard, General Manager in Calgary of the Trusts and Guaranty Company, the receiver already appointed by the Court. The substance of their conversation was as follows:

"Horace," Bennett said, "I hear you've been appointed receiver of all the assets of the partnership?"

"That's right, R.B."

"Well, then, get on with it. Carry out your duties. Take the assets into your possession. You're responsible. Get them under your lock and key now. Everything, and at once."

And Horace Howard had no alternative but to comply. That was what he must do if the order was to be taken at its face value. So for three days the offices in the Clarence Block were systematically stripped of every item of partnership property they contained, down to paper-fasteners, and every item removed was thereafter securely locked and guarded on the attic floor in the Southam Building, two blocks away. Clients' papers might be released to any of those involved in the partnership action on the client's own written authority. Otherwise everything stayed under the eye of a rather grim woman caretaker until such time as a further order of the Court should release it. Bennett's anger did not abate. After the partnership property had been taken away and stored, he sent for Howard and asked him if everything had gone.

"Yes, R.B.," Howard replied. "Everything except some drapes on the windows that weren't worth taking down."

"You're wrong," Bennett replied. "The brass plate, Lougheed and Bennett, is still outside. Take that down too."

Howard's recollection is that it was down and stored away within ten minutes.

With Bennett's return to the practice of law in Calgary those involved were able to declare their allegiances. On the one side was the firm of Lougheed, McLaws, Sinclair and

Redman, on the other Bennett, Hannah and Sanford, with whom were associated Might, Nolan and Chambers. The clients of the former firm made their choices (Bennett declined to make any approach to the Bank of Montreal; it had been a client of Lougheed in 1897, he said, and a client of Lougheed it should remain). And Bennett settled down to draft his statement of defence in the action of *Lougheed, Redman,* v. *Bennett et al.* It was delivered on December 30th, 1922.

It is still on the Court files in Calgary, and after so long it is a curious, almost pathetic, document to read. It is not a well-drafted pleading, by legal standards. In it Bennett ignored a great many of the rules governing what a pleading should contain, and the language in which it should be expressed: he inserted one paragraph, No. 46, twenty-two typed pages long, which is the whole story of the partnership, evidence, comment and a certain amount of vituperation thrown in as well. Characteristically, it displays the two sides of Bennett, inconsistent and yet equally sincere.

He was bitterly hurt by the action. A month after he had left Canada for England, believing that by agreement all vital decisions would be deferred until his return, a man with whom he had been in partnership for twenty-five years had tried to seize the whole of the law practice they had built together (Brokovski, in his defence, made that allegation in that blunt way). He could believe quite sincerely that no gentleman, no member of the Privy Council, no man holding the office of King's Counsel, would stoop to such behaviour, and in Paragraph 46 he said so, as explicitly as he could.

But, while lawyers, and gentlemen, may trade insults in drawing-rooms, in clubs, and even in Court, they are not supposed to do so in pleadings. Bennett knew that any judge would most certainly order paragraphs 45 and 46 of his statement of defence to be struck out if the other side applied for that, and Mr. Justice Ives did exactly that, on Lougheed's application, later in 1923. But the defence set out in detail all that he felt. It said it more promptly than any trial could, and he can hardly have been unaware that its whole contents would be given the widest publicity once it was filed. He had been hurt, he was out to retaliate, and he did.

The fact remains that Lougheed, McLaws and Sinclair started the ruckus, and, whatever their reasons for acting as they did—and no one could possibly doubt that Bennett was at times an overbearing partner—they misjudged him badly when they chose their course of action. Nothing they could have done could have been better calculated to bring Bennett back to Calgary at once, and in a mood to devote his enormous energy to a contest to outfight and outwit them. It is hard to believe that he had made an irrevocable decision to settle in England when he sailed for his Privy Council appeal in the June, but if he had, Lougheed's cable destroyed the idea in an instant. The gage had been thrown down in a way that made it impossible, for him, to refute the challenge.

The dispute was not settled while Senator Lougheed lived; he died three years later. Bennett never set foot in the Clarence Block office again, nor would he deal personally with his former partners. The Senator made one attempt at a reconciliation. He sent word that he would like to see Bennett, and an appointment was arranged. They met, and talked, but Bennett was still adamant. He told Alice Millar to sit near the door and leave it open, and she remembers the quiet voice of Lougheed saying: "If that's how you see it . . ." That was how he did see it, yet it is typical of his complex character that she also remembers how disturbed he was that evening to be told that the elevator operator in the building had gone off duty and that Lougheed had had to walk down the six flights of stairs.

The partnership action dragged on, proceeding in fits and starts, as juniors were prodded into action by seniors, with the papers and records, even the office furniture, of the former partners, under lock and key. The individual partners in the former partnership had their own claims one against the other. Might, for instance, entitled to a share in the profits, had been dismissed on ten minutes' notice. What was his claim for damages worth in dollars and cents? They were able to reach a settlement; all claims of that kind were finally abandoned, and, when Lougheed died, all that remained to be settled were some claims by and against the former partnership, the ownership of the forty-six shares in the *Albertan*, and the disposition of the chairs and desks Lougheed and Bennett had once used.

After his father's death, Clarence Lougheed sent word to Bennett through Horace Howard that he would like to settle matters if he could, and in the end they were. Bennett undertook responsibility for the outstanding claims against the old firm. He took the library and the *Albertan* shares, and the receivership ended.

The Senator was not so unyielding. It is said in Calgary that the results of the 1925 election were coming in while he lay very near death. He asked his secretary who was in the room how Bennett was doing, and the secretary told him that Bennett was in, that his opponent had conceded. "Isn't that fine," the Senator replied. A week later he was dead.

PART TWO

PART TWO

Chapter Eight

CUSTOMS AND CONSTITUTIONS

I F the reader has borne with this narrative to this point, he may well have come to the conclusion that the man under review was at best a second-class politician, never destined to succeed in his childish ambition to head his country's government, perhaps a little unusually unlucky in his political life, but a man very like scores of others whose names are listed in *Who Was Who* and who are quite forgotten even before they are dead, and I think anyone with that impression has a good deal of justification for holding it.

In 1925, Bennett was fifty-five. By good fortune as well as good management, he was a very wealthy man, without care or responsibility, able to please himself almost without restriction in where he lived and what he did. Forty years had passed since he had left Hopewell Cape for Normal School in Fredericton, New Brunswick, and he seemed to have changed completely from that shy and in some ways uncertain young man.

In business and in his profession he had been remarkably successful. In contrast, in politics he had been a rather outstanding failure. He had spent six years in the Commons under the shrewd eye of Sir Robert Borden and had got nowhere. He had been given a second chance by Arthur Meighen and he had not even been able to win back his old seat in his own city. In his political philosophy, he had no claims to any originality; on the contrary, he seemed to cling to a conception of 'Empire' that was quite outmoded. He did not really belong to the changing post-war world. If he were sensible, a candid friend might have told him, he would be content with what the gods had given him and settle down to enjoy all his money could buy—comfort, travel, society, respect, but not responsiblity. In short, Bennett seemed to be through.

And yet five years later he was Prime Minister of Canada, head of a Conservative Administration put into office with an absolute majority in the House of Commons by the popular vote of all adult Canadians.

Was the record of his first fifty-five years totally deceiving, or was he still a political misfit, given this unmerited success by no more than a sheer fluke? Had his talents always been adequate for this supremacy? Had there been some change in his life at that time which in some miraculous way enabled him to reverse the course of his fortunes and gain the lead in what might be called the last temporal lap of his life?

As is commonly the case with human beings, it would be dangerous to suggest that questions such as these can be answered by a plain 'Yes' or 'No', but I do suggest that a decisive factor in what happened thereafter was the dissolution of the Lougheed-Bennett partnership.

Lougheed's actions, above all their method and timing, must have come as a very sharp shock to Bennett, and he needed such a shock if he was to make any really effective public use of the rest of his life. Until that cable reached him in London, he had been in a defeatist mood, one increased by the finality of the Supreme Court decision over his election appeal, but possibly one beginning to mellow into acceptance under the influence of London in summer and the prospect of exchanging Calgary and a suite in the Palliser Hotel for an English country house and English country house society.

It had been a very near thing. If nine voters in Calgary West the year before had switched their votes from Shaw to Bennett, if twenty-five of his supporters had used the official pencil to make the official cross on their ballot papers, if Lougheed, or McLaws, or both, had been content to wait until the October, the story would have been very different. Elected as an M.P., as a former Minister sure of his position in the inner councils of the party, he might willingly have left Calgary, and the law, early in 1922, to be content with the role of an elder statesman. Defeated but treated with frankness by Lougheed and Sinclair, he might have looked at England that summer with far more positive intentions, and perhaps have left Canada for England seventeen years before he did. One of the fascinations of Bennett's life is how often, and to what extent, his future was determined by a hair's breadth of chance. Lougheed reawoke, with extreme violence, his instinct to fight back, and once he had begun to fight he found that he still liked it.

That is my explanation of the energy he put into everything he tackled after his return to Calgary in August, 1922, into his work for the new partnership of Bennett, Hannah and Sanford, into the effort needed to make quite sure that he would recapture Calgary West when the time came to try again. It no longer mattered that he had money enough to be idle. He discovered that his ambitions had been dormant, not dead.

The years between 1922 and 1925 were perhaps the most satisfying in his professional life. He now had partners in whom he had complete confidence, and to whom he felt a corresponding sense of gratitude, and all his life he had an urge to help in every way those whom he regarded as his friends. He was extremely busy. The fields of law that attracted him, and in which in consequence his abilities shone, were banking and constitutional problems, and he fought a number of such cases, if need be to the Supreme Court of Canada. And now he had in Alice Millar a secretary who met his needs perfectly.

She had joined the firm during the war years as a stenographer, but Bennett soon saw in her the personal assistant he needed. She was devoted to him, and his affairs were her main interest throughout his life. She was able and completely trustworthy. He could leave in her care the details of any matter of business, professional or otherwise, with confidence that nothing would be either overlooked or neglected. At the same time she was a cushion between him and the rest of the world, and the demands of his time and energy that could have swamped him had they been left to descend on him unchecked.

But she never allowed herself to become partisan; she had too much sense of justice and too much sense of humour. Once while Bennett was away from the Calgary office one of his students, with more energy than discretion, made a spring-cleaning of some of the old papers in the office library. On the morning of Bennett's return—he could be a very early arrival there, on occasion—she intercepted the young man as he came into the office.

"Get out," she said in an urgent whisper. "Go away. Take a day off. Do anything, but for Heavens' sake don't let him see you."

The young man was startled.

"What on earth's the matter?"

"Haven't you been tidying up?"

He nodded.

"Well", she went on. "You threw a pile of old speeches into the garbage too, and he's spotted that already."

Alice Millar understood him as well as his sister Mildred did.

One day in Ottawa, after he was Prime Minister, Mildred came into his suite in the Château Laurier after a shopping expedition and incautiously told her brother that she had bought a new hat, and how much it had cost. It provoked one of his sudden bursts of temper, to which Mildred listened patiently. After he had gone, she turned to Alice Millar and said:

"Millar [she always used her surname], don't ever walk out on Dick. We're the bumpers on his car. We save him a lot of damage."

The date set for the 1925 General Election was October 29th, and when the day ended Bennett had reversed his failure in 1921 and was once more member for Calgary West, without fear of any recount. He had polled 10,256 votes to the 6,040 cast for his nearest opponent, and he was never defeated again in that riding.

When he had left the House eight years before, his leader, Sir Robert Borden, had already formed his union Government and was to fight the election of that year, 1917, on the conscription issue. He faced a divided Liberal Party, of which Sir Wilfrid Laurier was still the leader, but which had suffered some serious defections to the Union side. It was a bitter campaign; the Liberals said that the Conscription Act and Wartime Elections Act that accompanied it were devices designed to win an election, not a war. Sir Wilfrid himself, with a sharpness that was not entirely in character, wrote immediately afterwards:

"It has been my lot to run the whole gamut of prejudices in Canada. In 1896 I was excommunicated by the Roman priests, and in 1917 by Protestant parsons." When Bennett returned to Parliament Hill, his leader, Arthur Meighen, was ready and poised to strike down another Liberal Government, led by a very different man, W. L. Mackenzie King, his weapon being an accumulation of evidence of wholesale corruption in the Department of Customs and Excise.

Meighen had developed considerably as a politician in these eight years. He had sat in the House continuously for seventeen years, the last four in opposition, which suited his talents. His reputation in debate was of the highest. He was fluent and ruthless, brilliant in exposition, devastating in attack. He had always had a wide range of reading, particularly of Shakespeare and the classical English writers, and a wonderful command of language. He was consistent and fearless; he would defend his convictions on the need for some tariff for the protection of Canadian manufacturers to the farmers in his native Manitoba as unequivocably as he would proclaim his belief in the need for conscription to the habitants of Quebec. He preferred to meet any issue head-on.

Unfortunately for him, the defects that marched with his qualities remained. The solutions to problems that came from his own mind were not only right; they hardly required further argument, even amongst his colleagues. To him politics was a matter of intellectual persuasion, and if a problem could be broken down into its components and then presented in that form he tended to assume that acceptance of his solution would follow automatically.

Compromise did not appeal to him. Like the man in British politics whom he most resembled, Sir Edward Carson, Meighen was proof of the fact that the qualities that make a man an outstanding lawyer do not necessarily lead to comparable success in the political field.

Meighen enriched Canadian life by his ability, by the beauty and directness of his language, by the clarity of his mind, and by the depth of his principles, and by his sense of duty. But, measured against the single standard of political effectiveness, he was a failure. His first term as Prime Minister was not outstanding, and he twice led his party to defeat, on the second occasion having first allowed himself to be outwitted by his major opponent. His strength had tended to become rigidity, and a certain arrogance had crept into his estimates of his own powers.

Max Freedman, the Canadian journalist, wrote this in his appreciation of Meighen after Meighen's death in 1960:

"Mr. King feared Mr. Meighen, who felt nothing but contempt for his opponent. It apparently was no adequate compensation to Mr. King that he could defeat Mr. Meighen in an election. He could never remove from his mind the torment and shame of being inferior to Mr. Meighen in debate. When he heard during the Second World War that Mr. Meighen was seeking entry to the House of Commons through a by-election, he was in a panic. Nervous and frightened, Mr. King warned his friends that the election of Mr. Meighen would force an early crisis on conscription. Mr. Meighen always believed that he was defeated because the Liberal organizations, on orders from Mr. King, threw their support to his C.C.F. opponent. . . ."

King was a man of entirely different character. In 1925 he was far from being the able and experienced administrator that he later became, but even then the key to his character was his sense of personal mission. He, like Bennett, was a man with a personality moulded, or twisted, by his mother. On his mother's side, he was the grandson of the rebel, William Lyon Mackenzie, a failure. He was the son of an Ontario barrister, a man who, in his wife's eyes, was equally a failure. William, the son, had not only been driven to strive for success; he had been persuaded, with a certain amount of rather sanctimonious self-examination, that he was destined for success. Inevitably, he recalls to mind Disraeli's complaint about Gladstone: that he did not so much mind the old gentleman producing a fifth ace from his sleeve, but he did object to his assertion that God had placed it there.

A major characteristic of King was his power of concealment, concealment of his personality, of his ends and, so far as he was able, of the means he employed and intended to employ. Few people could like him; he provoked either respect or revulsion. Where Meighen by instinct strove for, and could by talent succeed in finding, the utmost clarity in his thought and words, King used speech to conceal himself from his audience. All politicians tend to become egoists; King became one of the most complete, and that characteristic was accompanied by what his opponents regarded as an immense capacity for self-deception. If anything advanced the career of King, it was to the benefit of the Liberal Party, and (later; not so strongly in 1925) what advanced the fortunes of the Liberal Party was equally clearly in the best interests of Canada as a whole.

The 1925 election left King in office, but dependent upon the support of the remaining Progressives for his power to stay there. His first act was to see the Governor-General, Lord Byng of Vimy, and attempt to clarify the terms on which he could hope to continue in office. What did transpire between the two men at that interview has been the subject of bitter argument ever since. Bruce Hutchison, in *The Incredible Canadian*, put his interpretation on what each understood as a result:

> "To King it meant that if he could get a majority in Parliament he was entitled to seek dissolution and another election when he pleased. If he could not govern, and only if he could not govern, he was obligated to make way for Meighen. To Byng the famous conversation meant that the Prime Minister had given a binding contract by which he must make way for Meighen at any time, without dissolution or election, if King once lost the confidence of Parliament."

Whatever the arrangement, however secure King felt he had made his ultimate line of retreat, he still faced the first session of the new Parliament with many other problems on his mind. First among them was the scandal boiling up around the Customs Ministry—one not made any easier to handle by the fact that he himself had been defeated in the election and had had to seek re-election elsewhere.

King was aware that the substance of the charges the Opposition would make against his Government would be that he had tolerated and condoned a state of corruption within that Department that had not been equalled in the history of the country, but he did not know, then, exactly how much the Conservatives had found out. He could claim in defence that, the previous September, he had rid his Cabinet of the Minister in direct control of the offending Department, Jacques Bureau, and replaced him by a younger man, with no record to live down, George Boivin, but even over that move he had compromised what principles others would have said he should have had. Bureau had not been sent into obscurity. He had been elevated to the Senate; he was not without some influence left in Quebec. King cannot have felt at ease when H. H. Stevens, Vancouver, later to be Bennett's Minister of Trade and Commerce, opened the debate on February 2nd, 1926, on an opposition motion of censure.

Meighen had chosen Harry Stevens to take charge of his Party's investigation into the scandals surrounding the Customs Department, and he had made an excellent choice. Stevens was then forty-eight, eight years younger than Bennett, and might be described as a professional politician if that description did not usually carry with it some derogatory implication. He had been born in Bristol, England, and brought to Ontario as a child at the age of nine. Three years later his family had moved to and settled in Vancouver. He had had little formal education, and his business activities were subordinated to his interest in public affairs. At thirty-three he had won a seat as Alderman on the Vancouver City Council, and the following year had secured the nomination as Conservative candidate for one of the Vancouver Federal ridings, mainly, it was said, because the other possible contenders for the nominations considered the position of the sitting Member to be so secure that they had not bothered to contest a nomination to fight what looked like a hopeless battle. The election came in 1911, the swing to the Conservatives carried Stevens to Ottawa, and there he remained undefeated until 1930.

Bennett knew him well; they had shared the same office in Parliament Hill after 1911 as new Members together. Stevens had a very thorough grasp of practical affairs and a great capacity for assembling and sifting facts. When they came to serve together on the Investigating Committee of the House they made a useful team. Bennett, with his experience of handling witnesses in Court, could hammer home the essential facts that Stevens' enquiries had unearthed.

This is not the place to attempt any survey of the details of the scandals themselves. They happened over thirty-five years ago, and now perhaps hindsight would compel anyone to accept that the combination of the factors then present, the prohibition of the manufacture and sale of alcoholic liquors in the United States, the existence of a source of unlimited supply of those liquors in Canada and the West Indies, the availability of centres of distribution in what might be called 'friendly neutral' zones in the Bahamas and the French islands of St. Pierre and Miguelon, off the coast of Newfoundland, together with the seagoing skill and experience of the coastal inhabitants of the continent, was bound to create both an illicit traffic in this commodity and corrupt some at least of the public officials charged with the duty of suppressing it. The charge against the Liberals in 1926 was not primarily based on their failure to anticipate and guard against that. It was based on the allegation that they had allowed the corruption to fester and spread, to creep upwards to Ottawa and into their own party ranks, and, knowing all that, had still failed to take action to cut themselves free from it. The poachers had not turned game-keepers. The gamekeepers had been dismissed and the poachers hired to replace them. That was the substance of the Conservative case.

Once Stevens had launched his onslaught, the detailed nature of the allegations made it impossible for the Government to take any other action than to move immediately for the appointment of a Select Committee of the House to investigate the charges. The Committee was appointed, consisting of four Conservative Members (Bennett and Stevens were two of them), four Liberal Members, with a Progressive, D. M. Kennedy, of Peace River, Alberta, as Chairman. It began an investigation that lasted five months. Its proceedings drained away much of the vitality of the House itself, but King (returned to the House in March as Member for Prince Albert,

Saskatchewan) at least contrived to gain some ground in the interim. He secured a vote of confidence at the conclusion of the debate on the Speech from the Throne of 111 to 102. He introduced a measure to set up an old age pension system for the first time (which the Conservatives in the Senate threw out). His Minister of Finance produced a Budget that, with its tax and tariffs cuts, would serve any party well in an early election, if one were to come, and he personally worsted Meighen in a debate on the results of the Imperial Conference of 1923. By the time the Customs Committee had finished its work, King's Government had been sustained by sixteen separate votes on matters of confidence. He had, so he claimed, discharged the obligation he had undertaken to the Governor-General. He had shown he could govern. He was entitled to a dissolution of Parliament, if and when he requested it.

The Customs Committee began its sittings on February 9th, and sat through until early in June. It met on 115 occasions and heard evidence from 225 witnesses, who individually and collectively disclosed an amazing degree of corruption within the Customs service, including payments made to party funds and a personal intervention by the former Minister, Jacques Bureau, to save one of the main operators in the illicit trade, Moses Aziz, from serving a jail sentence. Its proceedings culminated in a struggle by the Conservative Members to include in the final report, and by name, those Members of the House whom they felt the House itself should censure, and an equally determined effort by the Liberal Members to prevent anything of the kind from happening.

This time, Fortune was favouring Bennett. He had again been thrown into an intense fight almost as soon as he arrived in Ottawa, but under very different circumstances from the fight he had encountered twenty-five years before on his arrival in Edmonton. For one thing, he was a more experienced and mature man. He had that much more knowledge of affairs and practice in the handling of witnesses giving evidence under oath. For another, this time there was a great deal more concrete material to use in the committee room. Even more important, he was no longer a lone Member fighting a government, nor a restless young man fighting his own party leaders.

He was a member of a team under firm leadership, which is exactly what he needed to be at that time.

The report of the Committee was made public on June 18th, 1926. So far as Bureau was concerned, and his Department, it was an emphatic condemnation: ". . . the Hon. Jacques Bureau, then Minister of Customs, failed to appreciate and properly discharge the responsibilities of his office. . . ." But on the question of how far the Government as a whole was involved—which meant, in effect, how much King had known and chosen to ignore—the report was silent. So, too, was Kennedy, the Chairman, and in that fact lay the core of the battles of the next three weeks. The Chairman was a Progressive, and there were twenty-four other Progressives in the House. Both Liberals and Conservatives would vote as party interests demanded. What decision would the Progressives make?

The battle proper began on the 22nd. On that day, Mercier, a Liberal, moved that the report of the Committee be accepted. Stevens, as leader of the attack from the Opposition benches, moved an amendment which specifically censured King as Prime Minister, and his Government, for failure to take prompt remedial action in face of the situation they knew existed. If the Stevens amendment were to be carried, the Government would not only be defeated on a major issue and be compelled to resign; the House would be dissolved and the Liberal Party would face the electorate with the Customs scandal as the centrepiece in the campaign. That was not a situation that King intended to allow to develop if he could possibly do anything to avert it. The final decision rested on the Progressives, and in turn the decision of each would be deeply influenced by the decision of their leader, even more by the decision of the leader of the Labour group, Woodsworth. Woodsworth was, in reality, the voice of conscience for the left wing of the House.

Woodsworth was an honest and conscientious man, but his dilemma was acute. On the one hand, King's programme since the session had started had appealed strongly to his political instincts and objectives; King had seen to that. The Liberals had promised old age pensions; Conservatives (Bennett amongst them) had opposed them. King had promised that this ugly episode within the Customs Department was over, that the lesson had been learnt, that the Liberal Party would rise purged by this ordeal. What had the Conservatives to offer when it came to the general policies of government? A different set of beneficiaries from public funds? High tariffs? Greater concessions to the manufacturing interests? Woodsworth, dismayed by this naked glimpse of the uglier side to political power, still could not bring himself to strike a Liberal Government down. Instead, he proposed a second amendment, that a Royal Commission should be set up to continue the work of the Committee and complete the reorganization of the Department. The Conservatives, aware that if carried this would destroy the element of censure in the Stevens amendment, claimed that it was out of order. The Speaker, exhausted by the long debate, adjourned the House at 1.14 a.m. on the morning of June 24th, and promised his decision in the afternoon when the House reassembled. His decision was that the amendment was in order.

Again a long day was spent in debate, mainly between King and Meighen. Again the House adjourned at one in the morning of the following day, the 25th, to reassemble in the afternoon. Still the issue was in doubt. Woodsworth had not persuaded all his colleagues. Kennedy, Chairman of the Investigation Committee, had already heard enough to place him with the opposition. Another Progressive, M. N. Campbell, denounced Woodsworth for what he described as both apostasy and appeasement. Finally, at midnight on the 25th, the division was called. The Woodsworth amendment was lost by 115 votes to 117. Ten minutes later, a further amendment, equally damaging to the Government, was challenged, this time by the Liberals. The Speaker ruled this sub-amendment out of order. His rule was at once challenged by Meighen, and the House, by a vote of 118 to 116, voted against the ruling, Woodsworth, this time, failing to support the Government. Hours later King attempted to adjourn the House; again he lost, by 114 to 115. Finally, at 5.17 in the morning of the 26th the House, exhausted, carried a fresh adjournment motion by one vote, 115 to 114. The day was ended, and King had the following day, Sunday, in which to decide both the next move of his Government, and, to a large extent, the fate of himself. The Progressives were slipping from his grasp. How could he escape from an election fought on the one issue that was producing his defeat in the House?

King's decision was to ask the Governor-General for a dissolution of Parliament, forthwith, before the final votes on the Report and the Stevens' amendment could be taken. Lord Byng's decision was to refuse the request for an immediate dissolution. There was a leader of a second party in the House who must first be asked if he would attempt to form a government. In the face of that, King's second decision was to resign as Prime Minister. When the House assembled on the Monday afternoon, he informed it that His Excellency was now without advisers and that Canada was without a government. This was a situation without precedent, and, since men who raise party advantage to the heights that King did are fortunately rare, one that is not likely to happen again.

A very great deal has been written on the events of that week-end, on whether King or Lord Byng was 'right' in what they did, and I do not propose to embark on a discussion of that here. I think one conclusion can be drawn: Lord Byng as Governor-General was not in exactly the same position as the Monarch himself.

In the United Kingdom, the King, or Queen, is more than an institution, part of government by 'King in Parliament'. He, or she, is a person having personality and character, held in a position of power both by tradition and loyalty and by personal relationships with those immediately around him. King George V could send for Baldwin and not Curzon, and both men, as well as Parliament and people, accepted that he had such a choice. It is doubtful if Canadians at that time would have acquiesced in the same freedom of action if exercised by the Governor-General in Ottawa, a man who was English, a member of the House of Lords, appointed by London at a salary for a term of years. It is obvious from King's conduct that he drew a sharp distinction in his mind between the duty he owed the monarch and the duty he owed to the Governor-General then in office.

It may well be that, thirty years later, the position has

changed again. Canadians expect their Governor-General to
be Canadian like themselves, and if some comparable situation
were to arise they would expect their Governor-General to be
resolute enough to use all the discretions vested in him by
tradition. But if he did, he would in our eyes be acting more as
an element in the Constitution of Canada than as a representative of a distant monarch.

No one has ever doubted either the sincerity or the integrity
of Byng. By the book, the Crown has a discretion to refuse a
request for a dissolution; as the Crown's representative, the
discretion was also his, so he believed. And, on balance, it is
likely that King was equally sincere in his request for an
immediate dissolution; he felt that he deserved to be allowed
to fight the election that would follow as a Prime Minister,
and not as the leader of a battered party forced into opposition
(not that 'sincerity' is a very appropriate word to use of King;
he could so easily persuade himself to believe what was ad-
vantageous). The use he made of Byng's decision in the days
that followed was almost certainly an afterthought. But
King's decision to resign and leave the country without any
government, to shuffle the whole burden of the next decision
on to someone else, was a party political act, intended to
embarrass the Conservatives, cost what it might to the position
and the prestige of the office of Governor-General.

Meighen was likewise faced with a conflict between immediate party interest and his wider duty to the institutions of
government. He was leader of the party in opposition, and no
man remains leader of an opposition party for long if he lacks
the ambition to be Prime Minister. Obviously, the Governor-
General, having refused a dissolution to King, would send for
him and ask if he were willing to attempt to form a government. What should his answer be? Acceptance would provide
the country with a government and place him in office. But
would it place him in power? That was extremely uncertain.
In the first place, constitutional law required then that any
member of the Commons appointed to office must resign his
seat and seek re-election. If he completed a normal list of
Cabinet appointments, he would automatically reduce his
immediate voting strength by the same number. Secondly,

whilst he might be able to rely on sufficient Progressive support to defeat the Liberal administration on a vote of censure, for how long could he rely on it for positive support for his own government? He did in fact succeed in making a tentative arrangement for support during the remainder of a truncated session, but the degree of party discipline amongst the Progressives could not give any such compact an air of solidity.

Alternatively, he could accept office and ask Parliament to adjourn to give time to hold the essential series of by-elections, but that motion might or might not be passed. If it did, it would leave both the Customs enquiry and the rest of the business of the session wholly in the air. About the one positive advantage that might accrue from the acceptance of the Governor-General's invitation would be the right to conduct the election, when it came, as Prime Minister; the advantage would not include the power to determine when the election would be held. That would remain the prerogative of the Progressives.

So much for party considerations. What of the wider issues? King had left Canada without any official government at all. If Meighen also declined to form a government, to whom could the Governor-General turn next? He could not leave the country without an Executive Council. Might he not be forced into the humiliating position of having to send for King again, and beg him to take office, even if he had to grant him the dissolution he had just refused? Or might he, equally humiliated, be compelled to turn to Woodsworth and ask him to form at least a nominal government, whilst the two major parties fought out the next battle for supremacy between them? King might have placed Meighen in a dilemma. Whether intentionally or otherwise, he had placed the Governor-General in a far more serious one. For Meighen, it was not so much a matter of saving the face of Lord Byng as an individual. It was a matter of saving from ridicule the whole conception of constitutional monarchy within the Empire. King might show complete indifference to that. Meighen could not. That was the constitutional crisis, and, complex as it was, it required immediate decisions from Meighen. So far as Bennett was concerned, once again chance determined the part he would play in it.

The session had already brought Meighen and Bennett much more closely together than they had been ten years previously. They were each more willing to recognize in the other virtues as well as faults. For one thing, the rivalry had gone. Meighen was the acknowledged leader of the Party and Bennett was, and could be, no more than one of his lieutenants. Nor was Bennett now the overly impatient man he had been when both Meighen and he were competing for advancement under the eyes of Borden. Bennett had come in fact to be the Deputy Leader of the Opposition, but he had earned that place by his work in the House that session.

Chance intervened in this manner. The Conservative leader in Alberta was Bennett's old friend and colleague, A. A. McGillivray, K.C., of Calgary. McGillivray had earlier secured from Bennett a promise that he would come back to Calgary to speak at the Conservative summer rally there, and the date of the rally had been left to the Alberta Executive to arrange. It so happened that the date chosen in Alberta was June 26th, the Saturday, and to reach Calgary from Ottawa by that day—train being the only means of travel available—Bennett would be compelled to leave on the night of the 23rd.

He was extremely reluctant to go, and Meighen was even more reluctant to release him. Although as the week began it was impossible to predict exactly how the battle would develop, it did seem as though the final engagement with King had been joined. But Bennett would not break a promise if he could possibly avoid doing so, and McGillivray would not release him from that promise, even when Bennett wired him so requesting. As a result, Bennett was in Calgary when the crisis reached its climax between the Saturday and the Monday.

Meighen took what counsel he could in the time available, from Borden and from the remainder of his shadow Cabinet in Ottawa, Sir Henry Drayton, Stevens, Tolmie and Chaplin. He was already very aware of the perils of his position. He knew that King had declined to consult with him as Leader of the Opposition on what the next step should be and, further, that he did not accept that the Governor-General had any right to consult with Meighen, either. In reality, his consultations with his colleagues were a step he was bound to take, but not one necessary to enable him to make up his own mind. He had decided where his duty lay. Even his half belief, half hope that the Progressives would support him to the extent of carrying through the rest of the essential work of the session was perhaps no more than a protective colouring given to the naked risks he was running. Yet when he had explained to his colleagues the reasons for his actions, they agreed with him. On the Monday he returned to the Governor-General and was sworn in as Prime Minister.

Up to this point, Meighen's judgments and decisions had been understandable, and entirely defensible. The wisdom of his next move may be doubted.

Basically, he had accepted office so that his country should have a government, and by doing so he had, at least impliedly, accepted that the need for a government was greater than the need for that Parliament to resume its debates on the controversies still before it as though nothing had changed. A motion that Parliament should adjourn in order that the members of Meighen's new government might secure re-election (as the Constitution still required) would have been a defensible act and one which it would have been hard for the Progressives who had supported him to reject. Certainly it would have been a step that could have been simply explained to the country itself.

Instead, Meighen chose another plan—one that laid him open to the charge that he had failed to give his country a legal government at all. His mind seemed intent on the pursuit of what was fast becoming the inessential, the motion censuring the Liberals, to the detriment of what should have been his first objective, the establishment of his own authority as head of the Government of Canada.

Once he himself accepted office, his party in the Commons lost both his actual presence and leadership on the floor, and a vitally important vote. To avoid the loss of any more of the party's voting strength, he requested the Governor-General to appoint five of his colleagues, Drayton and four others, who were already Privy Councillors, as acting Ministers. Since they were to be acting Ministers only, it was claimed that it would not be necessary for them to vacate their seats. So evolved, the plan looked a neat arrangement, intended to allow Parliament to proceed with its business, but, like so many apparently neat arrangements, its appearance could be twisted to resemble a mere subterfuge; as it was by King.

Bennett said afterwards that had he been in Ottawa that week-end Meighen's decision over the acceptance of office would have been different. That may be doubted. It is unlikely that anyone could have deflected Meighen from a course of action dictated solely by duty as he saw it. But in another way Bennett's absence was a serious disaster. Meighen had to name his acting Ministers at once, and to one of them he must hand over immediate leadership in the House, with all the responsibility that entailed. Had Bennett been physically in Ottawa at that moment, ready to meet the House on Tuesday, it is almost certain that Meighen would have given him that responsibility, and quite certain that Bennett would have accepted it. As it was, Meighen asked Stevens to act as leader, but Stevens declined on the ground that Drayton had the greater claim as the more senior, and Drayton was chosen. It was an unfortunate choice.

On the Tuesday, when the House met and the parties had changed places across the floor, King again tried to reverse the verdict on the Customs scandal. That achieved partial success. A Conservative move to have it ruled out of order failed. On the Wednesday, he tried to pry the Progressives away from the Government side by moving a non-confidence motion based on the prospect of higher tariffs to be expected from a Conservative government. That was a failure, the Liberals mustering no more than 101 votes to the Government's 109. It was a move too transparent to succeed. But later in the same day he hit upon the one effective road to a real diversion. He challenged the validity of the Government itself. Other than Meighen, he said, not one of the Ministers on the other side of the House was validly in office. Not one had taken the oath of office. Not one was in receipt of salary from his office. They were, he claimed, nothing but a casual collection of Privy Councillors who had assumed the right to give orders in the name of the Government of Canada. If that is permissible, he said, what guarantees have we for the future liberty and freedom in the country? Here at last was an effective weapon.

The debate lengthened and grew more bitter, and finally, at 2 a.m. on the morning of the Friday, July 2nd, the Liberal motion declaring that the Meighen Government had no right to be in office was carried by 96 votes to 95. Fourteen Progressives voted with the Liberals, and three with the Government. The decisive vote came from a Progressive, T. W. Bird, of Melrose. Bird had earlier paired with a Conservative member who had fallen sick, but when the division was called he voted, and voted against the Government, inadvertently, he claimed, but none the less effectively. It was in that way that this Parliament ended. That afternoon, Meighen informed the House that he had requested a dissolution of the House and that the Governor-General had acceded to his request. His temporary Government had had a lifetime of four days, from Tuesday, June 30th, to the Friday of the same week. Now he was free to form a more regular government. Now he was free to fight an election as Prime Minister, not as Leader of an Opposition. But he had lost a great deal of ground in the process.

Bennett always blamed himself for having left Ottawa, and Meighen, at that particular moment. He believed that, had he led the House that last week, he could have prevented the constitutional crisis from arising, and if he had he would have reversed the course of political history in Canada; without the constitutional issue to use, the Customs scandals would have defeated King, in more ways than one. Such a defeat could easily have been the end of his political career as leader of the Liberal Party. Grant Dexter, then parliamentary correspondent for the *Winnipeg Free Press*, in a letter he wrote to me some time before his death said:

"I asked him [Bennett] why he thought he could have prevented the constitutional issue from arising. He replied that any competent House of Commons man, given the Customs and other scandals, could have prevented Mr. King from ever being heard on the subject. He would have roared out his denunciations, refused to answer silly questions about the shadow Cabinet, and so on.

"I watched R.B. in Parliament from 1926, when he entered the House, until 1936, when I went to Europe for three years. I am a good Liberal, but I am very much inclined to think he was right. He was exactly the kind of debater that could have done this."

King won the election that followed, and by doing so made his own position as leader of the Liberal Party secure beyond challenge. His party won 118 seats, the Conservatives 91, the Progressives and Liberal-Progressives 20, and in Alberta the United Farmers of Alberta won 11. Meighen not only saw his party defeated; he himself lost his seat in the Commons for Portage la Prairie and never again sat in that House. On September 26th he handed over the seals of office. Already he had decided to resign the leadership of the party.

His decision so to do was final. He confirmed it to his Cabinet colleagues at an informal luncheon at the Ottawa Country Club immediately after the election and before his Government resigned, and the general feeling among the group was that the party should be urged to hold a leadership convention within a year and that Hugh Guthrie should act as House Leader until then. In the October the party met in caucus, accepted Meighen's resignation and confirmed the temporary arrangements for the interim period. The final decision was to hold the leadership convention at Winnipeg in twelve months' time.

Thus Fate destroyed, at the comparatively early age of fifty-two, the political career of the one man who had seemed to stand solidly between Bennett and the summit of his ambitions.

The constitutional crisis of 1926 was obviously the turning-point in Bennett's political career. Since 1925 his luck had decisively changed. He had had an unusual chance to show his mettle in debate, in the House and in Committee, under conditions that favoured his talents and under the full light of publicity. By chance he had not been directly involved in the decisions Meighen had taken at the climax of the crisis itself, and he had in Meighen a political rival whose whole instinct was to put country and party above private ambitions. Once Meighen had made his decision to resign, his successor in that leadership would know for certain that Meighen himself would never seek to reverse it.

But if Bennett had had good fortune in the way the chances unrolled themselves before him, it was his own qualities and personality that enabled him to make the best advantage of them. He had certainly not been the inevitable successor to Meighen at the time of his return to the House in 1925. Drayton might have destroyed his own chances during that crucial week when all the responsibility was on his shoulders, but there were others, Stevens, Guthrie and Cahan, each of whom had every right to claim the position. Amongst them, Bennett was the comparative newcomer. As it was, Stevens decided to support Bennett; the others ran and were defeated. A year later, on October 12th, 1927, at the leadership convention in Winnipeg, Bennett was chosen to head the party at the decisive second ballot:

Bennett	780
Guthrie	320
Cahan	266
Manion	148
Rogers	37
Drayton	3

He had secured two more than the 778 votes needed to give him a clear majority.

When Prime Minister, Bennett was often accused of an arrogant aloofness, of leaving too wide a gulf between himself and the rank and file of the party, as though that had always been his characteristic. But it should not be forgotten that he won that leadership with the support of party members who had served with him under Meighen between 1925 and 1927. They had seen him in action for long enough to know his failings as well as his virtues, and when they came to Winnipeg for the convention, and to strike a balance between the contestants, they showed that they believed he was the leader the party needed.

One passage in Bennett's acceptance speech says a great deal about the man, and his mood at that moment:

"I must renounce all these things that I have held most dear in my life heretofore, the legal claims, the business

claims. . . . I realize that I must renounce these things.
Politics have been more or less an incident thus far in my
life. You have determined for me that henceforward so long
as I have health and strength I must dedicate my time, my
talents, such qualities as I may have and the fortune that
God has been good enough to give me, to the interests of my
country, to the great party that I am privileged to lead. . . ."

This quotation from the editorial comment in the Vancouver
Sun indicates some of the doubts others held over the Party's
choice:

"Has this rich autocratic bachelor the qualities that would
ever permit him to assume leadership of the Canadian
people? There are snobbish elements that would welcome
his elevation to such a post. There are financial interests that
might find profit in raising him to political power. But the
mass of Canadians, in east or west, will never find in· this
cold, aloof, intellectual the sympathies and sincerity essential
in the Prime Minister of the Dominion."

Chapter Nine

THE CLIMB TO THE SUMMIT

ON August 7th, 1930, just over a month after his sixtieth birthday, Bennett became Prime Minister of Canada, in succession to Mackenzie King, and was sworn into office as Secretary of State for External Affairs and Minister of Finance in addition to the major office of state. That ceremony completed, he at once set in train the detailed preparations needed both for the special session of the new Parliament he had promised to call that fall and for the Imperial Conference to be held in London later in the year.

He then felt free to attend the annual conference of the Canadian Bar Association (he was President that year) and to travel to Quebec to greet the large contingent of lawyers from the United Kingdom who were attending, Lord Dunedin and Sir John Simon among them. At the annual dinner of the Association in Toronto, he made his farewell to his profession.

"This is my valedictory at the Bar. I say that somewhat sadly, for life for me has been very pleasant in the practice of my profession, which has done great things for me. I shall endeavour to discharge my duties to it."

And, no doubt thinking of the responsibility he would have in the future for appointments to the Bench, both federally and across the provinces, he went on:

"I recall a conversation I had with a great English judge not long ago during which I realized that he had left a practice worth $150,000 a year and he had accepted only $25,000 on the Bench. He gave us his reason for his action: 'It is one of the traditions of our profession that when we have attained to eminence we then shall serve our day and generation on the Bench.' I hope that some such sentiment as that will fill the hearts and minds of Canadian lawyers (so that) they too may be willing to submit to material sacrifice and render service to the State that has done so much for them."

From Toronto he travelled to Calgary, where, on August 22nd, he was entertained to a triumphal banquet by the Calgary Conservatives. He was guest of honour at a non-political dinner in Winnipeg, Manitoba, on the 27th, and from there he came back to Ottawa. All his new Ministers had retained their seats by acclamation in the by-elections following their appointments, and Stevens, defeated at Vancouver, but none the less appointed Minister of Trade and Commerce, was returned at a by-election in Kootenay East, British Columbia, where a seat had been found for him, on the 25th.

Bennett was now at the peak of his political career. He had brought the Conservatives back to office, with a majority over all the other parties in the House combined.

He had won the election mainly on the issue of unemployment. The campaign had begun well in advance and King had prepared his plans very carefully indeed. Believing that the election issue would be the customary one of tariffs, with characteristic care and thoroughness he had planned his strategy to meet that as the major threat to his party. For once, elaborate preparation hindered rather than helped. In the event, for the voters of Canada the real issue was unemployment, and, when that proved to be quite unmistakable, it was King who lacked flexibility enough to change his ground with adequate speed. He may be forgiven for his misjudgment at the start, for the winds of economic distress did not strike sharply until towards the end of the year. Save for a marked and significant fall in the production of grain crops (the wheat harvest of 1929 was only 299 million bushels, compared with 566 million in 1928), Canada's economy had not begun to falter until 1930.

In the summer of 1929 the two leaders made elaborate speaking tours of the country, very much as pugilists parade the ring before the contest starts. Bennett began in June. In July he was in Ontario, moving westwards. He spent two weeks in Calgary, without any major public speech, and went on into British Columbia. He spoke at Spillimacheen on the 26th and at Salmon Arm on the 27th, concentrating on the loss to that fruit-growing area from the fruit and vegetables dumped, as he called it, in Canada from the United States. In West Vancouver three days later, his main subject was New Zealand butter, in Nanaimo, on Vancouver Island, the coal industry.

In Port Alberni, on the west coast of the Island, on August 2nd he explained his position on 'Empire Free Trade'. Asked if he favoured it, he replied: "No; because that would sacrifice the industrial life of the industrial parts of the Empire." It was not until the following January, before the session opened, that he touched on unemployment specifically. Again his remedy was that Canada should process more of her own raw materials. "Thousands in the United States," he said, "have been given employment fabricating Canadian goods. They've got the jobs and we've got the soup kitchens."

The same tactical pattern continued into the 1930 session. The Liberal Budget was admirably designed for an election year, provided it were held in times when the Liberals could rely on their usual response to the usual Conservative attack. It added a great many items to the 'free list' for imports from the Empire into Canada (Bennett claimed that many of these additions were items which Canada had not imported from any Empire country in years), it increased duties on the import of butter, vegetables and fruit, and cut the internal sales tax to 1 per cent.

Bennett took every opportunity to drive home his tariff and preference programme: "I am for the British Empire next to Canada," he said on May 6th during the Budget debate and: "To grant trade preference to another state or empire without founding those preferences on a mutually helpful treaty is unsound business, profitless and filled with ill will and misunderstanding." But, as the Toronto *Mail and Empire* said of the Budget: "For unemployment, that most formidable of problems, the problem that occupies the minds of all, with the exception, it would seem, of the Government, the Budget affords no solution."

When that Parliament was dissolved at the end of the session,

E

polling day was set for July 18th, 1930, and the campaign
proper began. Bennett's opening, and keynote, speech was
essentially simple. The Conservatives, he said, believed in
Canada first and an expanding trade within the Empire; the
Liberals did not. Canada had the resources, the men and
women, the skill, the endurance, the capacity for hard work,
all that was needed to triumph over all her present difficulties.
The prime task was to use her resources within Canada—to
create employment at home, to keep out of Canada the products
made by other men in other nations. There was no element of
surprise in this. Bennett had urged it on the public day in and
day out. He believed it, and his sincerity was such that increasingly the public came to believe in him. He was at least
positive.

In contrast to Bennett's approach, King was on the defensive,
and none too happy in that attitude. His talent as a speaker
lay in the creation of atmosphere. By talking round and about
a subject at length, he could create the impression that this
particular topic was one very close to his heart, that he fully
appreciated the urgent need for action, and that he had clear-
cut plans for the action that should be taken. He had also
remarkable skill in the choice of words, so that he usually
escaped making any definite commitment. King could conjure
up in the minds of his audience a picture of an eager Theseus at
the mouth of the Labyrinth, conscious of the threat presented by
the Minotaur within, and determined to rid his fellow-countrymen of the ever-present danger that faced them whilst the
monster remained alive. But once he disappeared into his maze
of words, no Ariadne left a threat to guide his audience to its
centre. King might certainly appear to set off on the mission,
and his audience might attempt to follow him, but both were
likely to reappear some time later, from different exits and with
very different explanations as to why nothing had been done
inside.

Unemployment had crept in to the last session of the dissolved Parliament. A deputation from the west saw King in
February and pressed him for a statement of Government
policy. King was evasive, and tried to persuade them that a
comprehensive unemployment plan was a satisfactory answer

to their present troubles. The suggestion was taken up in Parliament by Woodsworth, who put a question to King asking if he intended to take the initiative in calling any conference on unemployment insurance. Again King backed away. Insurance, he said, was necessarily a matter for provincial governments, but, he went on, in his best and most cautious parliamentary style, if the provinces made a move and "it appears that the Federal Government can be of assistance in helping to bring about uniformity as between the provinces . . . we shall be glad upon invitation to take the matter under consideration." It was hardly a rousing response to a cry of distress. Finally, almost at the end of the session, on May 29th, King advanced a tentative step forward. He announced that he would call a conference on unemployment, to consider this question of co-operation between the federal and the provincial governments and the municipalities, but only after the General Election which he had, by then, announced.

It is curious that King was so blind to the potentially explosive nature of the situation around him. As the summer advanced, the normal seasonal improvement in employment in Canada could not conceal how threatening the prospect had become. In the past, King's principal attribute as a party leader had been his skill as an opportunist, his ability to sense what was or could become a suitable issue to make his own, to find a cause worth appearing to lead. True, he did not want to involve any federal government he headed with responsibility for unemployment; it was so much more satisfactory to leave the problem with the provinces and the municipalities. He could sense—as became the fact during Bennett's administration—that it would be a problem from which no credit could ever be extracted and only disaster be anticipated. But it is strange that he did not realize before he did that it was no longer safe to stay in the sidelines. The risks that followed from dissociation were becoming greater than those involved in active participation.

Be that as it may, he had made his first and most serious blunder in the Commons during the debate on April 3rd. He had been pressed hard by all the Opposition to do more than he had over unemployment, to step from out of the shelter of

Federal exclusiveness and give some aid to the distressed provinces. He declined:

"So far as giving money from this Federal Treasury to the provincial governments is concerned, in relation to this question of unemployment as it exists today, I might be prepared to go a certain length possibly in meeting one or two of the western provinces that have Progressive premiers at the head of their governments . . . but I would not give a single cent to any Tory Government. . . ."

That produced some reaction from the Opposition, and cries of 'Shame' from both Bennett and Stevens. King saw no red light. "What is there to be ashamed of?" he replied. "You ought to be ashamed of that," was Stevens' retort, and King, angry, proceeded to hammer the mistake home.

"My honourable friend is getting very indignant. Something evidently has got under his skin. May I repeat what I have said. With regard to giving money out of the Federal Treasury to any Tory government in this country for these alleged unemployment purposes, while these governments situated as they are today with politics diametrically opposed to this government, I would not give them a five-cent piece."

The cry of 'Buddy, can you spare a dime?' had fallen on deaf ears. For once, King's ability to conceal his thoughts with words had failed him, disastrously: 'Not a five-cent piece' is an easy sentence to remember. It was the nature of King, of course, to attempt to explain his lapse away. He wriggled and twisted and produced an entirely fresh version of his retort. But *Hansard* was too much for him.

When he began his election campaign proper, again he attempted to avoid this issue. In his opening speech, his keynote speech at Brantford, Ontario, a lengthy one, there was no reference to the rising unemployment figures for the country. No doubt some members of his party commented on this, for in his next speech, in Ontario at Peterborough, he admitted a problem existed. By the time he had moved eastwards into Quebec, he agreed that it was serious. It was only when he had gone as far as the Maritimes, well into the campaign, that he realized that his promise to call a conference in October was hardly a useful contribution to an election campaign due to end in July. At that point, he turned to attack the provinces for having failed to ask him for help. That produced a rejoinder from J. E. Brownlee, Premier of Alberta, in which he said that his Government had prepared all the data needed to show the seriousness of the position in his province for submission to Ottawa in the preceding February, but that all the ministers concerned were too busy to attend any meeting at which it could have been presented.

In a contest of this kind, Bennett had the advantage. He had no political past to defend. He radiated a positive confidence and determination for the future. He had no uncertainty over what he would do were he to lead the next government; he could advocate tariffs and Empire preferences convincingly because he was totally sincere in his belief that they contained virtually the whole answer to the problem facing his country.

Bennett's thoughts on Empire trade were not the consequence of a shallow emotion. As he said in a letter to H. R. Drummond-Hay, a Winnipeg lawyer, on November 27th, 1928: ". . . it would be quite impossible for this country to maintain its industrial life if we had complete free trade with Great Britain." Tariffs and preferences would compel industry to use Canadian resources in Canada. I think I might quote here from a speech he made in 1929:

"The first question which faces the people of Canada is whether we are to continue as a nation. This is not a matter of deciding for or against the secession of Saskatchewan, or for or against the continued union of the successors of John A. Macdonald and those of Georges Etienne Cartier. . . . The attempt is being made to picture that these things might happen. . . . That is all mere chicanery—the old trick of setting up a straw man in order to knock him down.

"The real danger to national unity does not lie in resolutions for secession, nor in appeals to race prejudice. Those are but the symptoms. The disease is the misunderstanding of the truths of our history . . . , and the germ was planted by the publication, some years ago, of the now famous study in which a professor of economics, now a Minister of the Crown, tried to prove that the people of Nova Scotia paid unduly for the privilege of being Canadians. This example was too tempting, and the whole course of discussion of public affairs in Canada since has been a series of unending attempts to divide the nation into 'haves' and 'have-nots'. . . .

"The problem is how to keep the nation healthy and prosperous, not how to poultice any of its parts. If all is well on the Pacific coast, all will be well in the Maritimes; if Ontario and Quebec are prospering, then the Prairie Provinces must be prospering too."

To what extent he was right or wrong in his approach is another matter, which may be discussed later. The one man in the capitalist world who, in that era, did apply drastic, and not unsuccessful, methods to end the economic problems his country shared with all the Western world was Adolf Hitler, and even in 1930 he was hardly a man whose example many Canadians would have chosen to follow.

Not that Bennett escaped the commission of some blunders during the campaign. He made his major mistake in the heat of the battle, the claim that he would 'blast his way into the markets of the world', and it was long remembered. It was a boast, and boasts are often boomerangs. It is said that this particular phrase was not his own, that it was written into a speech for him, and that he brought it out without giving due thought to its potential dangers. But once made, he did not consider attempting to repudiate it. It represented the mood in which he was fighting, and the mood in which he felt he could succeed when head of a government. "So I will, when the Government is mine, continue to blast a way through all our troubles and difficulties," he said later in Vancouver. "What else would I be there for? To cringe to others with soft words and to recoil from each rebuff? That is not Canada's way. That is not my party's way." It was a proud and defiant man speaking, but a fighter.

Polling day came, and the Conservative Party emerged holding 138 seats, an absolute majority in the House. The party had virtually swept the three Maritime provinces. It dominated

Ontario, with fifty-nine seats to the Liberals' twenty-two (one United Farmer survived in that province). It had captured twenty-five out of the sixty-four seats in Quebec. It held Manitoba almost solidly, and it had the advantage in British Columbia. In Bennett's own province, Alberta, the U.F.A. strength had been cut to nine, with the Liberals holding three seats and the Conservatives four. In Saskatchewan, the Liberals held eleven, the Conservatives eight, and the Progressives two. The final results gave the Liberals eighty-seven seats, the U.F.A. and the U.F.O. ten, the Progressives, of various shades, five, Labour three and Independents two. Many of the Liberal Ministers had fallen; the Conservatives had lost Stevens and Colonel MacRae, the party organizer, in British Columbia.

That was the road to the summit.

Chapter Ten

THE EMPIRE THAT NEVER WAS

THE scene from the summit in August, 1930, was challenging, but Bennett had then no reason to believe that the situation was already far more beyond control than it appeared to be. On the contrary, he believed—he had fought an election in the belief—that he had a remedy for the ills that beset not only his own country, but the Empire itself. Coincident with that was the fact that now it was he who, as Prime Minister of Canada, would be the spokesman for his country when the Empire met in conference at Westminster in two months' time.

I would find it hard to believe that even one of Bennett's bitterest political enemies would be unwilling to share, in retrospect, some of the immense satisfaction Bennett must have felt when he sailed for this meeting; the man who would not must be somewhat lacking in humanity. To speak for his country at such a gathering, and to do so with the belief that he could offer a real solution for the malaise of the times, would have been a splendid moment for any man. For Bennett, imbued from childhood with a reverence for this whole concept of Empire, it was a crowning mercy.

It was, of course, bound to fall short of that anticipation, but the moment has come, I think, to consider what Bennett meant by, and felt about, the Crown and this 'Empire'.

Towards the Crown itself, Bennett felt a deep sense of personal loyalty and obligation. In the spring of 1935, the Commonwealth joined together to celebrate the twenty-fifth anniversary of the Accession of H.M. King George V to the throne, the Silver Jubilee. The centre of the celebration was a Thanksgiving Service in St. Paul's Cathedral on May 6th, and Bennett, as Prime Minister of the oldest Dominion, rolled through the decorated and cheering streets of London with General Hertzog, Prime Minister of South Africa, in the second carriage of the Prime Ministers' procession, experiencing at first hand the welcome a London crowd can give to a thanksgiving and a pageant.

But for Bennett personally the climax of the journey from Ottawa came with the week-end he spent at Windsor Castle immediately following his arrival, on April 26th. The guests that week-end were mainly from the Royal Family: the Archbishop of Canterbury and Bennett were the only two from outside that circle. Bennett was lodged in the Edward III Tower. Amongst his papers is the draft, in his own hand and much revised, of the letter of thanks he wrote, and in that draft there is the following paragraph:

"Perhaps you would permit me to add that I valued very highly the opportunity so freely given to discuss with my Sovereign matters of concern. I state the simple truth when I write that I came away from the Castle with an even deeper feeling of affection and devotion for my King and Queen, and I shall continue to aspire the more earnestly to serve the Crown to the best of my ability, sustained by the conviction that my Royal Master expects His servants to do the best within them."

Those words express far more than their formal meaning. They express the deep gratitude of a man for all that life had given him, for the fulfilment of his dreams—dreams that had possessed him from his days as a schoolteacher in New Brunswick, dreams compounded of a passion to serve and a passion to succeed. Sixty-five years of life had led him to power, and, on that occasion, to the centre of his political faith, the strength, unity and purpose of an Empire unique in the history of the world. Ambition might have begun to fade. A few weeks before a heart attack had served him with rough notice that he was mortal, that his time might be nearly spent. But the desire to serve remained.

Bennett's own conception of loyalty is made very clear in a letter, dated June 4th, 1944, he wrote to J. S. Bickersteth, then Director of Army Education at the War Office in London (who

was nominally in control of my activities at that time). Bennett
had just given a lecture on 'The Future of the Empire' under
the auspices of that Directorate. He wrote to Bickersteth:

> "I have no objection to His Majesty being called the
> King 'of Canada', for he is King of Canada equally as he is
> King of the Fiji Islands. What I objected to, and still object
> to, is that it should be suggested that Canadians owe no
> allegiance to the King of Great Britain, for my oath of alleg-
> iance is to the King as defined by the Constitution, which is
> 'King of Great Britain, Ireland, and the British Dominions
> beyond the Seas'."

That was a clear and understandable statement of his belief.

But the British Empire was a far more complex concept. It
included loyalty, and all that Bennett understood by that word.
On another level, it was a political relationship between many
peoples, each independent and yet each within the circle, and,
so he believed, it could include an economic relationship
between them as well, as intricate as the other. In all these
Canada was deeply involved. Bennett saw in each element of
this relationship an instrument that could sustain and strengthen
the others, and he had very definite ideas on what should be
done to increase the effectiveness of them all.

He had talked of tariffs and preferences during the election
campaign. A tariff was justified if it strengthened Canada as a
unity, if it created employment and increased opportunities for
employment within Canada by inducing the employers of
labour to use and process Canada's immense natural resources
within the country where they were to be found, and, of course,
tariffs did that by raising the market prices of imported competing products. That is the classic defence for tariffs: protection
of the home market.

Preferences were the other part of the same system. A preference could not exist unless there was first a tariff, and since
Canada's exports consisted mainly of unprocessed or semi-
processed natural resources, a system of preferences within the
Empire would enable them to find wider markets more easily,
and more profitably, for the Canadian exporter.

Bennett, of course, sensed that the decline in international trade already then apparent would hit Canada as hard as any country in the world. The task for his government was to secure as firm a hold as possible on the markets that still continued to exist. Before the last Parliament had dissolved, the United States had set up the Hawley-Smoot tariff wall along Canada's southern boundary, and there were no preference loopholes in that. Among the world markets that were left, what could be better than that provided by the Empire itself?

He had already rejected from his mind the concept of 'Empire Free Trade', for the reasons he had given at Port Alberni in 1929, and to the continuing disappointment of Lord Beaverbrook. Canadian industry was not strong enough to withstand the full impact of unchecked competition from the United Kingdom. But an association of nations which imposed a common tariff barrier against all imports from outside, and yet which reduced the rates of those tariffs in respect of trade between themselves, would be one that should be able to flourish even in times of deepening dislocations in world trade. That would be a consistent—indeed, an overdue—development from their political relationship. That was his plan, and his hope, and certainly it was a plan that made a very strong appeal to the countries, and to the peoples, of Western Europe some twenty-five years later.

But it would be incorrect to leave the impression that Bennett saw the Empire primarily in economic terms. True, a group of countries that had unity in trading practices and objectives would be all the closer to one another in consequence, but for him the ultimate objective of the association was not to be expressed in material terms at all. In his view, it could only be described as a spiritual aspiration.

His mind followed the reverse route from that taken later by those intent on organizing a common market in Western Europe. He did not wish to see the project culminate in the creation of a single political entity or government. He believed that this unity was already there, that it was in fact the starting-point, not the terminus. He hoped that this unity of sentiment would be strong enough to permit true political individuality amongst the members of the association. If that unity of sentiment was strong enough, then the independence of each dominion would not damage the larger concept of Empire.

It is always hard to recapture an emotion. With 1930 we have now come to times which many have lived through, myself included. I do not share Bennett's beliefs and emotions concerning this Empire that never was, but I understand them, I think, for I, too, was once a political romantic.

I began as a juvenile jingo. My first readings were heavily impregnated with the illustrated weeklies that had appeared during the South African War, and which my widowed aunt had carefully cherished, and in those the British Tommy was the rough angel of Kipling's verse and the Boer a symbol of the powers of darkness; even his marksmanship had a diabolical quality to it. The first cracks in that simple vision appeared in 1919, with the Black and Tans. I lived in Liverpool; I saw them on leave and I read about their activities in Ireland in the *Manchester Guardian*, and I began to realize that a British Government could be as ruthless and as bloody-minded as any other. The process of disillusionment progressed still further during the 'non-intervention' farce of the Spanish Civil War and rushed its terminal point at the time of Munich in 1938.

I had joined the Territorial Army in Britain earlier that year with rather inchoate intentions of defending my country in the war that was obviously coming. I found within six months that those in charge of that country considered it proper to sacrifice the Czechs and the Slovaks to tyranny in order to buy time for themselves. I was ashamed, and I am still ashamed, of the bargain they made on my behalf. It was an honour and a deep satisfaction to serve during the subsequent war with the men who made up the ranks of the British Army, but for the last twenty years I have never felt anything but an abiding hostility towards those who make up what is now known as the Establishment in Britain. I suppose my crossing to Canada was a rather belated escape from their arrogance.

But during all that time I had only one country, for to the Englishman the Empire, or the Commonwealth, was an appendage to his own country. Bennett was always a Canadian, never a colonial thinking of himself as an exile. He had one country, Canada, to serve and protect. But he had this Empire over and above it. His conception of Empire involved another set of relationships, for his country as well as for himself, equally real, because of his conception of loyalty, but an extension of all his hopes and ambitions for Canada itself.

His view of that Empire did not materially change during his life. He could speak of it in terms that today have jingoist overtones, as he did during the debate on the Naval Bill in the Commons in 1913, on February 25th:

"I support the Second Reading of the Bill, first, because we are an integral part of the British Empire; secondly, because the naval supremacy of that Empire is menaced; thirdly, because it is our duty and our privilege, as a self-respecting people, to assist in the maintenance of that supremacy; fourthly, because co-operation in naval defence is essential to efficiency; fifthly, because it makes for and will do much to ensure the world's peace; and, lastly, because it makes for the consolidation of a united British Empire, and is a step towards Imperialism."

But emotion never clouded the clarity of his judgments. Over two years before, on November 13th, 1910, he had written to Max Aitken:

"If the Empire is to endure, the self-governing nations which compose it must in some way be federated. Unless there is a recognition of common interests, common traditions, and above all common responsibilities and obligations, and too within the lifetime of this generation, independence is inevitable, not only of Canada but of all the nations that now make up the Empire."

And in what was probably the last article he ever wrote, for the May, 1947, issue of the *Imperial Review*:

"It is obvious that with respect to matters that affect each of the Dominions some common policy must be evolved. It is quite clear that it is impossible to maintain the partnership relation unless the policy is one supported by all the nations of the Commonwealth. It is obvious to every citizen that we cannot have a partnership with the other nations of the

Commonwealth and promote and support separate policies. There must be united action for a common purpose. . . .

"In the words of the late Lord Milner: 'The only possibility of a continuance of the British Empire is on a basis of an absolute out-and-out partnership between the United Kingdom and the Dominions. I say that without any kind of reservation whatsoever.'

"In these critical days, is it not the duty of the senior partner to call an Imperial Conference for the purpose of dealing with the difficult and complex problems connected with the maintenance of the British Commonwealth of Nations?"

In his Peter le Neve Foster Lecture to the Royal Society of Arts in London in June, 1942, he said:

"While it was agreed that the Dominions must have an adequate voice and influence in the direction of the Empire's foreign policy and relations, the problem as to how 'continuous consultation' is to be maintained is still unsettled, and relations is an extremely serious responsibility. Admittedly, the Dominions now enjoy that right. Yet no method has been evolved to provide for continuous consultation between Imperial Conferences.

"The late Lord Tweedsmuir, when Governor-General of Canada, in a speech at Montreal in October, 1937, celebrating the 10th anniversary of the foundation of the Canadian institute of International Affairs, said that a Canadian's first loyalty was not to the British Commonwealth of Nations, but to Canada, and to Canada's King, and those who denied this were doing a great disservice to the Commonwealth. The nations of the Empire must think out their own special problems. Every nation must have a foreign policy in the sense that it must consider its position *vis-à-vis* the world at large. I wholly disagree with that view."

But nothing shows the contrast between his attitude to this special relationship within the Empire and that of the Liberals in the period between the wars better than a short debate in the Commons on the last day of the 1938 Session, July 1st, the last debate there in which Bennett took part. The United Kingdom Government had put out feelers for a programme of training R.A.F. pilots and air-crew in Canada; it was the forerunner of the programme that did begin two years later. King had strong objections to it, on various grounds, and was trying to keep it from public discussion, but rumours of the proposal had been published in a Vancouver newspaper, and Bennett raised the subject in the Commons when the House was in committee. King was a little pompous, as he often was when on the defensive. He said:

"Confidential and informal exploratory conversations with respect to training of British air pilots have taken place, but nothing has developed which it was felt warranted a statement of policy. . . . May I say a word with respect to the idea of having the Imperial Air Force set up flying schools in Canada to train their pilots; in short, a military station put down in Canada, owned, maintained and operated by the Imperial Government for Imperial purposes. I must say that long ago Canadian governments finally settled the constitutional principle that in Canadian territory there could be no military establishments unless they were owned, maintained and controlled by the Canadian Government. . . . A reversal of that principle and that historical process at this date is something the Canadian people would not for a moment entertain . . . no country pretending to sovereign self-control could permit such a state of affairs or its implications and consequences."

Bennett was aroused in his old vigour:

"To say that any partner in our Commonwealth should not, if it so desires, be given every opportunity to establish training fields for the safety, not of themselves, but the Commonwealth, is destructive of the whole theory of 1926 and 1930. . . . When the ancient partner on whom we have leaned all these years is not to be permitted to provide effective means of maintaining, not her life, but the life of Empire and Commonwealth, then I say it is time for us to take stock of the situation. . . . If it was the last word I ever uttered in this House, or with the last breath in my body, I would say that no Canadian is worthy of his great heritage and his great traditions and his magnificent hopes for the future who would deny to the old partner who established us the right in this country to create those centres, which she may not have at home, to preserve her life and the life of every man who enjoys freedom and liberty under the governing aegis of that flag."

At which Lapointe, Minister of Justice, interjected: "I knew the flag would be the last word," to which Bennett replied: "Certainly, and proudly so."

Those were very nearly the last words Bennett spoke as a Member in the Parliament of Canada. I am sure he was glad they had been on that subject and had taken that form.

I have used these quotations because, on this subject, Bennett should speak with his own words. In the fall of 1930 he was setting out for the Imperial Conference, from which would come both the Statute of Westminster and the Ottawa Economic Conference of 1932, with a very definite conception of what this British Empire should be, and of how its economic circumstances could be improved. He had both plans and visions, and immense determination to work towards their fulfilment.

The wonder is that Bennett's visions are neither dead nor discredited. The economic plans have gone. The Commonwealth certainly never became an economic unit, and the fiscal and trading arrangements made at Ottawa in 1932 are now of little more than historic interest. In these thirty years, as with the rest of the world, the political aspect of the Commonwealth has changed with frightening speed, and with it the status of the white man himself. In Africa at least, his function has been almost reversed from that which he regarded as his in the old Empire. To some Africans it is he who is now the burden. Certainly he is becoming either a hired expert or an embittered expatriate.

But for Bennett political systems and economic bargains were no more than facets. Underneath them lay the intangible things, the common interests, common traditions, and common responsibilities and obligations (to repeat the phrases he had used in 1910) which must be shared by all the countries of the Commonwealth if that association is to have meaning and continuing vitality. Bennett's sentiment of equality has, today, taken on a different form, but who would say it was not still the centre of discussion and concern at the Commonwealth Prime Ministers' Conference in March, 1961?

Chapter Eleven

THERE AND BACK AGAIN

B ENNETT came to office as Prime Minister approximately
halfway between the collapse of the United States stock
markets in October, 1929, and the crisis in Europe that,
amongst other things, forced Britain from the gold standard in
1931. In Canada unemployment was steadily rising; already
the total was 117,000 and it was expected that the figure would
rise to 175,000, possibly even to 200,000, before the coming
winter was through. But what Bennett did not know on that
August day was that the first crisis he would meet would
concern wheat and the prairie farmer, that the farmer co-
operative wheat pools in the three western prairie provinces
were already encountering difficulties beyond their powers to
meet unaided.

Canada's wheat harvest in the 1928-9 crop year had been the
largest ever produced, but an August frost had reduced its
grade. That year, Argentina had had a good harvest of high-
grade wheat, which had depressed the price obtainable for the
Canadian crop and influenced the prairie pool organizations
to hold back a large portion of their crop from the market.
Their carry-over to the 1929-30 crop year was 45 m. bushels,
a substantial burden for them to finance, but at least by doing
so they had maintained the price of the wheat actually sold. In
August, 1929, the price at Winnipeg was averaging $1.73 a
bushel, but by February, 1930, it had fallen to $1.15 a
bushel.

That fall in price had produced its own chain of reactions.
The banks lost confidence that the wheat carried over was a
good security for the loans they had made to the pools against
it, and began to press either for a quick sale or some further
guarantee. That brought in the governments in the three

provinces, who were asked to provide the guarantees the banks requested. They could not refuse, but, having done so, their own fears mounted. By the end of 1930, it was clear that Canada must face the fact that not only was the world demand for wheat already down by over 300 million bushels, but also that the market price for the crop that could be sold might well be below a dollar a bushel.

But in the August that was no more than a possibility. The special session of Parliament in the September, called as Bennett had promised, was short, and passed only three major Acts, none of them concerned with wheat. The first was an Unemployment Relief Act, voting $20 million to be spent in federal public works: "Palliative in its nature, to deal with an acute present problem"—so Bennett described it. The other two provided Bennett with implements for his programme concerning tariffs, and they included an amendment to the Customs Act which permitted an increase in the maximum rate for 'anti-dumping' duties from 15 per cent to 50 per cent. The session ended on September 22nd, and Bennett was free to cross to England for the Imperial Conference.

He sailed as soon as the session ended; his sister Mildred sailed with him, her husband, William Herridge, acting as his personal assistant. Two senior Ministers were included, Hugh Guthrie, Minister of Justice, and Harry Stevens, Trade and Commerce, and the balance of the delegation were technical advisers. John I. McFarland, newly appointed adviser on wheat, was one of them.

Besides the Imperial Conference, Bennett had a number of other duties and missions to carry through. One was to receive an honour which appealed to him deeply, membership of the Privy Council in the United Kingdom, the original body of His Majesty's advisers, to which he was sworn a member on October 27th (and for which he bought the appropriate court breeches and silk hose in London at the cost of eight guineas). Another was to accompany Mildred to Southampton, on October 10th, where she launched the R.C.N. destroyer *Skeena*, built for Canada in Thorneycroft's yards. Another was to present to the United Kingdom Government a bronze bust of Sir John A. Macdonald, to adorn his old home, Earnscliffe,

Ottawa, purchased by the United Kingdom Government for its High Commissioner in Canada.

At the beginning of November he was guest of honour at the Cutlers' Feast at Sheffield, Yorkshire. Two weeks later he made a flying visit to Ireland, to Dublin, where he was presented with a reproduction of the Armagh Chalice, and from there on to Belfast and Edinburgh, from which he returned with the honorary degree of LL.D. from three universities—Trinity College, Dublin, Queen's, Belfast, and Edinburgh. At the end of November he made a brief official visit to the battlefields in France, including the Canadian War Memorial on Vimy Ridge, and before he returned to Canada he fitted in some shopping in London, including, from the Times Book Club, Moneypenny and Buckle's *Life of Disraeli*, Kipling's *Book of Words*, the *Pageant of Parliament*, the Webbs' *My Apprenticeship* and an anthology of modern verse. But the Conference did not leave anyone too much leisure.

The 1930 Conference was as important as any in that series. On the constitutional side, it produced the Statute of Westminster, and it saw the beginning of the end of the association of the Irish Free State with the Commonwealth, mainly on question of appeals from Irish (and other Dominion) Courts to the Privy Council.

The Irish memorandum to the Canadian Government on these appeals, sent in anticipation of the Conference, contained this phrase: "The existence of an extra-state institution claiming, without any form of democratic sanction, to exercise jurisdiction in the matter of the internal affairs of the Irish Free State remains a menace to our sovereignty." That made the Irish position very clear and the Irish delegates did not budge from it.

Over the drafting of the Statute of Westminster Bennett was not in any great difficulty, although he had to walk warily. He had to avoid giving offence to those who regarded the British North America Act and the Colonial Laws Validity Act (which had to be repealed if the Statute of Westminster was to mean anything at all) as bulwarks of Canadian provincial rights. Howard Ferguson, Premier of Ontario, had said that he did, and he had given strong support to the party in the last election. So had C. H. Cahan, now Bennett's Secretary of State. Only six months before, when in opposition, he had said in the House that a repeal of the Colonial Laws Validity Act would vest in the Parliament of Canada the right to repeal a large number of statutes which "form the very basis of civil rights in each and every Province". On the other hand, Bennett knew that he must avoid even the appearance of being less interested in securing Canadian independence than were the Liberals: that was an accusation King would always be happy to make. He was properly cautious. For instance, on November 28th he attended a meeting of the Committee of Imperial Defence, a body that he regarded as purely a part of United Kingdom government. On the following day, Maurice Hankey, as secretary of the Committee, sent him a copy of the minutes of the meeting. He immediately replied:

> "As you are aware, Canada has never accepted membership of the Committee of Imperial Defence, and the question of the position she should now take in respect thereto is one requiring careful consideration of my Government. From a literal reading of the first page of the minutes it must be taken that I am now one of the Committee. As this is, of course, contrary to the facts, I would suggest . . . that my name and that of Mr. Herridge . . . be deleted from the minutes."

In the event, neither Bennett nor the provincial governments had real cause for alarm. Bennett's view on the constitutional achievements of the Conference are summed up in two sentences from a statement he made at Halifax, N.S., in December, 1931, when the Statute of Westminster had just concluded its final stages in the United Kingdom Parliament: "The day of the centralized Empire is passed. We no longer live in a political Empire." Then he added what was, then, a vital consideration: "I found people looking forward to the Conference [that to be held in Ottawa the following year] in the belief that we will lay at Ottawa the foundation of a new economic empire in which Canada is destined to play a part of ever-increasing importance."

The economic results of the conference and of the Ottawa

Conference of 1932 are now matters of historic interest, and
not much more. Here all I think I need describe are their
consequences to Bennett. From the start he was in an aggressive
mood; he had to be because in 1930 he was, in effect, asking a
Socialist Government in Britain, one with strong Liberal and
Free Trade traditions, to impose taxes on British imports of food,
in order that preferences might be given to Canada, and to
discourage imports of lumber from Soviet Russia, a country
with which they were anxious to promote trade, in order to
better the prospects of Canadian producers. It could be no easy
task, but surely the times were bad enough to compel any
government to think out afresh its approach to tariffs?

Bennett broadcast a talk, on October 15th, over the B.B.C.
network, in which he explained as directly as he could the
bargain he hoped to make. He said:

"... If I ask this country to buy our Canadian wheat, which
we must and will sell in the highest and most stable market,
and give you nothing but thanks in exchange for this practical
service, you would soon tire of it. Similarly, if Canada gave
you a preference for your goods in her market and got
nothing but your acknowledgment of this preference in
return, I fear it could not long continue. But if there is an
agreement, inspired by sentiment and buttressed by definite
and lasting and mutual advantage, then it will not fail. . . .

"Canada has suggested a plan by which this may be
brought about. I shall not refer to the reception our
proposal has received. In the near future it will be either
accepted or rejected. We can only await the decision. It will
be a momentous one, for I believe, and, believing it, I
consider it my duty to say, that if this opportunity for closer
economic relations is not seized it may not come again.
This, I need to tell you, is in no sense intended as a threat.
It is rather a prediction which, unhappily, I believe to be
true. . . ."

That was the kind of bargain he could justify at home. It was
the electorate in Britain who would, in the end, decide for or
against his proposals. Frankness to them was very desirable.

By the middle of the November, the contest was reaching its

climax. Bennett had reached certain firm conclusions about the other delegations and the personalities in them, those of the United Kingdom included. Ramsay MacDonald he regarded as unimportant, save as a phrase-maker; J. H. Thomas was a rough customer, but intellectually a lightweight. His major opponents were Philip Snowden, the Chancellor, and behind him the host of anonymous experts drawn from the Civil Service—men dedicated to the proposition that Britain should never make a commercial bargain with any country (Empire included) which was not in Britain's favour unless driven so far into a corner that escape was impossible (they were most skilful exponents of the practice the late W. C. Fields rather crudely described as: 'Never give a sucker an even break'). The strongest lever Bennett could use was the reluctance of a United Kingdom government, even a socialist one, to appear to desert the cause of Empire union and equality at the very moment when the Statute of Westminster was being launched, but it was not sufficient. Snowden's principles were as deep as Bennett's own, and as the time for the ending of the conference drew near Bennett made a careful appreciation of his position. If immediate victory was not possible, then immediate defeat must be avoided. To ensure that, it was important that he should keep Scullion, of Australia, whose problems were very like his own, firmly in his camp during the closing phases of the meeting.

The United Kingdom Government had circulated a draft statement on policy, rejecting the tariff policy proposed by Bennett but offering an undertaking not to reduce existing preference margins for three years. Bennett prepared a reply, quite short and quite blunt. It invited the Dominion delegations who agreed with the Canadian stand to set up study groups to consider means of implementing the principles involved, and proposed that the Conference be adjourned to a time and place at which those groups could meet and work out mutual arrangements between them. To that invitation Bennett added a concrete invitation that when the Prime Ministers assembled again they should do so in Ottawa. He finished with his final challenge: If the United Kingdom was not prepared to consider imposing the necessary tariffs, those Dominions that would should proceed without her. In the speech he delivered the following day he made the challenge quite direct.

"First we must approve or reject the principle. I put the question definitely to you and definitely it should be answered. There is here no room for compromise, and there is no possibility of avoiding the issue. There is a time for plain speaking, and I speak plainly when I say that the day is now at hand when the peoples of the Empire must decide, once and for all, whether our welfare lies in closer economic union or whether it does not. Delay is hazardous. Further discussion of the principle is surely unnecessary. The time for action has come."

His forcefulness, and his timing, were effective in avoiding a complete rejection of his plans. After a final forty-eight hours of intense activity amongst the delegates, the concluding session was able to pass a resolution (unanimous save for the Irish) covering three main points. It was agreed that the economic section of the conference should stand adjourned until the following year, and that it should meet in Ottawa, on Bennett's invitation. It was agreed that its main purpose when it did meet would be to discuss the Canadian proposals, and it did accept that the question of the imposition of taxes on imported foodstuffs by the United Kingdom should have a high place on its agenda.

Bennett had hardly been a conciliatory figure at the conference, and even in his formal speech at the last, plenary session he could not resist a jibe at J. H. Thomas:

"Mr. Thomas is not a professional man, but his mastery of many of the difficult details of subjects which he could not be expected to understand except as a result of a very great deal of study has, I think, commanded the admiration of us all."

A few days later J. H. Thomas, speaking of Bennett's proposals in the House of Commons at Westminster, used the word 'humbug'. It provoked two letters which Bennett kept. One was from Thomas himself, written from the House of Commons:

Nov. 27th, 1930

My Dear Bennett, In the hurry of an exciting debate I have just used the word 'humbug' in referring to your proposal of 10 %. I am sure you would be the last person to think that I meant *you* were a humbug in making it! but I write this in case you see the reports and think the expression was ill-chosen.

Yours very sincerely,

J. H. Thomas.

The other was from Rudyard Kipling, whom he had found time to visit:

Bateman's,

Burwash,

Sussex.

Dec. 2, 1930.

Dear Mr. Bennett, Believe me, every decent-minded citizen in Great Britain feels personally humiliated by Thomas's latest performance—not to mention MacDonald's 'humour', and Snowden's researches into the dictionary. That's why I kept off the subject when you were down here. But the thing gave you your opening, and you have used it to admiration. Your indictment—which, to be just, you wouldn't have framed if Thomas hadn't been the precise degree of cad that he is—has turned a dummy conference into a direct and vital issue: and we are all grateful and cheered.

Good luck to you.

Most sincerely,

Rudyard Kipling.

Bennett retained a deep liking and respect for Philip Snowden. In many things they were as far apart as men could be. Lord Tweedsmuir, in *Memory Hold the Door*, describes Snowden thus:

"I rarely met a man whose character was so four-square and compact, so wholly without loose fringes. He was like one of his stony, grey, Yorkshire moors, grim at first sight, but hiding in its folds nooks of rare beauty. . . . He had a corrosive irony in handling opponents but he was bitter only about creeds, never about human beings. . . ."

It was ironic that the one opponent with whom he would have liked to have crossed swords again was the one with whom the crisis of the following year dealt most harshly. The tornado of August and September, 1931, tore the political career of Philip Snowden to shreds.

In the short run, Bennett had met with considerable success at the Conference. He had compelled the United Kingdom Government to face the fact that there was considerable feeling within the Commonwealth for an extension of British tariffs against other countries, and that it was no longer possible for a United Kingdom Government to disregard those feelings simply because it was the Government of the United Kingdom. Further, he had so manœuvred events that his proposal to hold the next stage of the argument in Canada could hardly be rejected. At the same time, he had carefully stopped short of the point at which differences between Commonwealth countries would become an open breach. No one had been compelled to take a stand on principles from which it would be impossible or inconvenient later to withdraw (save the Irish Free State, whose delegation had no doubt contemplated such a development in advance with pleasure). In the end Bennett had not insisted that his plan must be accepted. The United Kingdom and South Africa had not said that tariffs on imported food could never be imposed. The way ahead to which he had pointed was still open.

But this tactical success concealed the strategic defeat. Throughout the meeting he had insisted that this was the last moment in time at which it would be possible to make an economic unity of the Empire, and how right he was. All his life he had believed that was desirable. When he sailed for England, he had believed it was still possible. Six months after his accession to leadership of his country he knew that his major dream for his country had been shattered.

Furthermore, this tactical success had other disadvantages. Because the issue had not been forced to a decision at that time the delegates left the Conference still inclined to assume that tariffs on foodstuffs or no tariffs on foodstuffs was not a major issue within the Commonwealth and the key to economic recovery. Bennett could not have foreseen that the Economic

Conference would in fact stand adjourned for two years, not one, nor that on August 3rd, 1931, the date originally suggested for its resumption, the United Kingdom itself would be facing a far sharper economic crisis than any encountered for decades. By the time the delegations assembled again in Ottawa, the landscape had changed.

In August, 1931, the United Kingdom was swept from her moorings to the gold standard and no one was quite sure whether the improvised sheet-anchor that became known as the Sterling Area would hold. France sheltered behind her breakwater of gold and foreign currency reserves, and had no intention of venturing out simply to go to the aid of anyone else. Germany was beyond the point of no return in her march into Nazism, although a great many people were not disposed to face all that fact implied, and the United States, licking the wounds inflicted by the loss of her loans and investments in Europe, was only a matter of months away from the climax of her internal disorders. The delegations duly convened in Ottawa at the end of July, 1932, but the irony implicit in their reunion was that events had moved too fast for them all.

Britain's crisis in August, 1931, had left deep and still-open wounds. Philip Snowden had fought on two fronts with Yorkshire tenacity, to end as an ex-Minister in the House of Lords, like a dismasted ship swept over the reef into the fatal tranquillity of a lagoon. Ramsay MacDonald and J. H. Thomas had remained in office, but with something of the status of barbarian chieftains in a Roman triumph; MacDonald hardly realized what had changed, and Thomas did not care. The new powers in the National Government were Stanley Baldwin, and the Chamberlains. In February, 1932, Parliament had given that Government the right to impose a general tariff of 10 per cent on all goods entering the United Kingdom other than those on the free list (which included wheat, meat and wool), and goods entering from the Dominions had only been exempted from this new tariff temporarily on the urgent representations of Bennett's Government. In theory at least, the United Kingdom was already halfway along the road to meet Bennett, but it was now much further away from the spirit behind the proposals he had first made.

The Commonwealth countries in 1930 can be compared to the ships of the Spanish Armada as they stood at the mouth of the English Channel at the end of the month of July, 1588. Whilst their captains might experience temporary disagreements between themselves over details, each was confident that there was a master plan which would lead them all to victory. By 1932 they were in the position of those same ships some three weeks later. Victory was not even a possibility. The paramount duty of each captain was to look after the safety of his own ship. To risk that in an attempt to aid another would no longer be heroic; it would be disloyalty to his first charge, his own crew.

During the nineteen months that had passed since the delegations left London, Canada's external trade and balance of payments had suffered in two ways. In common with other Commonwealth countries exporting raw and partly manufactured materials, she had seen their prices fall far more drastically than those of fully manufactured articles. Bennett gave these figures to the 1932 Conference:

"Prices of raw and partly manufactured materials have fallen 47·3 per cent since August, 1929, whereas prices of fully and partially manufactured articles have declined only 26 per cent. Farm products have been particularly hard hit, the decline averaging 56·4 per cent, wheat, the staple of the Western farmer, has fallen from an average price of $1·50 a bushel in 1926 to 55 cents in June 1932, a drop of 63·3 per cent. . . .

"Of special importance is the fact that our export prices have fallen more than our import prices. Thus, between 1929 and 1931 our index of export prices declined 30·5 per cent, whereas the import values index fell only 22·5 per cent. In other words, it took 11 per cent more exports last year to buy the same quantity of imports as in 1929."

An equal hardship had been imposed by Britain's departure from the gold standard. The fall of the value of the pound sterling in terms of the United States dollar had dragged the exchange rate of the Canadian dollar down with it. At one stage the Canadian dollar was worth only 75 cents on the

New York exchange market, and when the conference opened it was still at a level of approximately 85 cents. As Bennett pointed out, this decline had enormously increased the real burden on Canada of the cost of servicing her foreign debts.

During the fiscal year ending March, 1933, he told the Conference, Canada would have to find, net, approximately $340m. in U.S. currency, about one-third to meet maturing loans and the balance in interest. In terms of the 1929 value of the Canadian dollar in the United States, that burden represented a payment of approximately $500m. In 1929, a record year, the total value of wheat and wheat flour exports from Canada had been $494m., almost sufficient to meet all payments due to the United States. In 1932 the total value of these exports had been no more than $135m., barely more than a quarter of the cost of interest and debt payments. 62 per cent of foreign investments in Canada were owned in the United States and between 1924 and 1931 the United States had subscribed 41 per cent of the public issues of Canadian bonds, as compared with 2 per cent contributed from Britain.

Another concern to Bennett was the extent to which Soviet Russia, encouraged by the Labour Government that had fallen in 1931, had made inroads into Canada's position as an exporter of raw materials to the United Kingdom. In 1931 the United Kingdom had spent some £32m. in purchases in the Soviet Union. She had bought from Soviet sources 21 per cent of her wheat, 38 per cent of her sawn soft woods, and 34 per cent of her pit-props. She was buying from Russia three times as much as she sold to her. She was paying cash for her purchases, and giving credit on her sales. All the commodities she was purchasing from that quarter could have been supplied by Canada, and Bennett hoped that the National Government that had replaced the socialists would be less inclined to favour the Russians. Instead, he received the blunt answer that Russian prices were lower. Neville Chamberlain, in his diary (recorded in Sir Keith Feiling's *Life of Neville Chamberlain*, Macmillan & Co., Ltd.) under the date August 4th, wrote:

"Bennett came . . . to bring his offer. He adopted a very aggressive tone . . . declaring that we had amongst us official advisers who were interested in the import of Russian fish and lumber. . . ."

An adequate comment on that is to be found in an earlier entry in the same diary, under the date, July 24th:

> "Sir Atul Chatterjee came to see me. . . . I explained that we ourselves while aware of the serious menace to prices of Russian action . . . had financial commitments which would be jeopardized by such drastic action as a total prohibition of Russian imports. . . . Bennett attached great importance to action against Russia, but . . . we could not agree to prohibition."

In short, in these two years since 1930 the mood of the world, and of the men at the head of the countries of the Commonwealth, had changed considerably. They were more harassed, more desperate and more selfish. They did not come to Ottawa ready to discuss any grand plan, or principles in general. They came to drive hard bargains in detail, and that is what they did.

The conference assembled on July 22nd, 1932, and concluded its business some four weeks later, on August 20th. Bennett headed the Canadian delegation, and was surrounded by his own Ministers. The United Kingdom delegation was led by Stanley Baldwin (the Prime Minister, Ramsay MacDonald, remained in London,) and he had with him J. H. Thomas (the only one who had also attended the 1930 Conference), Neville Chamberlain, Chancellor of the Exchequer, and Walter Runciman. The Australian Government had changed, and S. M. Bruce was head of its delegation. Dr. O. D. Skelton, permanent head of the Canadian Department for External Affairs, acted as Secretary. Socially, it was a brilliant affair; Bennett was determined that the Commonwealth should appreciate Ottawa.

But the rifts were apparent from the start. In the opening statements, while Bennett asked Britain for an extension of both tariffs and preferences, Baldwin replied that he hoped that tariffs would be lowered, not raised. And so began what proved to be a marathon session for the negotiation of individual trade agreements between individual countries, dealing in detail with the hundreds of items contained in the Customs Departments' lists.

In such an atmosphere it was inevitable that Bennett should be drawn into the thick of the battle. He was under the spotlight in his own capital. Some of the colleagues at his elbow were urging him to be more aggressive than he was; so was his own Conservative Press. The Press of the United Kingdom, still mainly free trade in principle, was solidly behind its delegation in its refusal to consider any tax on food. And there, Bennett considered, was the main issue; would the United Kingdom tax food coming in from outside the Empire in order to give the food-producing countries within the Empire a preference by allowing their exports to Britain in free? In the background was Lord Beaverbrook, still fighting for Empire Free Trade, firmly convinced that this was the occasion to make a stand for it, and still believing that Bennett was the man to make that stand. Early in the Conference Bennett cabled to Ferguson, the High Commissioner in London, requesting him to see Beaverbrook and try to persuade him to modify his attitude. It threatened the success of the Conference, he said. Beaverbrook agreed: "I will do as you desire" was his message in reply through Ferguson. But he was not convinced. For him, Baldwin was still too attractive a target.

In the end, the Conference left some hard feelings behind it, and to a degree Bennett was responsible. It was almost certainly a mistake for him to have accepted the chairmanship of the Conference. He did not appreciate the importance the British would attach to a display of impartiality in that office, and their consequent irritation when Bennett acted both as Chairman and as a powerful and aggressive champion for Canadian interests. That was certainly Chamberlain's view. He wrote in his diary on the final day of the Conference:

". . . Most of our difficulties centred round the personality of Bennett. Full of high Imperial sentiments, he had done little to put them into practice. Instead of guiding the Conference in his capacity as Chairman, he has acted merely as the leader of the Canadian delegation. In that capacity he has strained our patience to the limit. . . ."

Chairmanship might be a matter of prestige, and as the host dominion Canada had the privilege of claiming that right. Ramsay MacDonald, then Prime Minister in the United Kingdom, had been Chairman of the 1930 Conference. But presiding at such a conference is not only a matter of prestige; it is also a matter of personality. MacDonald had left the argument of the British case in 1930 to others, partly by inclination, partly as a matter of policy. At Ottawa, the main activities were trade and commercial bargainings on a very practical level, and it is hard for an individual to build up an appearance of impartiality and concern for Imperial unity and sacrifice in the council chamber when he is, in the smaller committee rooms, before and after, haggling for dollar and cent concessions on this item or that.

Bennett had too simple—and perhaps too arrogant—an approach to that kind of situation. In the interests of Canada, the Canadian case for concessions must be fought as strongly as possible. Quite apart from his ultimate responsibility as Prime Minister, he was, he felt, the strongest figure on the Canadian side. Therefore he should do the fighting. In that he was probably right; believing that he should not have taken the position of Conference Chairman for himself as well. It is unlikely that he ever considered that the two roles would in any way clash, or would have appreciated why, to some minds, they did.

But that was not the only action that had strained Chamberlain's patience. Once again Bennett's weakness for accepting partisan statements without immediate and automatic check led him into an unpleasant situation. The details of the proposed trade agreements between Canada and the various countries attending the Conference had been worked out in advance, mainly by Stevens, with the aid of his department and Customs. There were over a thousand separate items in the Canadian tariff list, and each had to be considered. After the Conference got under way, a parallel process continued, but this time the consultation was between the Canadian and the British technical experts. Amongst the items on the Canadian list were steel plates. The information the Canadian experts had was that steel plates above a certain size were not made in

Canada, and that it would therefore be possible to place on the free list plates above this size. This was done, and agreed with the United Kingdom delegation. But a Canadian steel manufacturer saw Bennett personally and assured him that plates above this size could be made in Canada, and by him. Without enough investigation, and after the list of items had been agreed with the United Kingdom delegation, Bennett altered it, to remove from the free list the plates he had been told could be made in Ontario.

This action shocked the United Kingdom delegation. What was worse, by their standards, was the fact that Bennett attempted to bluster his way out of the dilemma. Left to themselves, the United Kingdom delegation might have broken the negotiations off there and then on this account; it was Ramsay MacDonald in London who, when advised by cable, instructed them to accept the agreement as altered rather than return in failure. But Baldwin and Chamberlain never quite forgave Bennett for that action.

They had other reasons for suspicion; were not Beaverbrook and Bennett lifelong friends as well as fellow-Canadians? Both Baldwin and Neville Chamberlain had spent a considerable portion of the preceding two years in an entanglement with Beaverbrook over Empire Free Trade, an argument that at one stage had put directly in issue Baldwin's leadership of the Conservative Party and had left Neville Chamberlain torn between his loyalty to his leader, his loyalty to his party, and his own very real ambitions. Neither had cause to love Beaverbrook at that moment.

Above all, the men at the head of the United Kingdom delegation had no trace of Bennett's romantic views of what the Empire, or Commonwealth, could become. They agreed, of course, that the Empire was an admirable institution as well as a sacred trust, but in matters of trade and commerce they were responsible first and foremost for, and to, their fellow industrialists and attendant trade unionists and their own voters. Again, they were very different from the men of the Labour Government Bennett had encountered in 1930. They belonged to the true Establishment. They belonged to the governing classes; they had known it all their lives. It gave

F

them confidence; it produced a certain blindness. It would be an over-simplification to say that they thought first of Britain, secondly of Europe, thirdly of the Colonies (which included Canada) and fourthly of the rest of the world; in 1932 Baldwin had only just begun to think of Europe again, and the rest of the world was far away at the back of his mind. But, unconsciously, they saw the world through Edwardian eyes, when the dominions had been daughters, not adults.

It was Neville Chamberlain who bore the main brunt of the battle with Bennett. Baldwin was not deeply committed in the Ottawa negotiations. As with Bennett, he could keep his feelings on two levels, and reasonably separate. In his biography of Baldwin (*Stanley Baldwin*, Rupert Hart-Davis Ltd.), G. M. Young has said:

"His experience had convinced him that while Free Trade within the Empire was an ideal, Freer Trade was a practical policy."

By 1932 Bennett, too, was limited to the practical policy. He wanted freer trade in the food and raw materials that Canada had to sell; Baldwin in the manufactures the British were anxious to export. For Bennett the real test of ability and strength would come in the negotiations over the schedules and rates in the trade agreements themselves. By temperament, Baldwin could leave those details to others without distress either at doing so or over the final result.

Neville Chamberlain was a man of a different mould. No man becomes Prime Minister of any country unless he possesses strength of character, but Chamberlain was a man of far more rigid a mind than Baldwin. He was the inheritor of the great Chamberlain tradition, the son of Joseph Chamberlain, the radical turned imperialist. He was a man who had spent extremely formative years on an isolated island in the Bahamas, attempting vainly to grow sisal, and who, failing by his own standards, had cost his father a fortune. He had come into politics by way of municipal life in Birmingham, and his first bid for a career had been ruined, so he felt, by that arch-empiricist Lloyd George. At last he was nearing success—in his filial duty, in the protection of the industries of the Midlands, where lay his heart, in his fiscal policies within the United Kingdom, and in the overtaking of his more brilliant brother. He lacked imagination. He knew little of Canada. He had little experience of Canadians. He could not project his mind into Canadian problems. His antagonist, Bennett, was better informed about Britain than he about Canada, but a man equally resolute in defending his country's interests. Bennett and Baldwin were far apart in upbringing and temperament, but they could have agreed to differ. Bennett and Chamberlain were closer in experience and business background, but for that very reason they were less likely to agree over the matters arising at Ottawa, and an amicable disagreement was beyond their capacities.

In his essay on Neville Chamberlain in his book, *Politics* (Hamish Hamilton, London, 1958), R. H. S. Crossman has written:

"If he came to believe himself indispensable, if he was dictatorial and indignant of opposition, if he preferred weak men around him and was a poor judge of persons, these are all failings which he shared with his successor [Winston Churchill]. They are almost inseparable from supreme responsibility. . . ."

Those words might also have been written of Bennett.

In retrospect, and against the background of those last seven years before the Second World War, the Conference was successful within the limits the delegates had finally to accept. It led to an increase, both absolute and relative, in the market for Commonwealth produce in the United Kingdom. Apart from the continued depression in sales of Canadian wheat, as much a matter of falling production as of falling markets, and the collapse in the demand for newsprint, Canada's trade with the United Kingdom recovered more quickly thereafter than her trade with her other, larger customer, the United States. But it was not the conference Bennett had hoped it might have been.

When Bennett came to office in 1930 his habits of mind

were those of his Conservative contemporaries all over the
Western world. They believed that the stability with which the
century had started had suffered no more than a temporary
interruption in 1914. That war had been a clumsy and unnecessary mistake. It had cost Europe a great deal in blood
and treasure. Perhaps a part of that Europe, Russia, had been
lost for ever as a result of the October Revolution, but the rest
could be restored, the old institutions rebuilt, the old techniques
of government and international trade refurbished. The gold
standard was the keystone to that arch and tariffs were an
accepted implement by which the balance of trade was
regulated. Hoover, Baldwin, Bruening and Bennett were all
backward-looking men. So, too, of course, were their socialist
contemporaries. They were the images on the reverse of the
same medal.

For the first ten years after that war those beliefs could be
defended perhaps with increasing difficulty, but not without
some facts to use in their support. After 1929 they could not.

In 1930 he had thought that a new economic Empire
could be built, and that he would be one of its architects.
Before ever the 1932 Conference began he knew that this
dream was impossible of fulfilment. Henceforward he must be
concerned with the problems of Canada alone, and he would
learn as much from the United States as from Britain. Economically speaking, the United Kingdom was now just another
customer.

It is just possible that had Bennett found at Westminster in
the fall of 1930 a Prime Minister of the United Kingdom with
a vision to match his own an Empire Economic Union might
have come into being. Twenty-five years later Western Europe
found its way along that path, although as a result of even
greater pressures to move. But Bennett found nothing of the
kind. Instead, he found Ramsay MacDonald, Philip Snowden
and William Graham, and a government more concerned to
foster trade with Soviet Russia than within the Empire.

By 1933 belief that there was any path leading back into the
security of the past was no longer maintainable by anyone, and
for most of the men in command bewilderment followed. Their
efforts had not been total failures. They had averted complete

disaster. Trade was improving, but it looked increasingly unlikely that it would automatically climb back to the levels of 1929, and in the meantime Germany had deserted their camp. Professor W. Arthur Lewis, the *Economic Survey, 1919–1939*, has written:

"The failure of the World Economic Conference [in 1933] marks in a minor sense the end of an era. It was the last economic conference before the war; the last major effort to cope with economic problems internationally. From 1933 countries abandon hopes of international revival and concentrate on greater restrictions on international trade. From 1933 the divergent domestic policies of the nations become more important than the international economy, to the extent even that the world market disintegrates into many different markets with different price levels and restricted interchange. Indeed, the whole climate of economic opinion alters; up to 1933 world statesmen and economists focus their attention on international trade and investment; after 1933 this interest diminished and economists hardly less than statesmen are preoccupied with domestic policies. Neither is the change confined to economic affairs. By 1933 the political situation had already begun to deteriorate."

They were the Dirty Thirties in many more senses than one.

But in North America the domestic policies that did emerge in 1933 had a dynamism to them that those in Britain lacked. As Maynard Keynes said in an open letter to President Roosevelt in the *New York Times* at the end of December, 1933:

"You have made yourself the trustee for those in every country who seek to mend the evils of our condition by reasoned experiment within the framework of the existing social system. If you fail, rational change will be gravely prejudiced throughout the world, leaving orthodoxy and revolution to fight it out. But, if you succeed, new and bolder methods will be tried everywhere, and we may date the first chapter of a new economic era from your accession to office."

There did blossom in the United States a remarkably vigorous

determination to make this economic system called capitalism
work again, even if it did need some extensive modifications
during the course of the attempt.

Even at the end of his four years in office, Bennett had courage
and energy enough to respond to this challenge, and to make
his own attempt to move Canada by reasoned experiment. In
1931 he lost hope that the Empire would provide a solution.
By 1934 he was turning his mind and his imagination southwards.

Chapter Twelve

MR. PRIME MINISTER

BENNETT certainly had come to Ottawa in August, 1930, with an immense sense of urgency, of power, and of determination to carry through the plans he had matured during his last years in opposition, but he also brought with him, as every head of state must, his own character, his whole background, as an inescapable part of the equipment he must use in grappling with the tasks that faced him.

Within six months, Ottawa was full of stories of the new Administration. A standard version ran thus:

Visitor to Ottawa: "Who is that man coming towards us?"
Ottawa Resident: "Mr. R. B. Bennett, the new Prime Minister."
Visitor to Ottawa: "Why is he talking to himself?"
Ottawa Resident: "He's holding a Cabinet meeting."

There can be no dispute that Bennett was a poor administrator. He was deficient in two qualities essential to success in the handling of a governmental machine: the capacity to delegate work and responsibility easily and wisely and the capacity to say 'No'.

To a degree, he was carrying with him into office the habits of a lifetime. From his first days in Calgary, any business he felt to be his had been, in matters of control, strictly a one-man affair. In his law pratice he had had other lawyers working for him; when they worked with him, it was on a particular case and for a particular end. He had controlled the E. B. Eddy Company because he owned it. From 1927 he had controlled the Conservative Party organization because he was paying a large part of its costs, a state of affairs good neither for himself nor the party.

In the conduct of political affairs, his experience of the need to work under discipline as a member of a team had been regrettably short, limited to the year 1926. Before then, in the 1911 Parliament, he had been the maverick, intent on jousting with Mackenzie and Mann, and with Meighen when he acted as their spokesman. After 1927, he was the leader, and the greater the sincerity he brought to the post the greater his conviction that he must make all the major decisions.

He had only held Cabinet office twice before—for three months in 1921 and for two months in 1926. On each occasion the House was either in adjournment or had been dissolved, and he and his colleagues had been more intent on their individual election campaigns across the country than on learning the techniques of working as a mutually supporting unit under the pressures of daily opposition attack from the other side of the chamber.

Bennett was never indifferent to the advice of other individuals, once he had come to accept their knowledge and their capacity to make a sound judgment. The history of his achievements demonstrates that. He trusted McFarland over wheat, and he had every reason to. He listened to advice, and made durable decisions on the basis of that advice, in the creation of the Bank of Canada, the Canadian Broadcasting Corporation, and in the negotiations with the United States for the St. Lawrence Waterway Treaty. His handling of Canada's stand in relation to Newfoundland and the United Kingdom when the dominion ran into its financial crises was firm and sound. But he was quite unable to create for himself an efficient machine for running the normal government of the country. He never seemed to understand the need for and value of a good staff.

The organization around him when he took office was far from impressive. True, the system had come down from an easier day, but he was not a man to hesitate to make changes when he saw they should be made. The Government of Canada lacked the equivalent either of the United Kingdom Cabinet secretariat or the network of liaison officers which enables a military command to function quickly and well. The standard office equipment for Prime Minister was two or more private secretaries—one bilingual—and a small staff of Civil Service stenographers capable of handling routine correspondence without direction, but no more. To that a Prime Minister might add one or more aspirant M.P.s to act as personal assistants, but their value was a matter of chance.

One employed by Bennett dictated, for Bennett to sign, a very moving letter of condolence to the lady he assumed to to be the suddenly bereaved wife of a Conservative M.P. Bennett signed this letter without reading it, and was exceedingly vexed when he received from the M.P. himself a chiding letter saying that he was in fact alive, but saddened to feel that his leader had not noticed his still regular attendance at Party caucus meetings.

What the office establishment did not have was a post carrying the status and responsibility of a chief of staff, or deputy minister. In fact, Bennett had in his own office only two people capable by temperament of taking some of the burden of routine activity from his shoulders. One was Dr. O. D. Skelton, Deputy Minister for External Affairs, who was available simply because Bennett held that portfolio as well as the Premier office, the other Alice Millar, whose status came from her own personality—nowhere else. They were very different beings, but they were equally indispensable.

It is, of course, likely that Bennett never realized the handicaps he permitted himself to suffer. For one thing, he was constitutionally unwilling to refuse to see anyone who wanted to see him. He felt it his duty to be available to every citizen who took the trouble to make his way to his office, and he liked to talk and to gossip. As a result, his waiting-room was always full, and there was no one there to weed out and send elsewhere those callers who had no real right to waste so much of the time of their country's chief executive. Even a minister who wished to see him alone might find himself stranded in the waiting-room, to take his turn with every casual visitor. Not all of them had sufficient time to waste in this way.

Written papers suffered from the same absence of an effective sieve. Bennett held to the belief that a letter addressed to him ought to be answered by him, and he did his best to do exactly that. But there was never sufficient time, and as a result there were often layers of unanswered letters, minutes and memoranda on his vast desk. He spent as much time as he could in dictating, and when he did he could still keep two stenographers fully occupied, such was his speed of thought and speech. But when papers did pile up, only he could sift the accumulation into some order of urgency. When he was away, there was a chance to distribute some of the unanswered letters to the department from which the writer might receive an early reply, even though it were not signed by the Prime Minister himself, but that was no solution.

His habit of mind had its reactions throughout the administration. If the chief thought he should be consulted over the whole field of activity, most acquiesced; it was easier, and less dangerous. In that way Bennett brought back on himself a volume of work that ought to have been disposed of by others.

For instance, in September, 1934, he was in Europe to attend that year's meeting of the General Assembly of the League of Nations in Geneva as head of the Canadian delegation, and to sign a new commercial treaty with France. He may have intended that the journey should provide a break from the routine of Ottawa as well, but he contracted influenza and spent a good deal of his time in Geneva in bed. None the less, whilst there, in touch with Ottawa mainly by cable, the problems referred to him for decision ranged from protests against the low tariffs on the importation into Canada of French berets (to which, even without his files, he replied in exact detail) to the question of whether the new Army barracks in Calgary should be heated by coal or by oil. No decision affecting a Minister's own constituency is ever unimportant, but some must be less important than others.

He did not even escape personal entanglement with the redoubtable Lady Houston (may her soul rest in peace). In 1931, an Empire broadcast had been planned by the B.B.C. for Christmas Day, but the arrangements came adrift. On December 23rd, Bennett received this cable from Lady Houston:

"Cannot you circumvent the trickery preventing England receiving Christmas messages from the Empire? Newspapers put blame on Canada. I think it emanates from Russia. Kindliest Christmas greetings. Lucy Houston."

He replied at once:

"If B.B.C. had originally taken matter up with High Commissioner or myself, arrangements would have been successfully completed. On being advised yesterday, took immediate action, but when arrangements completed was informed British Post Office and broadcast had dropped programme. Sincere greetings and best wishes. Bennett."

Yet, tardy as Bennett may have been in producing decisions, the cause was not an inability to make a decision. His mind was clear and firm, and, once a problem was squarely before him, he had no inclination to shirk a decision on it. If he failed to deal with everything, it was because he simply did not have time enough to do all he thought he should.

This self-sufficiency showed itself in many ways. Manion, his Minister of Railways, in his biography, *Life is an Adventure* (published whilst Bennett was still leader of the Party), says this of him:

"His Government personnel from 1930 to 1935 could, I feel sure, compare favourably with any Government in the last half-dozen. Like all Cabinets in Canada, where geography, race and religion, must come into the choosing, it contained some dead wood, but it also had at least half a dozen oustandingly able men.

"Yet Mr. Bennett's failure ever to give them collectively or individually due credit or meed of praise for their good work led many people to estimate them as a group of nonentities, and even had they been such, it would certainly not have reflected any glory upon the leader who chose them. . . .

"As a matter of fact, the story that he dominated his Cabinet, that he domineered over them all, was just so much balderdash. Most of us handled our departments without either his direction or interference, but his almost studied ignoring of his colleagues in public addresses and debates lent substance to the campaign of the Liberals against this 'rich, intolerant despot'—as they succeeded in getting the public to believe, and by it helping them to win the election of 1935."

Manion himself was not a nonentity. He did not prove to be

a great political leader, later, when he succeeded Bennett (perhaps chosen in part because he was so great a contrast). He was a cheerful, outgoing man, 'Bob' to everyone; as was said after his disastrous campaign in 1940, he had what Talley-rand called 'the terrible gift of familiarity'. But he was competent. So was Rhodes, from the Maritimes, first in charge of Fisheries, later, in 1932, taking over the Ministry of Finance from Bennett himself. So were Guthrie and Ryckman.

Meighen could take a more detached view. He did not return to office until he accepted appointment to the Senate in February, 1932, from which time, as a Minister without Portfolio, he led the party in that chamber. But he always maintained a certain detachment. As he wrote in May, 1941, to John Lederle, who was preparing a thesis for the University of Michigan on *The National Organization of the Liberal and Conservative Parties in Canada:*

"While a member of the Bennett Government and also Senate leader, I attended Cabinet meetings, but made no pretence of attending regularly. My object in attending was mainly to explain the attitude I was taking towards Government measures in the Senate and hear that attitude discussed. As a member of the Administration I was, of course, constitutionally responsible for all its actions, but I made plain in the Senate that I did not take that constitutional responsibility with the same seriousness as if I were a Minister in the Other House. . . ."

Meighen put his finger more directly on the temperamental gulf that had always existed between the two men in the speech he made at the farewell dinner tendered to Bennett in Toronto on January 16th, 1939, a few days before he finally left Canada:

"Mr. Bennett may forgive me, and he may not—there are some things for which he has never forgiven me—but platitudes of affection do not appertain to him. He is not, as Laurier was, so spontaneously affable a personality, so universally gracious and engaging that one likes him, sometimes follows him, though one believes him wrong.

"He is not, as Macdonald was, so intensely human and

companionable as to be loved even for his faults. He is, as everyone knows, a different stamp of man altogether. He is a product of this generation rather than of the last. He is a man of affairs, a man who has been in contact with realities, from his earliest years to this very hour.

"On the rough, ruthless battlefields of life, he has triumphed, and he depends, and does not fear to depend, upon his achievements for his following and his fame."

"This rich, intolerant despot"; "He depends upon his achievements for his following": These phrases illuminate so clearly Bennett's principal failing as a Prime Minister. It was an inability to communicate with others.

When talking to those who knew Bennett, I have found a marked contrast in the pictures they draw of him. One is of the distant, Olympian figure, the cold, aloof intellectual of the Vancouver *Sun* comment, the man who could not unbend even to please for a moment a devoted constituency worker. To many he seemed to regard himself as a most superior person, a Canadian edition of the Marquis Curzon, and the photographs of him at that time could be portraits of exactly such a man. They show a tall, rather stout figure, but one with erect carriage and immense assurance, invariably dressed in the most formal of men's fashions, a man who would wear striped trousers, tail coat, pearl-grey double-breasted waistcoat, Ascot cravat and a silk hat by choice. Such a man would not even look Canadian.

The other picture is of a man who could be, who liked to be, accepted as friendly and unassuming, at ease in any company, interested and concerned in the lives and activities of those around him, and anxious to help where he could. This was the man, so a C.P.R. employee told me, who ate with the greatest of relish and companionship a late meal of flapjacks and bacon cooked over a stove in the caboose of a night freight train from Fort Macleod to Calgary in which he had thumbed a ride, and who then rolled himself in a dirty borrowed blanket and slept on the floor for the rest of the journey. Since both pictures must be true, there must be some explanation for their apparent irreconcilability.

The most revealing illustration of Bennett lies, I think, in this story, told me by Eric Duggan of Edmonton, whose father, D. M. Duggan, was leader of the Alberta Provincial Conservative Party in the '30s. It involved his father, and it begins with a telephone call to his father from Bennett one summer afternoon.

Mr. Bennett was speaking, and at his most polite. Would it be convenient for Mr. Duggan to see him? Of course it was, and when Duggan discovered that Bennett was calling from Calgary, it was inevitable that he should suggest an appointment in Calgary, at Bennett's office there, for nine the following morning.

Duggan took the night train from Edmonton, which deposits (or did when it ran) its passengers on the streets of Calgary at 7.30 a.m. He took a room at the Palliser, washed, shaved, ate breakfast and still reached Bennett's office in the Lancaster Building five minutes before nine.

Bennett was in his room, and Alice Millar, as secretary and guardian, was at her desk by his door. The door was open and Duggan put his head inside his room.

Bennett was at his desk. He looked up sternly.

"Mr. Duggan, your appointment was for nine o'clock and it is not yet that time. I'm exceedingly busy today."

Duggan was disconcerted.

"If any other time would be more convenient . . ." he said.

"It would. Shall we say some time this afternoon?"

"Certainly."

"Very well. Five o'clock at the hotel."

Duggan filled in the day in Calgary as best he could. As he remembered it, it was exceedingly warm, and at four he was back in his hotel room, tired and bored. He took off his jacket and lay down on his bed. Five o'clock came and no Bennett. It was not until a quarter to six that Bennett entered, elegantly dressed as usual.

Duggan's patience was exhausted. He sat up, and exploded.

"Mr. Bennett, our appointment was for five o'clock. It is now a quarter to six. I've been here all day and I'm sick and tired of this kind of treatment."

Bennett stood there silent for a moment, tall and stern, and

Duggan wondered when and how the lightning would strike. Then Bennett laughed.

"I'm sorry," he said, "and I apologize. I have been busy, but I've no right to have behaved as I have."

Then, Duggan said, he took off his jacket and lay down on the other bed and began to talk, more freely, more intimately, than he ever had before or did later. Towards seven he reached for the telephone.

"Duggan, you'll have dinner here with me? And we'll make it a party."

He proceeded, with no prompting from Duggan, to call six of Duggan's best friends in Calgary and persuaded them to come to dinner at the Palliser at eight. He then ordered the meal.

It was, Duggan said, one of the gayest and friendliest evenings of my life.

This contrast between the outer shell and the inner humanity had been there a long time. Colonel Stevens, the historian of the Canadian National Railways, has this recollection:

"My first meeting with Bennett occurred when I was wounded in 1916. Both my father and I were overseas, and my sister, Victoria, was dying of diabetes in Edmonton, Alberta. I had six weeks' convalescence after my discharge from hospital, and I arranged to escort a demented soldier to Canada.

"When I reached Edmonton, Jimmy Reilley came to see me; he was then one of the City Commissioners and his brother, Charlie, was in my platoon in the P.P.C.L.I. He learnt I had paid my own way west and expected to pay my way back to Britain. He said that was nonsense, and he gave me a note to Mr. Bennett, then in Calgary, which he afterwards exchanged for one to Bob Edwards, of *The Eyeopener*.

"I went down on the night train. Edwards gave me breakfast, and then took me over to Bennett's office. Bennett sat glowering behind a desk at the far end of the room, and I remember thinking that he looked very formidable and that it was just as well that I had a sponsor.

"Edwards told him my story, but before he could make any request on my behalf the storm broke. Bennett said that control of patronage did not constitute a warrant for every 'Tom, Dick and Harry'—I remember he used that phrase—to come in on him, to the neglect of the main war effort, and so on.

"Edwards listened gravely, flicking the ashes from the cigar he still smoked. When the blast had ended, he said: 'You are quite right, R.B. But you have helped other chaps and you are going to help this one.'

"For a long minute Bennett stared back, and then the ghost of a smile showed at the corner of his mouth.

" 'Come back this afternoon,' he said. That afternoon I had a first-class ticket from Calgary back to Britain, which was rather more than I was entitled to, as a sergeant."

Bennett could be a companionable man. In Calgary there had been the Bennett table at the Alberta Hotel, the circle of families in the days of formal calls and afternoon teas, Bishop Pinkham, his daughters, and his son, articled to Bennett, who was killed in action in the First World War, to Bennett's great distress, and the Macleods, the children and grandchildren of Colonel Macleod of the North West Mounted Police, and the Crosses, the family of the founder of the Calgary Brewery.

Later there were the de Foras girls at High River, Alberta, the children of Count de Foras, an *émigré* who may not have been too successful as a rancher, but who had a wonderful instinct for hospitality; in Ottawa the formal dinner he preferred was the stag affair at which the talk would be of men and their business. Even in London there was a dining club, named the Bennett Club for him, that met once a week at the Savoy, and at Juniper Hill the constant stream of visitors, politicians, lawyers, civil servants—above all, men from the Canadian forces scattered around him in southern England. But conversation is not necessarily communication.

Bennett was not a conversationalist of the first order. He talked fluently and was extremely well informed on a great variety of subjects, but his sentences lacked the sudden flash of thought or turn of phrase that excites the listener and spurs him to excel in his turn. The same flat quality, almost an opaqueness, is to be found in his letters. They are a man talking from behind a gauze curtain; the meaning comes through, but half the personality is concealed. Why?

His life became set in a rigid pattern, that of a rich bachelor. His home was a hotel suite, in Ottawa at the Château Laurier, a section of one floor specially remodelled and redecorated for him, mainly at his own, very considerable, expense. His habits had not changed. He still ate heavily, with an increasing weakness for sweet things, and although he now served wine for his guests, he still did not drink or smoke. He was proud of his silver, his glass and his library, but work remained his obsession. His day in his office in the East Block on Parliament Hill began about 8.30 each morning, and rarely ended before midnight.

He still kept Sunday as a day on which no work was permitted, save in the most exceptional circumstances, and for him the Sabbath began at midnight on Saturday and lasted for twenty-four hours. It was permissible to read, and obligatory to read some chapters from the Bible. He had promised his mother that he would read at least six verses from one of the Gospels each day, and he still did.

His normal manners were courteous and considerate; it was not his habit to be rude to stenographers, messengers or staff. But he could be rude and offensive, and occasionally act the part of the bully. So much depended on the reaction of the man with whom he was angry; the quickest way to end an outburst of temper was to be unaffected by it. But, if he could be unreasonable, and occasionally vindictive, when the storm was over he assumed that things would be as they had been before. He found it hard to apologize in words, but he knew well enough when he should, and his apology was apt to take the form of an unexpected and handsome gift.

He had now a wide circle of acquaintances, and he was a regular correspondent. But had he any friends? Indeed, had individuals, other than his mother, ever mattered very much to him? Certainly, the number who had was very small; George Robinson, Max Aitken, and later Maurice Brown, of the Royal Bank of Canada. But there was also his family.

George, regretfully, he had written off. Despite his charm and ability, he was a failure, and was in virtual exile. Ronald was a sea captain, like his grandfather, and they could see each other but rarely. Evelyn was married and lived in Vancouver, at the other side of the country. The closest to him was Mildred.

Mildred was an excellent companion for him. She was some eighteen years younger than he, vivacious, attractive, intelligent if not intellectual, and deeply attached to him. She enjoyed his confidence because she was discreet enough to retain it. She lived in Ottawa, and acted as his hostess on formal social occasions. She came nearest to being a daughter to him, and after her marriage to William Herridge, Herridge himself seemed to fall into the role of son-in-law.

In character, Herridge was in strong contrast to Bennett. He was an Ottawa lawyer who had married a woman with a considerable fortune and he had a streak of the playboy in him. His first wife had died before he met Bennett, and they met because Herridge was a loyal and enthusiastic party supporter, glad to be of use to his party leader. But Herridge had an innate gaiety and charm, and an insouciance, that in their turn drew Bennett to him; at least here was a man with no obvious axe to grind. Herridge married Mildred shortly after Bennett became Prime Minister, and thereafter the links between them strengthened.

Bennett sent Herridge to Washington as the Canadian Ambassador to the United States and he remained there for the rest of Bennett's term of office. It was an excellent appointment, and Herridge was of great value to Bennett, and to Canada, both as an informant on the American scene and as an interpreter of Canada to the circle of government in Washington. Dean Acheson has paid his tribute to Herridge's skill and success during the crucial period of the New Deal. Over the years of his appointment, Herridge's influence on Bennett deepened, and it was at its zenith when Bennett came to formulate his own policies for Canada in the fall of 1934 and the spring of 1935. Herridge had an idealism that responded to the emotions and ideas bubbling in Washington at that time. He became a partisan for the New Deal and he pulled Bennett

at least a third of the way along with him. But by then Bennett
was willing to move. Indeed, he was convinced that Canada
had to move.

But in the end one is forced back to the belief that Bennett
must be described as a self-centred and self-sufficient man, and
that those around him sensed it. Robinson, Aitken, Herridge,
Brown, McFarland; he knew them all, he valued their aid and
their support, but it is impossible to believe that they were an
essential part of his life. He used men rather than enjoyed them,
and deep friendship is impossible under those conditions. How
tragic it was, one man said to me, that a man who had given so
much of himself to his country should in the end, when nearly
seventy, quit that country for voluntary exile elsewhere, and
still leave so few who felt any real distress at his departure.

If Bennett's nature had been cold and wholly self-regarding,
this would have been easier to understand, but it was not. In
politics, as has been said, one had no friends, only confederates.
One great handicap was that he had so few other interests and
outlets, so many limitations that militated against friendship
based on shared interests. He read extensively, but to inform
himself rather than to widen or release his mind. He had no
interest in sport or any form of outdoor activity. He was tone-
deaf, and so insensitive to the world of music, and his interest
in the visual arts was conventional and lukewarm. But even
that provides no complete explanation. There was a great
warmth in him. It was in its communication that he failed.

To my mind, the explanation can only be found in the
circumstances of his childhood; the unchanging nature of the
man himself after he left New Brunswick shows how early his
character was set, and how deep the mould. It was then that
shyness, loneliness and a sense of mission were firmly stamped
into his being, and time did not dissolve them. It did no more
than transform them into the brusqueness, the isolation, the
obsession with work that were his so noticeable characteristics
fifty years later. By the time he was sixty-five, the armour he
had built around himself was enormously thick, and to reach
others he must shout from across a wide moat. Why should
other men around him have bothered to try to understand a
man who always seemed so distant and so secure? In this,

King, his opponent, had all the advantages. He sat at the centre of a web, Bennett in the depths of a strong-point.

Superficially, an insensitive man; and yet dare one say that of this man whose life had been work for others as much as for himself, for clients in every kind of trouble, for his country in its most difficult period of depression? When one recalls other men who have been so obsessed, the ends they have sought, the empires they have built, and the use they have made of the power they grasped, Bennett deserves no sneer from those who may be tempted today to look back at him with mild curiosity and faint disapproval,

No ability to communicate, defective mechanism with which to share what he had; how these defects cut a man off, not only from his contemporaries, but equally from those who look back at him. Bennett could give loyalty, devotion and the most intense service to those he felt a duty to serve. He could give generously to those he felt had claims on him or his possessions. But he could not accept equality, and so the spaces closest to him were very empty indeed. That was his tragedy, as a man and as a politician.

Chapter Thirteen

DROUGHT AND DEPRESSION

IN Canada a great many people have talked of Bennett as a total failure as a Prime Minister. He did not defeat the depression. He did not, they say, blast his way into world markets. The '30s have remained a dirty word, and no one has yet forgotten what a Bennett-buggy is.

Depression there was. Arthur M. Schlesinger, Jr., in his book on Roosevelt, *The Crisis of the Old Order*, in two short paragraphs gives this picture of the effect on the farmer in the United States of the fall in world prices:

"The burden of agricultural adjustment thus fell not on production but on price. . . . Between 1929 and 1934 agricultural production declined 15 per cent in volume, 40 per cent in price; industrial production 42 per cent in volume, 15 per cent in price. . . . Corn slid down to 15 cents, cotton and wool to 5 cents, hogs and sugar to 3 cents, and beef to 2.5 cents. . . . Net farm income in 1932 was $1.8 billion— less than one-third what it had been three years earlier. . . .

"The farmer's obligation—his taxes and his debts—had been calculated in terms of the much higher price levels of the 'twenties. A cotton farmer who borrowed $800 when cotton was 16 cents a pound borrowed the equivalent of 5,000 pounds of cotton; now, with cotton moving towards 5 cents, he must pay back the debt with over 15,000 pounds of cotton. And, while the farmer's income fell by 64 per cent, his burden of indebtedness fell a mere 7 per cent."

The plight of the farmer in western Canada was rather worse. Canada's backbone, the prairies, was broken, not by the depression alone, but by depression and drought. At one time Bennett feared that the disaster was a permanent one, that the climate within the Palliser Triangle in western Canada was reverting to desert conditions and would never produce again any crop that needed more than a desert rainfall. The years of drought ended, as the world surplus of wheat ended, but not while Bennett was Prime Minister. He had no weapon that could summon rain from the skies.

In the west those were times when there was nothing to live on but hope; the hope grew very thin, and fear was just beyond. The miracle is that communities held together as they did. But the depression and the drought killed Bennett in the west. I think he knew it, and I don't think he blamed anyone for it. His defeat came in the east, where it was least expected and least deserved.

And yet Bennett's plans and actions over the marketing of what wheat was produced were, within the framework of what was possible, the most successful of all his efforts during his period in office. They were unorthodox. For their success they depended very much on the personality and capabilities of one man, the man Bennett chose to carry through the whole job, John I. McFarland—but they resulted in Canadian wheat farmers receiving consistently better prices for wheat exports than their counterparts in other wheat-exporting countries.

McFarland between 1931 and 1935 was in effect the Government wheat broker, operating on the international wheat market by the aid of Government guaranteed loans. He believed that wheat would retain its value, and he had courage enough to back that belief. By 1935 he had taken from the market and carried over, on Government account, some 213 million bushels of wheat or wheat futures, and his commitments to banks in respect of that carry-over were in excess of $80 million. Yet he concluded his operations with the liquidation of his borrowings, with payment of all interest and carrying charges on those borrowings, and with a surplus of $9 million.

Bennett came back from the Imperial Conference to find the Canadian wheat-producer already in serious distress. The three prairie wheat pools had already overpaid him, in terms of world prices, for the 1929-30 crop year. He had no prospect of further income for twelve months. The pools themselves were in mortgage to the banks, the banks were seriously worried by

potential bad debts of this size, and the provincial governments were pledging what credit they had to support the banks.
Australia, to aid her wheat-exporters, had devalued her currency by 25 per cent. Argentina devalued hers, and set up a
tight system of foreign exchange control to aid exports. And
Soviet Russia had entered the world market as a wheat-exporter
for the first time since the First World War.

Within two weeks of his return, Bennett had carried through
his first objectives. He had seen the representatives of the banks
and persuaded or forced them to undertake that they would not
jettison the 1929-30 crop year surplus on the world market,
already in a collapsed state. Instead, they agreed to leave it to
McFarland to market this surplus piecemeal as opportunity
offered. He announced the rest of his policy at Regina on December 30th. He reported what he had done in respect of the
1929-30 surplus. He promised to set up a finance corporation
with its main object the giving of credit to farmers to aid them
to diversify their activities and cease to be wholly dependent on
wheat (the corporation, named the Dominion Agricultural
Credit Co. Ltd., with a capital of $5m. subscribed by banks
and insurance companies, was set up the following month and
announced on February 2nd). He promised the three western
provincial governments free aid in the shape of food, clothing
and seed grain for those individuals in need.

At the same time he resolved to tackle another complaint,
one of old standing in the west: the belief of so many farmers
that the Winnipeg Grain Exchange was a parasitic organization
using brokers' money to force down the price of wheat when
bought from the farmer and to inflate the price at which it was
finally sold to the consumer. One of the main objects of the
farmer's suspicions was the market in futures; at best, he thought
it was gambling; at worst, a conspiracy to strip the producer of
all reward for his efforts. At the end of March, Bennett
announced that he had asked Sir Josiah Stamp, then serving
as Chief Executive officer of the L.M.S. Railway, to head a
Royal Commission "to inquire into and report upon what effect
if any the dealing in grain futures has upon the price received
by the producer". Lester Pearson acted as secretary to the
Commission.

The following June, McFarland's powers as government
wheat broker were extended; his task became in effect that of
giving general price support to Canadian wheat: the year 1932
was the worst one of the crisis. In the December of that year,
the price of No. 1 Northern fell to 38 cents a bushel, the lowest
price recorded for 400 years. McFarland held to his convictions
that he should hold off the market as much wheat as possible;
as he said in 1936 after his retirement, what finally adjusted the
balance and enabled him to sell his carryover without loss was
a series of successive short crops in the exporting areas—three
in North America, two in Australia, and finally, in 1935, one
in Argentina. He gambled in wheat futures, but the gamble
paid off in the end, and it was the wheat farmer who reaped the
benefit.

McFarland and his activities did not constitute the sole
attempt Bennett made to aid the wheat producer. In 1931 his
Government paid producers a bonus of 5 cents a bushel on the
crop of that year. In 1932, at Ottawa, he fought for and
obtained an Empire preference of 2s. a quarter (approximately
6 cents a bushel) on wheat. He was largely instrumental in
setting up the conference that produced the London Wheat
Agreement of 1933, and presided at it. That failed in its main
purpose—the application of quotas to each exporting country—
but only because Argentina later refused to be bound by the
quota to which her delegates had at the Conference agreed.

Bennett and McFarland worked in extremely close contact
during all the four years. They were in constant touch by
telephone or telegram; the sheaf of communications between
them is one of the largest amongst the Bennett papers. In the
end even the three Prairie Provinces, governments and wheat
pools, emerged without loss, being able to repay to the banks the
$21m. they had borrowed from the ultimate proceeds of the
sales of wheat. McFarland, on the other hand, was removed
from the new Wheat Board, set up in 1935, by order in Council
passed by King's Government within three months of its
assumption of office.

But McFarland could work no miracles. He could not make
wheat grow where no moisture existed to germinate the seed.
The year 1934 saw the western provinces at the end of their

tether. Distress had been cumulative and still no improvement was in sight. No western premier wanted to repudiate any public debt, or default in payment of the interest due on it, but their situation was parallel to that in which the farmer found himself. Revenue fell; the burden of interest remained constant.

In Alberta, the provincial expenditures were some $15 million a year. Out of that, no less than $7,159,000 went in payment of interest charges. In Manitoba the position was very much the same, interest charges absorbing some $6m. out of a total budget of $14,300,000. Saskatchewan was the province most badly hit. In the previous three years controllable expenditure had been cut in half, with all the hardship that that meant to the men and women in the province, and at the end interest on provincial debt was costing twice as much as the province could spend on all its other essential services. And yet everyone recognized the fact that, were the Federal Government to take over direct responsibility for the liabilities of a province, the end of provincial independence would be very near. The fate of Newfoundland in the same period showed that only too well.

Bennett first met the depression with the traditional methods of the day. Under his first Order in Council dealing with relief, passed on September 26th, 1930, $4m. was earmarked for payment to municipalities, on whom the direct burden fell, on the basis that the Federal Government would pay one-third of their costs, leaving the provincial government and the municipality each to pay one of the remaining thirds, and this pattern of aid held good over the next four years. The balance of the $20m. voted at that first session was assigned to expenditure on public works, in the main on the initiative of the municipalities, but with the Federal Government limiting its contribution to one-quarter of the cost of each operation. The results of that first year were encouraging. For an expenditure by the federal government of some $19m., public works of an estimated value of $90m. had been sparked into existence.

Up to the end of 1933 the Federal Government paid out approximately $100m. for direct relief to the unemployed (the largest sum was $42m. in 1931) and loaned or advanced another $46m. to the provinces, the largest share going to Saskatchewan. It had also spent another $29m. in Federal public works and had given Government guarantees in respect of another $92m. in loans for specific projects. These ranged from $60m. to the C.P.R. to a $660,000 advance to Algoma Steel Corporation to finance an order for 30,000 tons of steel rails for the C.N.R.

Bennett disliked direct relief, both in principle and because it divorced administration (which was provincial) from financial responsibility. He preferred that men should be at work, and in 1932 the Government set up relief camps for single, unemployed and homeless young men.

The proposal originated with the Department of National Defence, and the first three camps, set up in October, 1932, were intended to deal with three specific projects that the Department thought would be useful; they included clearing landing strips along the route of the proposed Trans-Canada airway and the construction and improvement of a number of air stations. The estimate was that there were between 50,000 and 70,000 young men eligible to use these camps, and over the first twelve months an average of 11,548 of them did.

It was an Army undertaking. The Engineers prepared the plans, estimates, and specifications, provided accommodation and supervised the works. The men were fed by the Army Service Corps, clothed by the Ordnance Corps, and doctored by the Medical Corps. Most of the administrative jobs on the projects themselves were filled by the men taken into the scheme; the Army claimed that not more than a dozen of its permanent personnel were ever employed full time in the scheme. Each man was given free accommodation and food, free clothing and medical care, and a cash allowance of 20 cents a day. No one was engaged for a fixed period; each was free to leave at any time.

But each man was liable to be discharged "for cause"; if he was, he became ineligible for re-employment under the plan, and this provision was one of the main causes why the scheme finally foundered. Yet the camps did provide thousands of young men with work and the chance to improve their skills, as well as their physique. They provided Canada with a number of public works that would not otherwise have been tackled. Five years later, many of those young men were to join the Canadian Army and turn themselves, voluntarily, into a fine, disciplined, fighting force. The scheme can hardly be called a failure.

In the end, of course, Bennett did not defeat the depression. What finally absorbed the unemployed men and women in Europe, and to an extent in the United States, were the preparations made for the Second World War, and in Canada at that time most Conservatives, and certainly every Liberal and C.C.F member, would have thrown up their hands in horror at any suggestion that Canada should join in that flirtation with death.

In 1935, the Conservatives in Britain fought an election on the basic claim that they had done very well, considering, and should be left to carry on. Bennett fought one in Canada on the cry: 'I can do better if you will back my fresh plans.' It is ironic that the Conservatives in Britain won and that the Conservatives in Canada lost.

But Bennett's record in government does not consist entirely of struggle with a depression. He is also remembered because he reintroduced an Honours List into Canada. He is not remembered as the Prime Minister who successfully negotiated a St. Lawrence Waterway Treaty with the United States, nor is he commonly praised for establishing the Bank of Canada and the Canadian Broadcasting Corporation, and it is difficult to feel that posterity has, so far, been entirely fair.

Bennett was entirely in character when he decided once again to submit names of Canadians to the Crown for the grant of honours. As he put it, rather stiffly, in a letter to J. R. MacNicol, M.P., dated December 4th, 1934:

"So long as I remain a citizen of the British Empire and a loyal subject of the King, I do not propose to do otherwise than assume the prerogative rights of the Sovereign to recognize the services of his subjects."

To him, the Crown was an integral part of being a Canadian, and the granting of honours was an integral part of the Crown. He would not have put it, as Lord Elgin did in 1853:

"Now that the bonds formed by commercial protection and the disposal of local offices are severed, it is very desirable that the prerogative of the Crown, as the fountain of honour, should be employed so far as this can properly be done, as a means of attaching the outlying parts of the Empire to the Throne."

He would have been more disposed to take the word 'honour' literally. There were people in Canada, as in the United Kingdom, who deserved to be honoured. Was there any reason for Canada to pretend to a form of sham republicanism and say that this method of recognizing a public service was undemocratic?

He was perfectly aware that public opinion in Canada drew a sharp line between the grant of an honour that was personal to the man or woman who received it, and an honour that was hereditary. The Canadian Privy Council had so reported in 1918, and all Governors-General over the previous fifteen years had agreed that this sentiment was still strong. He probably agreed with it; even though he himself accepted an honour that was, technically, hereditary, he was a bachelor when he did so and of an age when it was in the highest degree unlikely that he would leave any descendant in the direct line to succeed to it.

But he also knew that the preparation of an honours list is and must be the responsibility of a Prime Minister alone, that it would be a troublesome task, and that for every person pleased, he would run the risk of disappointing at least one other who did not see his or her name in the published list. All those things he weighed; it can only have been that he regarded the final decision he did make as much a matter of duty as of individual conviction.

And the persons he did recommend for an honour—Lyman P. Duff, Chief Justice of the Supreme Court of Canada, Arthur Beauchesne, Clerk of the House of Commons, Ernest Macmillan, a leader in Canadian music, Frederick Banting, the discoverer of insulin, C. E. Saunders, the father of so many of Canada's wheats—they hardly make up a list of party stalwarts. True, Miss Charlotte Whitton received a

C.B.E., but it was for her child welfare work in Alberta, not because she was Mayor of Ottawa or a Conservative parliamentary candidate. Today, of course, Canada should have her own honours and decorations, and it is hard to feel convinced that their almost total absence from public life is a sign of grace.

The St. Lawrence Seaway Treaty is another matter, and Bennett's persistence in his battle to reach an agreement with the United States is a reminder of his practical vision for Canada's future.

At the convention in Winnipeg in 1927 at which Bennett had been chosen leader of the party, the delegates had passed a resolution condemning the Seaway project. Montreal was against it, and no one else was strongly for it. Bennett always regarded Conference resolutions as useful guides and admonitions—he defended his 1935 platform on the ground that everything in it had been approved at Winnipeg eight years before—but they were not directives. During his administration, King, no doubt anxious to avoid taking any stand which might offend Quebec or Ontario, or both, had referred to the Supreme Court, in April, 1928, a series of questions on the dividing lines between federal and provincial rights in and over the St. Lawrence River, and its use as a waterway and as a source of power. This had gained him time, but little else, for the Court, when it did hand down its judgment the following February, failed to answer definitely all the questions submitted to it.

The Court having thrown the ball back to the political side of the net, the obvious next step was a conference between King and the two provincial Premiers, Taschereau of Quebec and Ferguson of Ontario. This took place in January, 1930, and on this occasion King must have been at his most obscure. Virtually all that emerged was an agreement that the two Premiers should draft a letter embodying the decisions they thought had been made between the three men. Taschereau sent the draft to King on February 4th, 1930, and it contained this phrase for signature by King as Prime Minister: ". . . I am authorized to state that the Federal Government recognizes the full proprietary rights of the Provinces in the beds and banks and water powers of all navigable rivers subject, of course, to the right of control of navigation by the Federal authority. . . ."

Faced with this interpretation of what the two Premiers thought he had agreed, King's repudiation was prompt and definite. If he had been prepared to concede that much, no conference would have been necessary at all. He replied: ". . . It is a position we could not possibly take, as it amounts to a renunciation of the Dominion's legal position. . . ." He then set to work to prepare his own draft of a document that could become the agreed statement; it was three times as long and infinitely more evasive. When confronted with this kind of situation, King very much preferred agreements in principle, with no inconvenient reference to detail. Another conference between the three was clearly necessary, but before it could take place King was no longer in office.

The Premiers of Quebec and Ontario were themselves in agreement in principle, and it was one not difficult for them to reach. Each of them had a natural urge to win for his province the maximum of advantage from any federal works on navigable rivers that could be obtained, and in particular that any power produced from dams or barrages on such rivers should come to them at the lowest possible price, preferrably for free. But when it came to the actual use to be made of the St. Lawrence, the two provinces were far apart.

Ontario's position was the more simple. The province needed power and was searching for additional sources of supply. Further, power in Ontario was distributed through the publicly-owned Hydro-Electric Power Commission. On the other hand, in Quebec a new installation had just been completed at Beauharnois, on a section of the St. Lawrence wholly within Canada. There were those in Quebec who feared that their province would not be able to absorb all this additional power at once, and that they must look for some market in Ontario if Beauharnois was to pay its way. And pay its way it must; it was privately owned. The thought that Ontario might obtain power from works on the international section of the river, and at a cost of no more than that involved in installing turbines and generators in a dam paid for by the Federal Government, was not at all attractive. But that was not the only thought in their minds. Beauharnois was the Quebec installation, but at this time that name had quite another significance to both Conservatives and Liberals in Ottawa.

Beauharnois as a topic had been raised in the House in May, 1930, by Robert Gardiner, of the Acadia Riding in Alberta, chairman of the U.F.A. group of Members. The original operating company had been created by provincial statute in Quebec, but it had moved into the Federal field when it acquired water rights in the St. Lawrence River, the right to take 40,000 cubic feet per second from the canal between Lac St. Francis and Lac St. Louis in the St. Lawrence Valley near Montreal. Gardiner had wanted a judicial enquiry into the activities of its promoter, R. O. Sweezey. In some manner, Gardiner suggested, capital assets which had cost some $1,280,000 in 1927 had now been capitalized at over $30m., and he demanded to know if there was any secret agreement between the Company and either the Government or the Opposition. Both denied that there was.

Bennett supported the demand for an enquiry, in terms which showed he knew a great deal of the background to Sweezey's activities (Sweezey had at one time attempted to negotiate with him to buy his Eddy holding), but the Government declined it. If there has been any malpractice, Lapointe, the Minister of Justice, said smoothly, the Attorney-General of either Ontario or Quebec should start the investigation. But the actual malpractices were at a rather higher level than that, and much nearer home. The truth began to emerge in the 1931 session, unearthed once more by Gardiner. This time there was an enquiry, offered at once by Bennett, and the Committee of the House that made it published its report on July 28th.

It was a fantastic story. The federal grant of water rights had been obtained when the General Manager of the Power Corporation was actually deputy Minister under the Liberal Minister, Dunning. The grant had been one of the factors that had enabled the promoters to raise from the public enough money to return the whole of their original cash outlay, to provide them with an immediate cash profit of $2,189,000 and to leave them owners of 1,000,000 Class A shares in the

Corporation (out of a total of 1,799,000 issued), which at one time had been worth on the market $17,000,000 and which were worth, even at the time of the enquiry, some $4,000,000, all free of charge. Out of this windfall—perhaps in anticipation of this windfall—the promoters had paid to the Liberal Party, through two Senators, friends of King, somewhere between $600,000 and $700,000 for that party's 1930 campaign (the Conservatives had received some $60,000 from the same source. Even King himself did not escape what he sadly called this 'valley of humiliation'. One of the exhibits in the enquiry was a hotel bill from Bermuda. The bill had been paid by the Beauharnois Power Corporation. King's explanation was that he knew someone had paid his bill, but he did not know who.

Bennett explained his actions as Prime Minister very clearly in a letter he wrote, on February 27th, 1934, to Robert A. Reid, a Toronto lawyer with whom he had carried on an intermittent correspondence most of his public life:

"Apparently you, like many others, do not realize that not Heaven itself can exchange the past—what has been, has been. The trouble is that we came into Beauharnois after the injury had been done, and every step we took had to be governed by that consideration. I confess that I have had stronger feelings about the Beauharnois situation than about most matters of which I have knowledge, but a fact accomplished is a fact accomplished. All you have to do is read the record and you will realize that by taking the action we did we at least did something to secure the canal for the St. Lawrence Waterway, if it is ever built."

Bennett had never any doubt that the whole Seaway project was one that would have immense advantages for Canada, in many ways. It should reduce transportation costs to and from the western provinces. It would provide new sources of comparatively cheap power, which certainly Ontario then needed. Above all, if the project could be started without delay, it would form an ideal public works programme, valuable in its own right when finished, valuable as giving at once a great amount of work. It was a project any government would be glad to put in hand at any time. And now the Liberals, in

Ottawa and in Quebec, had managed to cover the name 'Beauharnois', and the whole question of water rights on the St. Lawrence, with a thick film of political graft. He was in no mood to give the Liberals in Quebec overmuch consideration.

Once the enquiry was over and the report published, he began talks in Washington for the negotiation of a treaty along the lines of the existing technical reports which, fortunately, were decisive in what could be done and how it could be done. He was sanguine that he could reach agreement with the United States. He had also to deal with Quebec and Ontario. With Taschereau, in Quebec, he opened a rather desultory correspondence, one that was far short of any conclusive stage by the time he called his first conference, in March, 1932. His discussions with the Ontario Government were much more practical; he had worked out in detail what the province would contribute towards the total cost of the waterway in return for the power it would get from the dams, and he had reached almost complete agreement with Ontario by the time they met with Taschereau of Quebec.

That came as a considerable shock to Taschereau when they did meet, and his letter to Bennett after that meeting, dated March 26th, 1932, is a cry of anger from a man who felt that he had been betrayed. Behind his back, Ontario had bargained to obtain power at a price well below what Quebec considered its proper cost should be. Bennett's reply to that letter, written on July 11th, 1932, when the Treaty had been agreed in Washington and was about to be signed, was studiedly moderate in tone, but amongst his papers is the draft of a letter he did not send, answering Taschereau point by point, and in a corresponding temper. It was not for a Prime Minister to embitter relations with any province, but one sentence in that draft shows what Bennett's hopes from the whole project were:

". . . I hold the view that the St. Lawrence route is potentially the greatest waterway in the world, and furthermore that no Province in Canada will more greatly benefit from its development than the Province of Quebec."

As finally agreed in Washington, the Treaty provided that the work, and the cost of construction, should be divided equally between the two countries, and secured for Canada, for the first time, the right to build an all-Canada waterway, if she so desired. It also strengthened Canada's position with regard to the long-disputed abstraction of water from Lake Michigan at Chicago for sanitary purposes, by committing the United States Government to enforce a judgment of the Supreme Court of the United States, handed down the previous April, requiring the abstraction to be reduced.

But the Treaty was stillborn. It was signed in Washington on July 15th, 1932, by Herridge, as Canadian Minister to the United States, and by Henry Stimson. the United States Secretary of State, but, being a treaty, it needed ratification by a two-thirds majority of the United States Senate. That ratification was never given. Thus perished in the confusion of American domestic politics a project that might have brought great benefit to Canada twenty-five years ahead of the day on which the Waterway was finally completed and opened to traffic.

It is ironic that during the five years Bennett was Minister for External Affairs the one issue of major importance that arose, that of whether collective sanctions should be applied to Italy on her defiance of her obligations under the Covenant by her attack on Ethiopia, and if so what they should be, should have come in October, 1935, in the last week of an election campaign, when it was exceedingly difficult for any Canadian government to take a positive and perhaps decisive stand.

Tension over Ethiopia began to rise throughout the world at the beginning of that October. Despite the past, when faced with that crisis there was some measure of collective will left at Geneva. There were nations prepared to impose sanctions on Italy if she became an aggressor, and at that stage Canada was amongst them. Ferguson, High Commissioner in London, headed the Canadian delegation and, before the start of the Assembly, he had asked that the world should show that "the League was no longer to be scorned and laughed at". But Mussolini's defiance continued, and the stakes involved in any positive decision mounted. If the issue did become one of peace or war, what attitude would Canada take then? Who should decide: Parliament or Cabinet? But Parliament was dissolved and the Cabinet was scattered, its members deeply engaged in the election campaign. As a result, the answers given by Ottawa to the questions from the Canadian delegation at Geneva came for the most part from Dr. Skelton, who, as Deputy Secretary of the Department and in Ottawa over the whole period, was the one person with any authority who had both a comprehensive and continuous view of the scene and the power to make all but the most major policy decisions.

On October 8th, 1935, Dr. W. A. Riddell, Canada's permanent representative to the League, then at Geneva, cabled a full report to the Department at Ottawa. It was clear, he said, that as soon as the Assembly met, all member states would be invited to declare themselves at once on the main question whether Italy was guilty of a breach of the Covenant. He suggested that Austria and Hungary might abstain, and that the Swiss response would be guarded, but that, were Canada to abstain without explanation, the impression created would be unfortunate. Dr. Skelton prepared a memorandum on the situation for Bennett, and Bennett's instructions were that Riddell should not refuse membership of the committee on sanctions if it was offered, but should not try to seek it. At the same time he cabled Ferguson to say that the Canadian delegation should refrain from voting at that juncture; since this was a crucial moment in Canada's relations with the League, it was desirable that the new Parliament should be consulted.

Riddell continued to keep Ottawa informed of each development. Italy was condemned as an aggressor, and that without a long debate. The Committee to consider sanctions was set up, and Canada was offered membership of it. Ferguson accepted that membership provisionally, and nominated Riddell as his substitute, an action confirmed by Skelton on the 10th. At the same time, Skelton advised Riddell that Bennett still considered that no commitment should be made before the result of the General Election, now only four days away, was known. On the 11th, Riddell reported on the probable actions of the co-ordinating committee, and that the first would likely be the lifting of the embargo on the export of arms to Ethiopia. On the 14th he made it clear that it was here the moment for a decision by Canada on how she would vote when the proposals for the main decisions, on sanctions, came before the Committee.

There, for Bennett, the story ended; by the following day the results of the election were clear. He could no longer conscientiously make a decision of that importance, since his tenure of office as Minister for External Affairs was nearly at an end. Riddell was formally advised that the defeated Cabinet would not take a stand on any of these proposals in the remaining days in office.

The resulting developments were not a happy chapter in Canadian history.

Since the first session of the 1930 Parliament had opened, every day Bennett had been faced from across the floor of the House by King, Leader of the Opposition, a man growing older, more experienced, and more than ever determined to win back power for himself and his party, and as the 1934 session approached for both men the next major clash between them began to fill more and more of their horizons.

This time Bennett would fight the General Election as the Prime Minister in office. This time he would be responsible for the programme on which his party would stand, and he alone would decide the date of the contest itself. Since 1921, Conservative and Liberal Governments had alternated. If he could break that pattern with a second mandate for his party, he would have established very securely his reputation as a statesman and his position as a leader.

I find it very difficult to view King with dispassion, a personal failing, of course, the result, I suppose, of an insufficiently resolved romantic view of public affairs. Be that as it may, the image of him at this time I have in mind is that of a vulture, infinitely watchful, infinitely patient, unable to kill, but expert at destruction. Another is of King as the political miser, grubbing in every corner for another morsel of appreciation or support to whom the acquisition of a political nickel was worth as much calculation and effort as that required to earn a $100 bill. Nothing about him seemed uncalculated. If he moved a step in any direction, he first tried to make certain that when doing so he would win more support than he might lose. That, of course, is supposed to be the technique of politics, but how sordid politics become if they are no more than an affair of techniques!

Bennett never underrated King, as Meighen had. He had a great respect for him as a craftsman and as an administrator; if he were told that a departmental policy had been instituted by King he thought a long time before making any change in it. But by his actions Bennett seems to have taken a fair measure of King: that he was a general who would never lose a battle because of any failure to provide against all he could see, but who might be defeated because of an inability to appreciate correctly what was to be seen, or to estimate correctly what was not.

Each man had a burning need to succeed, but that did not make Bennett the less human. On the contrary, Bennett's mistakes and blindness are as natural as his abilities. He could flare into anger on a grand scale; King could be driven into anger, but even then there seemed to be something contrived about it. For me, King will always lack some quality of humanity. I believe he came closest to gaining it at the San Francisco Conference in 1945, when some of the insulation around his mind was torn away and he saw very clearly the powers in this world as they are, evil as virile and as resourceful as good.

In their final contest, King was the victor and Bennett the defeated, and for Bennett as for Meighen the defeat was final. Thereafter King was in office for a very long time. He was Prime Minister throughout a major war. During it he avoided most of the disasters that might have accompanied the demand for, and enforcement of, any form of conscription in Canada during that war. His welfare plans at the end of the war were nicely balanced—not too heavy for the economy, not so niggardly that those to the left of him could have real bite in their criticisms. He was an adept at this art of balance, of men as well as measures, and an extremely shrewd judge of men as political beings. He walked sedately down the middle of the road.

I have often wondered how damaging to Canada and Canadians this prolonged worship of the middle of the road will prove to be.

Chapter Fourteen

THE STEVENS MISADVENTURE

THE story of Bennett's final eighteen months in office begins with the story of the Price Spreads enquiry, and that itself began in the fall of 1933.

Harry Stevens, Minister of Trade and Commerce, was asked to make the closing address at the Couchiching Conference for that year, at the Labour Day week-end in the September. He was driven out there from Toronto, a matter of a little over an hour's drive, by Jim Walsh, the General Manager of the Canadian Manufacturers' Association, and on the way Walsh, as Stevens recounts it, poured into his ears the long story of the hardships and losses that the large departmental and chain stores were inflicting on the smaller retail merchants, in Ontario and Quebec particularly, by their cut-price methods of trading.

On his return to Ottawa this story was repeated by another caller, who gave him more details of the sweat-shops in the garment trades that had grown up in Montreal and Toronto, and in the smaller towns near them, to supply the larger city stores. In these stories Stevens saw both an injustice to be remedied and an issue that he thought could, and should, be made the foundation for a first-class political campaign.

To this end, Stevens saw Bennett and discussed what, if anything, the administration should do. Stevens had the zeal of a recent convert. Bennett was more cautious. Whatever the truth of the complaints, the issue raised directly the division between federal and provincial responsibility. The regulation of hours and conditions of work was generally a matter for each provincial government, and both Ontario and Quebec had statutes governing such things as minimum wages. Even if the provincial governments were failing to see that their own regulations were properly observed, how could the Federal

Government legitimately intervene? That was his first response to Steven's urgings, and as a result the end of 1933 had seen no decision as to action on a federal level.

Bennett was in Calgary at the New Year. He had been asked to speak at lunch at the annual convention of the National Shoe Retailers' Association in Toronto on January 15th, 1934, and, not wishing to return east so soon, he called Stevens and asked him to speak in his stead. No definite subject had been agreed upon, but during the week of the meeting, so Stevens's account goes, Stevens received at least three more allegations of hardship and unfairness caused by an excessive spread between the prices paid to producers and those subsequently charged to consumers, and he decided to make that the subject of his speech.

The complaints came from the milling trade, the clothing industry, and dealers in livestock. Bennett may have known in advance the subject on which Stevens had decided to speak, but he did not know how far Stevens intended to go in committing the Government to action. Possibly Stevens himself did not know until he was on his feet.

In his speech to the shoe retailers Stevens made the most of the material he had. He drew a picture of the individual primary producer, weakened by the long years of the depression, unable to gain strength by combination, and engaged in a very unequal contest with the buyer of his products. He called it exploitation. He described it as an abuse of the principles on which a healthy competitive society must rest, and he specifically referred to the departmental stores (without mentioning any single name) as amongst the worst offenders. He concluded by going a long way towards promising a full Government enquiry into the whole problem.

From the standpoint of public appeal, the speech was a success. It was enthusiastically received by his audience, and was front-page news in the Press. It produced an immediate response across the country. A meeting of merchants in Calgary pledged its support. So did the Premier of Ontario, the Toronto Retail Meat Dealers' Association, the city of Vancouver, deep in unemployment trouble, and sundry boards of trade. And individual letters and instances flowed in; they included several letters from women working in what were known as the needle trades in and for the departmental stores:

> "No matter how hard we work, it is utterly impossible for all the girls to make $12.50 [the minimum wage] during the week. Some make as little as $6 or $8 in the week."

Another girl wrote to say that those who made the blouses advertised in a Monday's paper as a 'Spotlight Special' for $2.65 each were paid no more than $1.50 for a dozen garments.

The response from the management side was different. The following is Stevens's account of the events of the day following his Toronto speech.

He returned to Ottawa, he says, by the night train. Early the following morning a visitor named Thompson presented himself at his office and stated that he represented one of the larger departmental stores. He then demanded an apology from the Minister for the unfair attack made by the Minister the previous day on the company he represented. Stevens's reply was that he had mentioned no store by name and that he had no intention of apologizing. "In that case," Mr. Thompson replied, "I shall go and see the Prime Minister," to which Stevens responded: "You do just that. And you know where his office is."

At 5 p.m. that day, Stevens's account continues, he received a call to go and see Bennett, and he went over to the Prime Minister's office. Bennett, he says, was angry, and before he had entered the room and closed the door Bennett had begun protesting, first at Stevens's attack on the store, and then, a more serious charge, that Stevens had made an important statement of Government policy on his own initiative without prior discussion in the Cabinet. Stevens denied that he had attacked any store by name or that he had made any policy commitment.

Bennett, so Stevens says, ignored the explanation.

"I suppose you know," he went on, "what happens when a Minister of the Crown makes an announcement of policy without the consent of his fellow Ministers?"

"Perfectly, Mr. Prime Minister," was Stevens reply, and at that the interview ended and Stevens left, to give an address, as he recalls it, to a group of the Glebe Anglican Church in the city.

The following morning Stevens wrote out a full account of the incident and of the events of the previous day, and attached to it a letter of resignation from his office as Minister of Trade and Commerce. His covering letter certainly contained one sentence calculated to sting:

". . . I fear that you have allowed certain problems of a more or less international or general character to so obsess your mind and your attention that it has made it impossible for you to appreciate some of these pressing Canadian problems which, while difficult of solution, are quite within the power of Parliament."

Bennet and Stevens were old political companions, but they were very different men. In Army terms, Stevens would have been an excellent company commander. He understood those under him, and how to get the best from them. He could grasp a plan quickly and carry it through with care and thoroughness. In parliamentary terms, he was a useful Minister and, Meighen excluded, the man in the Cabinet with the greatest all-round competence. He was not the man to make all the plans or give all the orders, but, properly handled, he could have been a continuing source of strength.

But, as events showed, Stevens needed more than sensible plans on which to work. He needed appreciation and encouragement in what he did, particularly when he felt he had been successful. He had a great respect for Bennett; he had fought alongside him in 1926 and he had worked for his election as leader of the party in 1927. Had Bennett been a man sufficiently aware of others around him to know when to offer a touch of good companionship, such as D. M. Duggan described, to be able to create a sense of understanding and equality, the history of the next year would have been rather different.

Bennett's nature did not work in that way. He made no direct approach to Stevens in response to his proffered resignation. Instead, he left it to Manion to smooth things over. The two men met amicably the following Monday, with Bennett possibly aware that it was for him to make amends, but if so the method he chose proved in the long run to be disastrous.

It was always difficult for Bennett to appear to climb down. Instead, the two men talked of the problems Stevens had raised in his Toronto speech, and the letter of resignation was tacitly ignored. It would have been far better if each had been franker with the other, for Stevens was not a man to hold back when he sensed he had the advantage. He saw in the complaints already made to him the source of a campaign which should make a considerable stir, and he wished to be at the head of it. He pressed for the appointment of a Royal Commission of Enquiry into price spreads.

Bennett was still dubious. There had been too many Royal Commissions already. As an alternative, he suggested a Select Committee of the House itself, of eleven Members and with Stevens as its Chairman. To that Stevens agreed, anxious to clinch the matter, but he still wanted to make his gain as broad as possible; he added the proviso that he himself should draft the terms of reference. Bennett let it go at that, and on February 2nd he himself moved the resolution setting up the Committee. The dice had been cast.

Bennett explained his actions in a letter to Charles McCrea, Minister of Mines in the Ontario Government, on February 10th, 1934:

"Until I read the manuscript from which he [Stevens] spoke, I was not disposed to attach to it the importance that I then did, and more particularly after I had seen the evidence that had been sent to him of conditions in various manufacturing establishments, not only as to the hours, but also as to the methods employed to compel the producers to sell their products. . . .

"I am hopeful that . . . we may be able to take some action that will be helpful to the country generally and disabuse the minds of the people that we are thinking only of the large interests. . . ."

Only Meighen in the Senate had a premonition of danger. In a letter to Bennett dated February 8th, he wrote:

"I think a lot of the complaints which have been made

have arisen at the instigation of [he then named a man]. In fact, I think he is the fountain source of the whole thing. Further, I am absolutely satisfied he is entirely wrong and acting purely from selfish motives. I think in this respect Harry Stevens has been badly misled, but I have no doubt at all he is acting in good faith."

In the light of the evidence given at the subsequent enquiry, clearly sweated labour, and sweated labour conditions, had crept back into the trades most prone to that disease, those of garment-making. In Ontario the minimum wage in this industry was then $10 a week (it was lower in Quebec), but in some workshops the volume of output set as the basis on which the minimum wage was calculated was that achieved by the most skilled workers, not the average. As a result, either the earnings of the less skilled fell below even the minimum or some workers had to put in unpaid overtime to be able to make the number of garments set as the standard for a day's work.

The complaints Stevens had received to that point touched only the surface. In its final report, the Commission found that the workers employed at home were the most exploited:

"Woman with daughter making boys' short pants for [a Montreal store] at 30 cents a dozen, less 5 cents per dozen for thread. Output one dozen per day. Those garments made under union scale cost at least $1.50 a dozen in labour."

It is understandable that the better-known departmental stores were dismayed at the prospect of an enquiry of this kind. They may well have guessed, even at this early stage, that a price-spreads investigation headed by Stevens would tend to have a certain unrestrained quality to all its activities. In fact, by comparison their employees were relatively well off. In Montreal, where wages generally were lower than those paid in Toronto, Eatons reported that 51·4 per cent of all their store employees were earning between $10 and $12.50 a week (18 per cent earned less than that figure), while the stores of their three principal competitors reported that only approximately one-third of their employees were within that bracket. In one of the four stores investigated in that city, 56 per cent of the total staff earned less than $10 a week. But if mud is thrown at any industry, some will stick to all in it.

Yet the calamities the enquiry subsequently brought for Bennett had very little, if anything, to do with the need or otherwise for an investigation. They flowed from the manner in which the Committee was set up.

It is arguable that Bennett made four mistakes, all important. First, he suggested, or acquiesced in the suggestion, that Stevens should be Chairman of the Select Committee of Enquiry. Secondly, he allowed Stevens to write the terms of reference for the Committee, and Stevens chose to write them very widely indeed. Thirdly, he ignored the fact that, if the enquiry disclosed any abuses at all, he would be driven into the maze of federal-provincial jurisdiction; in which field must action be taken? Finally, he seemed to have forgotten all about time.

The Select Committee was set up in February, 1934. A Committee free to probe price relationships in any industry in Canada it pleased (and the terms of reference amounted to that) could hardly hope to finish taking evidence before the House rose for the summer recess. Its members would then have to discuss the evidence and prepare their report, and they would need something of a vacation; that would carry matters on into the fall. Thereafter, unless the Committee whitewashed every industry it had investigated, both Parliament and the public would expect some legislation to follow. That legislation could not possibly come before Parliament before late in 1934 or early in 1935. In short, in matters of time, Bennett had already drastically limited his powers of manœuvre when it came to fixing the date of the next General Election, and his five years ran out in August 1935.

By setting this Committee to work as and when he did, Bennett made certain that Parliament could not be dissolved before some date early in 1935, unless he was prepared to face the charge that the Liberals would surely make, that the Committee had been no more than a bogus side-show, a diversion set up to draw attention away from the Government's other failures, an effort thrown into discard as soon as the Government found it convenient to go to the country. King, as Leader of the Opposition, would have been completely at home in such a campaign. Bennett had created for himself a dilemma with four horns, and he remained firmly impaled on all four of them.

The Committee opened its sittings on February 16th, and when Stevens submitted its preliminary report to Bennett on June 15th it had sat on fifty-three days and had by no means finished the taking of evidence. Under Stevens's chairmanship, and with the latitude he allowed to Somerville, the counsel for the Committee, enquiries had already extended well beyond the industries mentioned at the time it had been set up. Bennett showed no disposition to clip Stevens's wings. The session was nearing its end, and as the Committee was a Select Committee of the House it could not, without special authority, sit whilst Parliament was not in session. On July 7th the Cabinet resolved to convert the Committee into a Royal Commission, and so endowed it with an independent existence.

But even as the Cabinet did so, the fuse that set off the next explosion had already been lit and was smouldering. On June 26th Stevens addressed a private end-of-season meeting of some sixty-five Conservative M.P.s, the 'Study Club' on the work of the Committee. It met in the Parliament buildings. Stevens spoke from notes only, but a shorthand writer from *Hansard* was present, and he transcribed the speech from his notes. The speech included references to Simpsons' departmental store by name, and to Sir Joseph Flavelle, who had interests in that company and who was a powerful figure in the party. Three copies of the transcription were made, one of which went to Stevens for correction. After he had corrected it, the Chairman of the group, Brig.-General Stewart, M.P. for Lethbridge, had a stencil cut marked 'Confidential', and 100 copies were run from this. One copy went to each M.P. who had attended the meeting, and Stewart then handed the stencil over to Stevens.

The speech had been well received and some of the members who had heard it asked Stevens for further copies. Stevens sent his secretary to the head of the Bureau of Statistics with a request that the speech should be printed in pamphlet form. This was done. Stevens saw the proofs, and when he had approved them the Bureau ran off 3,000 copies. At that stage, so the Bureau Manager later said, no one had raised any

question of secrecy, nor had anyone given him instructions as
to distribution. On his own initiative, he sent a dozen copies
to Stevens's secretary, and, from a standing mailing list, mailed
a few, marked 'Personal', to a number of newspaper editors
known to be friends of Stevens. The whole operation took some
five weeks, and before the printing was finished Stevens had
left Ottawa for Winnipeg. On August 2nd a summary of the
speech, as issued in the pamphlet form, was printed in the
Toronto *Star* and immediately received editorial comment in
the *Winnipeg Free Press*, a champion both of constitutional
propriety and of the Liberal Party. Another copy reached the
President of Robert Simpsons', and on August 4th Bennett
received an exceedingly angry letter from him. Stevens, he said,
had got his facts wrong. Bennett immediately telephoned
Stevens for an explanation of what had happened; Stevens
explained that the pamphlet had been intended for private
circulation. Bennett said no more at that point, but he gave
orders that no more copies of the pamphlet should be issued.
They were not.

Bennett was still left with a first-class controversy on his
hands. On the one side, the Liberal Press, led by the *Winnipeg
Free Press* at its most judicial, belaboured Stevens, as Chairman
of a Royal Commission, for having published a one-sided
attack on concerns which, as yet, had had no chance to meet
the charges made against them, and Bennett, as Prime Minister,
for having used his authority to suppress a document of extreme
public interest. Probably Stevens never really understood the
nature of the complaint against him. Bennett did, quite clearly.
A Royal Commission was a judicial enquiry and it was a
paramount duty of any judge to keep his mind open until he
had heard all the evidence. What tied his hands even more
securely was the fact that Stevens had not got all his facts right,
either in his speech to the Study Club or the printed version.

It was one thing for a Cabinet Minister to belabour capitalists
for what they had done. It was acutely embarrassing for Bennett
when one of his Cabinet belaboured them for what they had not
done. It would have helped Bennett if Simpsons' did sue the
Winnipeg Free Press for libel, as they threatened, and he dropped
a gentle hint to that effect, but Simpsons' were at least as well

aware of public relations as he was. Bennett was left with exactly the kind of situation he liked least, one in which he was forced into inaction, As he wrote to J. T. (later Senator) Haig in Winnipeg, under date August 13th:

"The difficulty is that the statements in the document are incorrect, and when they are corrected it places the Minister in a very difficult position and the Government in a worse one. . . . There is never any difficulty in facing facts, but it is perfectly clear that if we seek justice we must do justice. . . ."

The one ray of daylight in the whole scene was that it was August, that Parliament was not in session, and that he himself was due to leave Canada at the end of the month, to head the Canadian delegation to the General Assembly of the League of Nations at Geneva. Given any degree of good fortune, the worst of the storm might have blown over before he was back in the October.

But this storm was not going to blow itself out so soon. A great many people—some of them, so Bennett was beginning to believe, under the pressure of a certain amount of organization on Stevens's part—regarded the enquiry as a well-justified probe into the activities of blood-suckers and sweat-shop proprietors, against whom Stevens was battling on behalf of the common man. The enquiry itself could not be dropped. It had gone too far and unearthed too much.

It was equally impolitic to consider demanding Stevens's resignation as Minister, even if Bennett at that stage had wanted to go so far. The same shrill comments would have been made; Stevens's head was being offered on a charger to placate the exploiters of widows and orphans. The Liberal Press was already in full cry, prepared to berate the Government, whether Stevens remained where he was or was asked to resign. In the meantime, it kept the fire under the pot well alight by a series of suggestions, couched in a dozen forms, that Stevens's days as a Minister were surely numbered.

Bennett's first mistakes had been made in a mood of regret for having lost his temper. His next actions were dictated by the fact that he had lost his temper again. He returned from Europe on October 19th, resolved that Stevens should, at the first meeting of the Commission after the summer recess, publicly make a correction of what had been untrue in his pamphlet, particularly in the reference to Flavelle, and when the Cabinet met on the 25th he put that to Stevens. Stevens neither agreed nor refused to make such a statement. Instead, he asked for time to think it over, and it was agreed that the matter should be deferred for settlement to the Cabinet meeting called for the following day. On the following day Stevens did not appear. Instead, Bennett was confronted with his written resignation as Minister and as Chairman of the Commission.

Both men were now extremely angry, for quite different reasons. Stevens was convinced that the request for the apology came from his (Stevens's) enemies within the Cabinet. But when the Cabinet meeting adjourned he had by no means reached any decision as to what his actions should be. What turned the scale, and produced the letter of resignation, was the fact that the following morning the Ottawa *Citizen* carried a front-page report of the Cabinet meeting, with the plain statement that the Cabinet had demanded that Stevens apologize to Flavelle. Then Stevens had cause for bitter resentment. One of his Cabinet colleagues—he suspected Cahan—had deliberately broken his oath of Cabinet secrecy and had given this account to the Press. It was in that mood of anger that he decided not to attend the meeting of the Cabinet that morning, but to resign there and then.

Bennett had equal cause for anger. Stevens had not had the courtesy to meet his colleagues again, to see whether, after a night's sleep, a situation potentially damaging to the party could not be resolved. Instead, he had resigned again; this time his resignation would be accepted without chance of recall. What is more, Bennett determined to set down in black and white everything about Stevens's handling of the whole business of which he disapproved. He spent some time that day in composing an extremely lengthy letter which read, when complete, like the closing address to a jury by a somewhat partisan Crown prosecutor. In one thing the letter was very clear. By inference, but unmistakeably, it accepted Stevens's resignation without hint of regret.

This letter was delivered to Stevens by hand on the 27th.

Stevens poured out an angry statement to the Press on the following day, and replied to Bennett's letter on the 30th. As a rule, any exchange of correspondence between Prime Minister and Cabinet colleague on the subject of a resignation from the Cabinet is conducted from both sides with the minimum of recrimination and the maximum of polite evasion of the real points of difference; the correspondents are usually aware, consciously or unconsciously, that they belong to the same party and may have to meet again around a table as colleagues. When they wrote these letters it was obvious that neither Bennett nor Stevens expected to be Cabinet colleagues in the foreseeable future.

Bennett dealt with the resulting situation with his customary decisiveness, as though quite determined to regard the break as final. He made no immediate appointment to replace Stevens as Minister of Trade and Commerce, but on the following Monday, October 29th, an Order in Council was passed appointing W. W. Kennedy, K.C., M.P., a Winnipeg lawyer, as Chairman of the Royal Commission in place of Stevens. The Commission went back to work, with Stevens still sitting as a member. But nothing in its further activities, or in its final report, could undo all the damage the party had suffered as a result of the episode. For every individual who understood Bennett's actions, and agreed with them, there was at least another who believed that Harry Stevens had been forced to resign because his fight on behalf of the underdog had begun to hurt the Bay Street and St. James's Street friends of the party. The average party member thought the whole business extremely unfortunate, regarded Stevens as the next most able man in the Cabinet, and expected the two men involved to settle their differences, certainly before the next election. But there was no reconciliation.

The sequel is tragic, in the true sense of that word, but let it be told in the words of Leon Ladner, Q.C., of Vancouver, for long a figure of influence in the party, as he wrote it out for me:

"About March, 1935, I had occasion to meet Honourable R. J. Manion, Mr. Sauvé, Postmaster-General, and Honourable Wesley Gordon. They asked me to see the Prime

Minister, and do what I could to persuade him to hold Mr. Stevens within the party, because if he left the party it would have a damaging effect upon the party's prospects of success in the coming election. I asked my three friends, and particularly Bob Manion, why they wanted me and not one of them to do this unpleasant job. The answer was that if any one of them did so, the reaction of the Prime Minister might be so violent that it would be weeks before they could recover normal relationship in carrying on their duties. After some persuasion, I accepted the undertaking.

"I had occasion to meet the Prime Minister on some business connected with the Post Office. The question was to find the psychological moment when I could refer to Harry Stevens. After our business discussion had concluded and we were talking in generalities, the opportunity arose and I approached him with what I thought would meet with a sympathetic reaction. I referred to the illness of Mr. Stevens lovely daughter, Sylvia, and how greatly it had disturbed him.

"With the mention of Mr. Stevens's name, Mr. Bennett rose from his chair and his fist came down with a thump on his desk. He exclaimed: 'That man has done me irreparable harm.' The look on his face expressed the intensity of his violent feelings.

"I paused for a bit to reflect on whether I had really found the psychological moment. While Mr. Bennett proceeded to criticize Mr. Stevens in an exaggerated and at times unfair manner so characteristic of his temperamental outbursts, I thought out my next step, as I could not possibly argue the merits of the question with him in his state of mind. Finally, when I had made no reply he said to me: 'Now, Leon, what can I do about it?'

"That was my chance. I knew that caucus was going to be called in about ten days' time and that no party Whip would invite Harry Stevens, who had resigned from the Cabinet and had been in such strong differences with his leader. The Whip, Tom Simpson, M.P. [Lindsay, Ontario], would be bound to seek authority from the Prime Minister before extending such an invitation, so in reply to his question I said:

'R.B., the next step is on you.' He replied: 'How do you figure that out? I have nothing to do with what Stevens does now.'

" 'In a few days caucus will be called,' I said. 'Everyone knows that the Whip must have your authority before inviting Stevens. Every newspaper correspondent in Ottawa will be standing at the caucus door to see whether Stevens enters the caucus room, thereby indicating that the rift in the family could still be cured, or whether on the other hand he did not appear, thus showing that you had thrown him out of the party.

" 'Surely, it is a part of wisdom on your part to invite him and leave it to Stevens to walk out of the party if he wishes to, or to attend caucus to indicate his position. After all, R.B., you are the leader of a Party of diversified, contradictory and at times unknown personalities. With respect, I think it is your duty to forget your personal animosities and feelings, and, having regard to the nation-wide standing of our party, and Mr. Stevens, to keep within its fold everyone who will remain loyal to the party, even though you, as leader, may have differences.

" 'Your failure to invite Mr. Stevens to that caucus will, in my opinion, have a far-reaching effect upon the unity of the Party throughout Canada.'

"He turned, looked out of the westerly window that covers the grounds in front of the Parliament Buildings and reflected for some minutes. Finally he swung round, looked me squarely in the eye, leaned forward and with a modulated tone of voice, said:

" 'Stevens will be invited, and, what is more, he will be welcomed.'

"Those are his very words. I remember them so well. I thanked him, complimented him on his breadth of view, his tolerance and his high sense of duty, shook hands and took my departure.

"I hastened at once to the office of Mr. Stevens, and found him there in an unhappy state of mind. As I entered the door, I said: 'Harry, are you going to attend the party caucus which is to be called in a few days' time?' He replied: 'I won't be invited,' to which I answered: 'If you were invited, would you go?'

"He paused and hesitated. I then said to him: 'Surely you are not going to miss such a good opportunity so far as your relationship with the Prime Minister is concerned? If you are invited and failed to go and the newspaper people at the door observe your absence, then the stories will go out and the people will know that you have walked out of the party of your own volition.

" 'On the other hand, Harry, if you are invited and go to caucus, and find you are not welcomed there, then the situation is just reversed and the public will be more sympathetic.' After a little pause, I said: 'I might as well tell you, I have just come from the Prime Minister's office and he told me that you would be invited and, what is more, you would be welcomed.'

"This surprised him, and he stated: 'Well, under those circumstances, I guess I ought to go.' I told him that there was no argument about it. He would be absolutely foolish if he didn't.

"A couple of days after, I left for Vancouver, and while in Winnipeg I read in the papers that the Honourable H. H. Stevens had attended caucus, stayed a few minutes and then went out.

"This was indeed strange and inexplicable. Later when I saw Mr. Stevens I asked what had happened. He told me that he had entered caucus, taking a seat right opposite the door at the centre. The Prime Minister came in with briefs and papers under his arm, hastened forward to the end of the room, sat down, made no reference to the presence of Mr. Stevens. After about fifteen minutes, with all his friends looking on and Mr. Bennett paying no attention to his presence there, Mr. Stevens felt that he was not really welcome and was not disposed to remain there in this embarrassing situation before his fellow members and associates. He left abruptly.

"Later, when travelling from Montreal, I saw Mr. Bennett in his private car and said to him: 'What happened about Stevens's attendance in caucus?' He explained that he came in, absorbed in the problems he was to discuss, had not seen Stevens or known of his presence there until he saw him get up and walk out. He told me that if he had known Stevens was there he would have stepped over and shaken hands with him, as he was anxious that Stevens should remain in the Party.

"A grave mistake had been made by someone. Perhaps it was the Whip, who had sent out the invitation to Stevens and should have taken great care to be present, or have someone present to make sure that each of these able and distinguished leaders in the Conservative Party knew that the other was present in caucus, and that the party's future might depend upon a hand-shake and a smile."

Chapter Fifteen

REAPING THE WHIRLWIND

THE climax to the relations between Bennett and Stevens was tragic; it came almost inevitably from the natures of the two men. Stevens was the practical politician. He thought that he had been doing a good job for the party right down the line, and that he had been stabbed in the back by colleagues jealous of his success. Bennett had come hard against a point he regarded as one of principle. Stevens had abused his position as Chairman of a Royal Commission, and he must put himself right with his conscience (or what Bennett assumed should be his conscience) by making public confession of his mistake. Of course, there were side issues. Stevens no doubt thought of his earlier resignation, and of the fact that in the end it had been ignored. Bennett no doubt thought of Flavelle; he was too important in the Party to be lightly insulted. Certainly there were those in the Cabinet who hoped to see any bridges that might provide Stevens with a return route burnt as completely as possible. But if there was to be a way out of the impasse, the responsibility for doing so was Bennett's.

He failed to find one. Had he thought of himself as one of a political team, *primus inter pares*, perhaps, but in that situation having more responsibilities than rights, he would in the end have taken on himself the burden of clearing the record over the unfortunate pamphlet. But Bennett was not that kind of man. He was Prime Minister of Canada. He must set the standards, and the others, most of all his colleagues, must conform.

It is easy to condemn Bennett's intransigence but, while politicians may not claim mercy, they are entitled to justice. Bennett was then in his sixty-fifth year. Necessarily or needlessly, he had carried an immense load during the past four years. That October he was recovering from his illness at Geneva; six months later he was to suffer a heart attack. He was physically and mentally tired.

Further, the normal pattern of his life contained very little that would naturally restore his resilience. He lived on the job; the Château Laurier, where he slept, the Rideau Club, which he frequented, and the East Block on Parliament Hill that contained his office, all lay within a quarter of a mile of each other. He moved in a closed circle. Of course, he could have broken free from it, but only if he had been otherwise than he was. He could not allow himself to shirk anything that was clearly a duty.

Besides, in a very real sense, the business of Stevens was not even his major preoccupation. Now the next election was close at hand and he alone, he felt, could settle the future programme of his party, its campaign platform. And that he did, in the two months between the end of the October and the end of the year. In fact he completed what was a complete re-orientation of his approach to Canada's future.

In the first week of January, 1935, he delivered a series of five broadcasts, under the title of 'The Premier speaks to the People', which dismayed many of his supporters, startled his fellow-countrymen, and provided the foundation on which the domestic policy of Canada over the next ten years was built. Nor was his policy a matter of oratorical statements and no more. In the parliamentary session that followed, his Government introduced and carried through no fewer than fourteen Bills which, together, put that policy and programme into effect—subject always, of course, to the decisions of the Privy Council on whether or not these Acts were within the powers of the Parliament of Canada under the British North America Act.

To quote in detail from these broadcasts would, I think, break this narrative—the key points are set out in an Appendix—but at least one can summarize the legislation put on the statute books in 1935:

(1) the Employment and Social Insurance Act, which contained a comprehensive scheme for federal unemployment insurance and was perhaps the most important in the series.

(2) the group of Acts which provided for weekly holidays in industry, machinery for minimum wages fixing and the limitation of weekly hours of work, all based on the Convention of the International Labour Conference of 1919.

(3) an amendment to the Farmers' Creditors Arrangements Act of 1934, a relief Act to enable farmers to avoid dispossession, modelled on one framed by Brownlee, of Alberta.

(4) the National Products Marketing Act of 1934 and its amending Act of 1935, which contained machinery for setting up Dominion Marketing Boards.

(5) an Act amending the Criminal Code, making it a criminal offence to cut or discriminate in prices in order to 'destroy competition or eliminate a competitor'.

(6) a Dominion Trade and Industry Act, which permitted trade agreements intended to modify 'wasteful or demoralizing competition'.

In addition, this Parliament set up a new Wheat Board, with statutory powers, to take over the operations McFarland had conducted during the previous four years, passed a Prairie Farm Rehabilitation Bill, a Dominion Housing Bill, new Relief and Public Works Construction Bills and a Bill setting up an Economic Council for Canada.

All the Bills in the series (1) to (6) above were referred by King to the Supreme Court of Canada within two weeks of assuming office. When the Supreme Court held that the Hours of Work Act and the Minimum Wages Act were *intra vires* the Parliament of Canada, King's Government appealed that decision to the Privy Council and the Privy Council reversed the Supreme Court's finding. The only survivors of the programme were the Criminal Code Amendment Act (not a very effective instrument) and the Farmers' Relief Act, to which King hardly dared risk any challenge. To complete the story, in 1940 the United Kingdom Parliament, at the request of King's Government, amended the British North America Act to permit the introduction into Canada of a federal unemployment scheme (it was added to the list of federal responsibilities contained in Section 91 of the British North America

Act). King was apparently prepared to do in war what he was not prepared to do during a depression. Of course, unemployment by then was considerably less.

(Bennett set out his views on the decisions of the Privy Council in a letter he wrote on February 26th, 1938, to F. W. Turnbull, K.C., of Regina, Saskatchewan, in reply to one commenting on the rulings:

"I agree with you that the judgments of the Supreme Court are ofttimes unsound, but never has that Court given reasons for judgments that are comparable, for unsoundness and incorrect citation, to the judgments given by the Privy Council on the legislation which we enacted in 1935. It is almost incredible that any judge could use the language of Lord Aitken. In fact, if a student did it, I incline to think he would be plucked. . . . Of course, to permit a body of men in England to make a constitution for us is absurd. You of course realize that the words 'peace, order and good government' have been treated as though they had no meaning at all except in case of national emergency, and trade and commerce have been whittled down to mean nothing. . . ."

He added a comment on the abolition of appeals to the Privy Council:

"I dare say you know I have always been opposed to the abolition of appeals to the Privy Council, hoping that one day we might be able to create an Imperial Court of Appeal which would take the place of the House of Lords in England and of the Judicial Committee for the other parts of the Empire. It is quite clear that no progress has been made in that direction. In fact, I'm afraid no one except Lord Haldane pushed the matter with any degree of vigour. . . .")

Bennett was a man who came alive in adversity. He reacted to Stevens's resignation, and all that he knew might follow from it, with the same capacity to thrust ahead as he had shown, twelve years before, when Lougheed had dissolved their law partnership. Both associations had been close. In each case, for Bennett, it had been the other man who had ended them, in a way that he considered unjustified and underhand. Each time he had been hurt, but it seemed that the deeper the hurt the deeper the draught he drew from his strength to fight back.

I think it is worth considering at this stage the objectives Bennett had in mind over this legislative programme and the distinction the Conservative feels must be made between what is now called the Welfare State and what must be called the Egalitarian State. Bennett was, of course, influenced by the activities of the New Deal administration in the United States, at second hand, through his brother-in-law, W. H. Herridge, Canadian Minister in Washington, who had lived through the New Deal from the time of Roosevelt's Inaugural. Herridge undoubtedly influenced the style in which the broadcasts themselves were cast, not perhaps to Bennett's real advantage. But Bennett was never shaken by all he saw or was told into any desertion of the classic Conservative concept of the State and its purpose. The Government of Canada was the product of a parliamentary democracy, a concept very different from that held in the United States, where the Government was the product of revolution and counter-revolution. That Canadian tradition was a part of his being.

The Conservative who inherits the British tradition has never feared a strong central authority. He has always feared that the strong central authority may use its strength for ends which should be alien to its essential purpose, and he has always endeavoured to guard against that. To the Conservative, the purpose of this central authority is to set the rules under which the freedom and enterprise of the individual shall have full play. Law and order, the rules governing the descent of property on death; those are the first. In the time of Elizabeth the First, the English added their celebrated poor law; the obligation of the people in each parish to provide for their own needy. So the list descends, to Companies Acts and Security Acts, to Workmen's Compensation Acts, to the Hours of Work and the Minimum Wages Acts, and to Bennett's Act to provide that industry should bear the cost of making provision for its own unemployed. All have one common theme. The State should accept the duty to preserve and augment the capital resources of the country. It should raise money for Prairie Farmers Rehabilitation Acts

and for St. Lawrence Seaway projects. But it should not use its
powers of taxation to redistribute the incomes of its peoples on
ideological grounds, in order that, while everyone has some, no
one shall have more than a set limit. That is the Egalitarian
State. That is the state the Labour government began to
create in the United Kingdom after 1945. That is the state
which the Liberals in Canada have toyed with, and which the
C.C.F. and its offspring would assuredly introduce if they could.
It is one Bennett would have instinctively shunned.

In the short run, it would have been far easier for Bennett to
have played a more cautious game during those last nine
months of the life of that Parliament, and it is possible that he
might have improved his electoral chances had he done so.
After all, it is always easy for a Conservative Party to refuse to
move from the old and the well-tried, for there is always a
body of Conservative opinion which does not like any change at
all. Play it safe, he must have been told over and over, the times
are too dangerous for change or experiment. Baldwin and
Chamberlain were saying exactly the same thing in the United
Kingdom at the same time, and, for reasons which had nothing
to do with them, their conceptions of Conservatism were not
rejected by the electorate until 1945. But by then it was a
socialist régime and the Egalitarian State that replaced them.
In Canada, King, by the use he later made of Bennett's programme, was able to ward off the socialist threat from the
C.C.F., despite that party's inevitable accession of strength
during the war. King's political instincts did not fail him.

One final comment: Bennett came to power when President
Hoover in the United States had still another two years of office
to run, and he left it in 1935, when already some of the glitter
of President Roosevelt's New Deal had rubbed off. When he
became Prime Minister, Bennett was very much the Canadian
equivalent of Hoover; they had much the same background of
experience in business and banking circles. But five years later
he went out of office as the Canadian Roosevelt, prepared to
go further in the reform of his country's institutions than King,
the so-called Liberal, ever thought of trying to do in the
remaining four years of peace. No other leader in a parliamentary democracy during those times was capable of such

development. The fact that Bennett was, I think constitutes his
great claim to honour as a Canadian statesman.

His programme failed. It failed as a legislative programme
because, under Canada's constitution, it could later be attacked
and destroyed piecemeal in the Courts. It failed as an election
programme for a variety of reasons.

First, it failed because it came too suddenly, with inadequate
preparation, and for this most of the blame must go to Bennett.
Once again his inability to communicate was a fatal handicap.
He had no good relations with the Press, and good relations
would have been of enormous value to him over the months of
November and December, before his broadcasts. He was too
aloof from the rank and file of his party. He had been the
solitary leader for too long; the image could not be altered that
quickly. And, perhaps to many more than be believed, he was
the symbol of honest certainty and stability, whose confidence
in continuity was more to be valued than any untried experi-
ments. Wilfred Heighington, when he wrote this later in *Saturday
Night*, may have been exaggerating:

> "The great asset of the Conservative Party . . . has been
> that of reliability. The moment that the Rt. Hon. Mr.
> Bennett took the microphone for those all-shattering speeches
> in January, 1935 . . . that priceless attribute disappeared in
> a veritable cloud of confusion, doubt and despair. The
> staunchest of party workers was blanched, the normally
> Conservative voter was dismayed, the great body of silent
> and unbiased electors wagged their heads."

But there is an element of truth in what he wrote.

Nor did Bennett have as much time left as he imagined.
His broadcasts ran over ten days, between January 2nd and
January 11th, 1935, from the C.R.C.O. studio in Ottawa, each
half an hour in length. Thirty-eight other stations across
Canada, from Sydney, N.S., to Vancouver, B.C., were linked for
these broadcasts, and by the time the fifth talk was delivered
it was estimated that some 8,000,000 Canadians were listening.
Bennett himself paid for this time on the air.

He followed these up by a series of speeches. On January 15th, he spoke in Montreal to the Young Conservative Club, his speech being mainly a recapitulation of the radio addresses. On the 17th the session opened in Ottawa and the debate on the Speech from the Throne began. On the 23rd and the 26th he was again in Montreal, speaking to the Board of Trade and to the annual meeting of the Canadian Construction Association, where he emphasized the importance of public works, and on the 29th he addressed the Board of Trade in Toronto:

"If we do not remove the exploitation of material things and of human beings, we are doomed. . . . I do not believe in socialism or communism, but I do believe it is not possible to prevent them becoming a part of our economic life unless we take the steps I have outlined."

Two weeks later, on February 16th, he journeyed to New York to address the Canadian Society there, and he returned through Kingston, Ontario, where, on the 19th, as Rector of Queen's University, he delivered a formal address to Convocation. Four days later he was back in Toronto, guest of honour at the annual banquet of the Young Conservative Club. Then the blow fell. A few days before he had contracted a heavy cold, but had refused to cancel the Toronto engagement. He returned to Ottawa by the night train and the following day he was ill with an acute respiratory infection. Two weeks later, on March 7th, whilst still convalescing, came the heart attack. His campaigning came to a sudden stop, not to be resumed until June, and then with a diminished vitality.

By medical standards, the attack was not a severe one. He was ordered complete rest, but after four weeks in bed he was allowed up as a convalescent. By April 16th he considered himself well enough to entertain the Press in his suite in the Château Laurier, and on the 18th he left for New York, *en route* for London and the Silver Jubilee.

The attack certainly left its physical effects. He was examined by Dr. R. S. Stevenson in Calgary in August, 1936, and the electro-cardiogram showed an irregular rhythm to the heart, with auricular fibrillation, left ventricular preponderance, but he had by no means been reduced to the status of an invalid.

In 1935, when in London, he had been examined by a Canadian heart specialist, Dr. Thomas Cotton (with whom he came to be on terms of personal friendship), who had written him:

> "I am very glad to assure you that I was not able to make out any sign of structural disease, either of the heart or of the other organs."

In April, 1939, he saw Cotton again, and was again reassured:

> "Nothing has occurred which need give you cause of anxiety."

But the attack, coming at such a crucial moment, set up its own chain of consequences.

When the heart attack struck him, Bennett was engaged in a decisive battle, within his own party, in Parliament and in public, and it was still undecided. He might claim, as he afterwards did, that the whole of the programme outlined in his broadcasts came within the four corners of the policy resolutions passed in Winnipeg at the conference that elected him leader in 1927, but there was a certain sophism in that claim. He was presenting his programme, as dramatically as possible, as the way out from the difficulties of now, of 1935. He had to fight inertia and scepticism—and plain resistance—within his own party. He had to fight the Liberals' cry that this was a death-bed repentance from a reactionary Tory. I believe that the heart attack cut his vitality in half when he needed it all. Not only did he lose the month of March and part of the month of April in convalescence; he lost the rest of April and some of May in London at the Silver Jubilee. As was said in the *Canadian Annual Review* for 1935-6:

> "That had given his opponents ample time to undermine his social reform platform. Just so, in 1911, had Sir Wilfrid Laurier lost the Reciprocity Election by attending King George's Coronation, thus giving the Conservatives six months in which to fight the trade compacts with Washington."

I think that Bennett came back from London already half-persuaded that he might have lost the battle during the three months of absence.

Certainly he came back in the May in a depressed mood. He told the Press in Ottawa on his return:

"I saw two specialists in London and they reported that my heart was organically sound. It was, however, a tired heart. Just what it will be capable of accomplishing remains to be seen."

He was more revealing in a letter, dated June 3rd, to Howard Ferguson, still in London:

"Dear Howard,—I really should not be at work, but there is nothing left for me to do, having regard to existing conditions. I doubt very much whether I will be able to go on. If I get half a chance to rest for six months, I will be all right, but as there is an election before that time, it looks to me as though I might have to retire. I will know definitely before prorogation."

But he came back to an Ottawa clouded with rumours centred around Harry Stevens, and, as always when directly threatened, his fighting spirit began to return.

The combination of Bennett's broadcasts and Stevens's continued exclusion from the fold—the Whip had been withdrawn, on Bennett's instructions, so the Chief Whip told Stevens—had left the party in a restless state, one that naturally increased during Bennett's absence. The election was now very near. How serious would the effect of the breach between Bennett and Stevens be upon the party's prospects? Must Stevens be brought back, even at the cost of defying Bennett, even at the cost, perhaps, of displacing Bennett? There was every reason for considerable internal ferment.

Stevens, by his own account, remained studiously aloof; at the start of the year he had no intention either of challenging Bennett or of quitting the party. He was told by John McNickle, Chairman of caucus, that if he came back everything could be ironed out satisfactorily. Without some gesture from Bennett, he declined to return. He was told that a group of seventy-two M.P.s had signed a round robin, requesting him to attend caucus and challenge Bennett's leadership. He refused to take up the challenge, even with that support. And on no less

than three occasions, so he told me, he was approached by
Ministers in the Cabinet, Manion, Gordon and Rhodes, each
of whom assured him that a strong group within the party was
anxious that he, Stevens, should replace Bennett as leader, and
that this could be brought about if Stevens would make the
first move and lead the campaign. To all these suggestions
Stevens turned a deaf ear. At the same time, by other accounts,
Manion, Gordon and Sauvé were searching for some means to
bring Stevens himself back into the fold.

Parallel to this, overtures were being made to Stevens to
desert the Conservative Party and to found one of his own to
lead. The first approach came from a group in Montreal, for
whom Beatty, President of the C.P.R., was one of the spokes-
men. Beatty told Stevens that the group he represented was
hostile to Bennett's leadership, that they intended to form a
National Party, and that they wanted Stevens to lead it.
Stevens declined, for the very good reason, so he believed, that
any party sponsored in St. James's Street, Montreal, or in Bay
Street, Toronto, would be doomed from the start. Later, in
Toronto, Stevens was given more detail. The group included
Sir Henry Holt; it had $3,000,000 at its disposal, and it could
offer Stevens financial security for the rest of his life if he so
wished. The last emissary from the group to see Stevens, Ward
Pitfield, of Montreal, hinted, so Stevens avers, that Stevens
himself might suffer financially if he declined. Stevens continued to say 'No'. But obviously a seed had been planted
in his mind.

Bennett cannot have been unaware of these manœuvrings,
once he was back in Ottawa in the June. He had never dis-
couraged gossip, and he must have heard rumours from a score
of sources. He made his own position clear. On June 19th,
speaking at a complimentary banquet of Conservative Members
of both Senate and Commons, he said that only a breakdown
in his health would induce him to surrender leadership of the
Party. At the last caucus meeting of the Session, on its final
day, July 5th, he repeated the same determination to the Press
on leaving the meeting, but in caucus itself he said bluntly:
"I'll die in harness rather than quit now." But the rumours
increased his alienation from Stevens.

For Stevens, June passed without any move by Bennett
towards a reconciliation; he was equally obstinate and had no
intention of taking the first step himself. He remained obsessed
with the problems that had been the subject of the price-
spreads investigation, and his final decision to agree to form
and lead a new party, the Reconstruction Party, was made at
least in part because he was offered support from a group
prepared to back exactly that policy. Warren Cook, of Toronto,
was its spokesman. It could offer little money; Stevens himself
bore a great deal of the cost of the subsequent campaign, to
his financial detriment. But it gave Stevens the platform he
sought. On July 7th, 1935, he announced the formation of the
party and his intention to fight the election under its standard.

For Bennett, July brought other troubles, outside Parliament,
in the shape of a serious riot in Regina. Men from the relief
camps in the west were 'marching' (by means of C.P.R.
equipment) on Ottawa, gathering more to their ranks as they
moved east. In June Bennett had decided that they must be
halted at Regina, and two members of the Cabinet, Manion
and Weir, the Minister of Labour, had gone out to meet them.
They returned with a small deputation from the marchers, but
the Cabinet rejected the men's demands. In Regina the
Federal authorities ordered that the men should leave the city,
where they had clustered around the freight yards, for a camp
at Lumsden outside, but they made no move to go. On July
1st the R.C.M.P. and the City police decided to arrest the
leaders, and their move precipitated a violent riot, lasting some
three hours, in which one policeman was clubbed to death,
about 100 other people sustained injuries, some serious, and a
great deal of property damage was inflicted on Regina itself.
The riot ended the march. The Provincial Government was
itself galvanized into action, and within a week had made
arrangements to return 1,500 of the men westwards to their points
of origin. But the incident startled the whole country. It was a
long time since anything of the kind had happened in Canada.

Bennett was shocked at this outbreak of violence. He had no
sympathy with or tolerance for those who could use force
to gain political ends. As he wrote to a correspondent, W.
Wilbur, of Belleville, Ontario, on July 4th:

H

"It is not the intention of this Government to allow such demonstrations as will interfere with the maintenance of law and order throughout the country."

But the riot had happened, a policeman had been killed, the centre of Regina had been battered by a mob of violent men, and the repercussions continued to spread; James Gardiner, the Liberal leader in Saskatchewan, for one, had no intention of letting the events of that day fade from public memory.

To Bennett it must have seemed that he was assailed from all sides, but now he could no longer use time as an instrument in self-defence. The fingers of the clock of the Parliament elected in 1930 stood at five minutes to twelve. It was formally dissolved on August 15th and the date for the election set for October 14th.

The formal campaign started in the September, Bennett opening it for the Conservatives with a fresh series of radio addresses, this time from Toronto. He left for the customary grand tour of the country on the 14th, heading west. He spoke in Regina on the 16th, in Calgary on the 19th and reached the Pacific at Victoria on the 21st. By the 28th he was back in Winnipeg, and from there he continued eastwards into Quebec and the Maritimes. On October 7th he spoke in Quebec City, in French, and was in Toronto on the 9th for a very well attended rally at the Maple Leaf Gardens. He ended his speaking tour in Belleville, Ontario, on October 12th, two days before polling day. He campaigned with something of his old vigour, defending the phrase 'blasting a way' into the markets of the world that had haunted him since the 1930 campaign:

"... By it I stand today. It was right then, when there were still one or two nations practising free trade. It is a thousand times more so now, when every nation has adopted a doctrine of economic nationalism."

There was little novelty in the issues dividing the two major parties. The interrogation mark that hung over the elections was Stevens and the new Reconstruction Party.

Stevens's party proved, in the end, to be no more than a party of single protest. It made its appeal to the farmer, to the non-organized industrial worker, to the small store-keeper, to the veteran. It had its parallel in the United States, in Father Coughlin, in Dr. Townsend. It was essentially negative. Why has the Government not done the things it ought to have done, the things it promised to do? That is always one of the cries of the opposition, but the Reconstruction Party was not the opposition. The Liberals were, and all that Stevens could do along these lines King could do better.

For Bennett, and the Conservative Party, the decision on October 14th was overwhelming, in terms of votes cast and seats lost. It was a heavy poll, 75 per cent of those registered voting. The Liberal vote was 2,076,394, the Conservative 1,308,688 and that for the Reconstruction Party 389,708. The Liberals had won 171 seats, an overall majority in the House. The Conservative total was reduced to 39, and the new Social Credit Party had 17 members, 15 from Alberta and 2 from Saskatchewan. In addition there were 5 Independent Liberals, all from Quebec, and two Liberal Progressives from Manitoba. Conservative representation in Ontario was reduced to 25 (the Liberals held 55 seats there), to 5 in both Quebec and British Columbia, and 1 in each of four other provinces (Bennett was the sole Conservative returned from Alberta), and there was one Independent Conservative from the Yukon. The fourth party in the race, C.C.F., had won 7 seats, all in the west. The Reconstruction Party had denied all the hopes of its founder. Only Stevens himself was returned.

Bennett had a presentiment that he was facing defeat, and no doubts on why. When he was in Calgary during the campaign, late one evening he went into the dining-room of the Palliser Hotel for a meal and saw an old Calgary friend, Frank Holloway, eating alone. He asked if he might join him, and they sat and talked, their conversation ranging far and wide. Finally, it came back to the election, and Holloway asked Bennett how he considered the campaign was going. Bennett's reply, as Holloway remembers it, was:

"I wouldn't say this to anyone else, Frank, but I think we've lost. And one man has crucified the Party: Stevens."

Bennett put the same thought a little more classically in a letter he wrote to R. A. Reid the following October:

> "Perhaps one might be able to use the words of Balfour regarding Peel: 'He committed the unforgivable sin; he broke up his party.' "

'If only—': speculation over what might have happened is always fascinating, except perhaps to the serious historian, who has his own troubles in trying to find out what actually did. And speculation over what might have happened if Bennett and Stevens had made up their differences before the summer of 1935 ended and had fought together on the same platform is all the more interesting, for that is a question a great many Conservatives did ask themselves, and their friends, on the morrow of the election. To have been defeated by a matter of 500 votes in a total poll of 10,000, and to feel that those 500 votes, or more, had gone in support of a man who had bolted the party a matter of three months before the election, was a galling experience; that was exactly what had happened to many Conservative candidates in Ontario, and they resented it. To them, leadership, somewhere, had failed.

No one can ever hope to calculate what the rift between Bennett and Stevens cost the party in terms of diminished enthusiasm, in the preliminary organization and on polling day, but it is possible to make some estimate of in how many seats the votes cast for the Reconstruction Party literally cost the Conservative candidate his victory; the results are somewhat startling.

The Reconstruction Party made a poor showing in most of Quebec, British Columbia and Nova Scotia, and it had avoided the prairies. Its greatest strength proved to be in the central area of Canada, in ridings directly concerned in trade and industry. In these, on October 14th, the balance between Conservative and Liberal voters was almost even, and it was very frequently the intervention of a Reconstruction candidate that turned the scale, generally against the Conservative. If the returns are studied in detail, in no fewer than forty-eight ridings, twenty-five in Ontario, seven in Quebec, five in Nova Scotia, three each in New Brunswick and British Columbia, and one in Saskatchewan, the combined total of the Conservative and the Reconstruction poll was sufficient to have defeated the victorious Liberal candidate. In six other ridings, all won by Liberals (save that in Nanaimo, British Columbia, where the victor was a C.C.F. candidate) another 250 votes added to that combined total would have placed the Conservative at the head of the poll. An additional fifty seats would still have left the Conservatives in opposition, but they would have cut the Liberal strength in the Commons to 121, and would have given the Conservatives 89 members on the Opposition benches.

It is equally interesting to speculate on how King would have handled a minority situation up to and including September, 1939.

"It was a damned close-run thing," as Wellington said after Waterloo. I have never heard the corresponding comment from Napoleon.

Chapter Sixteen

JOURNEY TO THE EAST

To me, the remaining twelve years of Bennett's life are something of an enigma, principally because I still cannot fully comprehend his final decision to quit Canada and settle in the United Kingdom.

Bennett's mood for a long time after the election contained a strong undercurrent of bitterness; it hurt him to feel that an administration in which he still felt pride was an object of hatred to many he believed he had served. In November, 1935, he wrote to Professor G. H. Clarke, at Queen's University, Kingston:

> "We did not expect to succeed in the election. On the other hand, we did not contemplate being disastrously defeated. . . .
>
> "I realize that people have endured great hardships in recent years and they had to find some way to vent their resentment against general conditions. This they did by voting against the government of the day. . . .
>
> "At least I have the satisfaction of knowing that I did not abandon the ship or seek to evade punishment by retiring last spring, as the state of my health rendered it advisable for me to do. . . . R.B."

Eighteen months later, in April, 1937, in a letter to J. H. Warren, of Toronto, he said:

> "I am afraid you do not understand the difficulties that I have to meet in my present position. I am fairly well off and I am now convinced that no man of means can afford to be head of the party. They expect me to provide money for everything and I have reached a stage when I cannot

reasonably be expected to do more. You will probably gather that I have a comparatively large income when I say to you that in the ten years I have been leader of the party I have paid income tax amounting to upwards of $600,000, and at the end of that time I have not only saved no money, but I still owe for party obligations $150,000. That certainly cannot continue. The results of the last election indicate that my services are no longer required and, while I have not arrived at any definite decision, I think it not improbable that I may make other arrangements for the balance of my life, be it short or long."

Three years later, in December, 1938, after his decision to settle in England was public property, a journalist submitted to him for approval an article on his life in which the following sentence then appeared:

"A great Canadian . . . is leaving it, not because he loves Canada less, but because England has for him a greater appeal."

In his own handwriting Bennett struck out the words after 'because' to the end of the sentence, and substituted these:

". . . he believes that his activities of the past militate against his usefulness to Canada as a private citizen."

This mood of bitterness showed itself in various ways, one, curiously enough, in the matter of the maintenance of the grave of Sir John A. Macdonald at Kingston. At the outset of the Winnipeg Leadership Convention in 1927, the delegates had passed a resolution accepting that the Party should make itself responsible for the upkeep of the Macdonald grave for all time, and a committee had been appointed to take care of the responsibility. Bennett had at once told the then Member for Kingston, Brigadier-General A. E. Ross, that he was prepared to pay over the capital sum needed for that purpose, and had been met with the polite rejoinder that this was a privilege Kingston itself would discharge. That seemed to have ended the matter, but in 1937 Bennett's recollection was rudely jogged by an official statement from the Liberal Government that it intended to take action to safeguard what it regarded as two nationally historic places, the birthplace of Sir Wilfrid Laurier and the grave of Sir John A. Macdonald, which, King added, was in a sadly neglected state. Since the cost of providing for the perpetual care of the grave was only $200, Bennett had some reason for assuming that King was interested in the grave for two reasons only: to provide an excuse for buying Laurier's birthplace from public funds, and to cause as much embarrassment to Conservatives as possible.

Bennett's mood of bitterness appeared in a resulting exchange of letters with General Ross. In March, 1938, Ross wrote to him and made some critical comments on party policy at the time of the 1935 election, and Bennett at once flared up. "It is quite clear to me," he replied on March 8th, "that you have not been reading the platform which the Conservative Party gave its leader in 1927. All the so-called reform legislation was embodied in the resolutions passed at Winnipeg. We at least endeavoured to give effect to those resolutions." He then passed on to the matter of the grave, quoted verbatim the resolution passed at Winnipeg, referred to the action of the Liberals in rescuing it from complete decay, and continued: "I do not know anything that has impressed me more with the ingratitude of public life than the way this matter has been dealt with." He concluded with one final, and angry, dig at Ross: "I should judge from the terms of your letter that you have joined the Liberal Party."

The General stood his ground, and refused to lose his temper. He reminded Bennett that he had worked for him at Winnipeg, gave an account of the efforts, and hesitations, of the Kingston group, and rebuked Bennett, not unfairly, for his jibe that he was now a Liberal: "As for the last part of your letter—and perhaps the wish that I join the Liberal Party—it is unworthy of your greatness." Bennett's reply on April 1st was less sharp, but still unpersuaded:

> "I am not unconscious of the fact that you supported me at Winnipeg . . . but, looking back upon what that has meant to me in effort and toil and sacrifice, I am not sure that you did me a service."

He went on to recount the steps he had taken over Macdonald's grave:

> "I do confess to you that I felt very, very badly about the matter. I was ready and willing to take such steps as might be necessary to provide perpetual care for this grave.... The net result is that the Liberal Party will now claim, and properly, that they provided for the care of Sir John Macdonald's grave from the public treasury, after the Conservative Party, having been in office for many years, did not do so."

He concluded with this bitter cry:

> "I am not unaware of my own limitations. I have made many mistakes, but I served this country as disinterestedly as any man who ever occupied public office, and I have never expected more than loyalty from those with whom I was associated. That I did not receive it may perhaps be a criticism of myself."

The reply touched some chord in Ross, but to him that was water under the bridge. Another war was not far away. Were the authorities prepared for that? he asked.

Bitterness is a poor guide. For many men, the time at which they are called upon to make their last major decisions is long since past at the age of sixty-five. Not so Bennett. In many fields, he had no cause for concern. He had a fortune sufficient to enable him to do what he wished, to live where and how he pleased. If bitterness had been his only guide, he could have snapped his fingers at the ingrates, and if he had retired to a life empty of any serious responsibility at once few would have criticized him for doing so. After all, he had served his time. He had given his country already far more of himself than most men ever do. If he had bought Juniper Hill in 1936 he would have been an easier man to understand. But he remained as deeply influenced by his sense of duty as ever.

Suppose he were to resign as party leader, who was to replace him? He still believed that the Conservative Party was the best practical guide for Canada. Ontario had been indifferent to his call for reform. Could Conservatives there not see that unless the Party did face the real problems of the day it was as doomed to extinction as the dinosaurs had been? His own province, Alberta, and Saskatchewan had gone adrift in pursuit of economic mirages of one kind or another. Who was to help them find the way back? And, when these questions arose in his mind, it is possible that he realized more acutely than ever before the barrier his egotism (although it is unlikely that he used that word) had thrown up between his own personality and that of the party.

Parties and leaders should be complementary entities, in the sense that an excessive inflation of the one tends to diminish the vitality of the other. A leader such as Bennett runs the danger of becoming a species of vampire, taking for himself alone what should be used to sustain both. By temperament Bennett would have fitted the position of a United States President better than that of a Prime Minister in a parliamentary democracy. King did not make that mistake; when the time came for him to go, as come that time must, his successor was there, and he was a man of his own choice.

In his survey Bennett looked on something of a wasteland, and one he had done little to change. Stevens had gone, and he could not be forgiven. Rhodes had gone, to the Senate. The most likely candidate was Manion. Manion would not be his choice, but then had he ever given serious thought to who his successor should be?

There was his own health. Until the age of sixty-five he had been a strong, vigorous man. Now he was no longer sure that he was, and like so many healthy men who reach that age before they are reminded, sometimes sharply, that they are mortal, he was more concerned over his heart than perhaps he had need to be. But to lead the party into attack again, whenever the time came, to start out once more on that ordeal, the speaking tour of the whole of Canada, that would be a most demanding activity. Even if he were prepared to risk killing himself in the effort, was it really to the party's advantage that he should be willing to take the chance? Dead men made poor leaders.

These were all real problems. Their solutions were not to be rushed. Responsibilities, once assumed, were not to be discarded simply to suit one's own inclinations.

He took his time in the making of his final decisions. He continued to lead his party in opposition for the three sessions between the start of 1936 and the summer of 1938, and he did not shirk the burden that necessarily imposed. In 1937, with Mildred, he was in London for the Coronation ceremonies of that year, and when they were over he crossed to Germany, to obtain while he was in Europe the best possible advice he could on his physical condition. In the end it was his health that was the deciding factor. He was told by all whom he did consult that if he returned to the kind of life he had led up to 1935 he would increase the risk of a second and possibly crippling heart attack.

Later that year he suffered a serious blow. Mildred died, suddenly, in a hospital in New York. Neither he nor her husband had believed that her illness was likely to be fatal, and neither was in the city at the time of her death. With that, Bennett's closest family tie was cut, and he lost the companion-ship of a woman who had come to play an essential part in his active political life.

When he returned to Canada in the fall of 1937 he told his immediate circle in the party that he intended to retire as leader, but he was persuaded to remain in command for the 1938 session. His final appearance in the Commons as a Member has already been related, but his last speech, in reply to the customary gracious end-of-session words from King and Lapointe, contained a characteristically sharp touch:

> "I think perhaps I had better say to my colleagues in the House that this is not the time to deliver a valedictory; and . . . I shall never forget your kindness at times or your cruelty at others. . . ."

Even to the last he kept his concern for Canada and the part his party should play in its affairs. That summer he was very disturbed that King should remain so indifferent to the respon-sibilities over Empire defence that he thought Canada should already be sharing. The candidate for the succession to Con-servative leadership with the strongest support was R. J. Manion, formerly in his Cabinet, but was Manion, who relied on support from Quebec, a man to be trusted with party leadership at such a time? Bennett thought not. At the leadership convention, with Meighen, he made a last appeal to the party to accept this old challenge, and he gave his support to another candidate, Murdoch MacPherson, a Regina lawyer who had been Attorney-General in that province, but who had not sat in the Federal House. But, although MacPherson made a remarkably strong showing in the second ballot, Manion carried the day.

Bennett did not resign his seat in the Commons for Calgary West until the last possible moment, on board S.S. *Montclare* as she lay in Halifax Harbour on January 28th, 1939, when he was on the eve of his final departure for Britain. Did he keep to the very last moment the hope that he would be called back? They were many who thought that he did.

But the *Montclare* sailed that January day, and he was on board, and as the low hills of Nova Scotia sank below the horizon his ties with the political life of the country in which he had been born and which he had served for so long were finally severed.

The events of these last nine years, from 1938 to 1947, may be quickly summarized. Bennett sailed for Britain in August, 1938, with the intention of finding a home there. In a memorandum he later prepared on the question of his domicile (the memorandum was written to establish that he had changed his domicile of origin in Canada to one of choice in Britain) he recorded:

> "It was suggested that I might settle in California, but for personal reasons I preferred to make my home within the British Empire. I even considered the possibilities of making a home in Australia or South Africa, but I concluded that they were too far from the centre of world activities to warrant my living there. . . ."

In that summer, to be at the centre of 'world activities' meant that he should be in Europe, and if he were to be in Europe the only conceivable place in which he could settle was England.

It was Lord Beaverbrook who brought him to Surrey. Bennett

visited him on his arrival in the September and learnt that Beaverbrook had just contracted to buy the property, Juniper Hill, that adjoined his own estate, Cherkley, above Mickleham, between Dorking and Leatherhead. Beaverbrook had bought this property to extend his own domain. He had no interest in the house itself, and when Bennett told him that he liked the house he willingly signed over to him his contract of purchase. Bennett left for Canada again in the November, having made his final decision on where to live in England, and he wrote to Beaverbrook from the ship under date November 19th, 1938:

"In 1935 I had intended, as you know, to retire, and had hoped to take up residence in England. But Stevens's action made that impossible and I had to remain. After the election I could not leave, but later the doctors advised that I should. . . .

"It pleases me beyond words to think that in my old age I am a neighbour in a strange land of the great man whom I used to know as a mere lad—of promise, I then thought—in the Old Manse at Newcastle and who amid all the changing scenes of life has never ceased to remember the old days and his ever grateful friend,

"Dick."

The property itself and the improvements he had completed in the house (he added a passenger lift and a small cinema projection-room and theatre) cost altogether some £40,000.

His purchase of an estate in England finally convinced his fellow-countrymen that his decision to leave Canada was a fact, and the invitations to speak, to visit friends and places perhaps for the last time, poured in. On his return he set off on a tour that carried him from Vancouver to Halifax and through so many of the places in which he had been known as a political campaigner. The tributes paid to him came from men of all parties; as he himself wrote later, with a touch of bitterness:

"I am quite certain that the politicians opposed to me would not have taken part in these gatherings had they not assumed that I was permanently taking up my residence in England."

His journey brought him many gifts; a silver salver from the St. John's Ambulance Association in Calgary and a silver cake-tray from the Calgary Branch of the Canadian Legion, a painting of the Dalhousie Law School, a silver waiter at Halifax and a silver rose-bowl at New Brunswick. There were, too, the farewell dinners, and the many expressions of friendship and respect. They all ended in January, 1939, when he sailed.

He spent most of the rest of that year supervising the work being done at Juniper Hill and in arranging his affairs in Canada, and in that he had the invaluable help of Alice Millar, who crossed with him and stayed in England until after his death. He was determined to become wholly a resident of Britain, even to the extent of paying United Kingdom income tax as soon as he could, and to equip himself properly to play his part as a well-informed occupant of one of Surrey's country estates. An early purchase, in May, 1939, in an antiquarian bookshop in Dorking, was a parcel of books: *Promenade around Dorking* (1822); *the Church of Mickleham* (1824); *Handbook of Dorking* (1885); and *The History of Dorking* (1884), all acquired at a cost of £2 5s. He considered it his duty to take his regular turn at reading the lessons in the Parish Church at Mickleham, and in 1942 he became a Justice of the Peace for the County of Surrey, taking his regular place on the Bench when the county magistrates sat. But even before he had moved into Juniper Hill on October 1st the England he had hoped to see, and share, and enjoy, was itself beginning to be submerged by the war.

His wartime activities were extensive, but not within the upper echelons of the Establishment. He served throughout as Chairman of London Advisory Committee of the Canadian Red Cross Society. At Beaverbrook's request, he made an investigation into the employment of interned enemy aliens, whose skills were vitally needed, by the Ministry of Aircraft Production. He represented the United Kingdom Government on the board of a company engaged in munitions manufacture and receiving considerable Treasury aid in consequence. He visited Canada again, once to make a speaking tour across the country. He belonged to a number of societies and made a number of addresses. In 1941 he received a peerage of the United Kingdom, a Viscountcy. The writ was dated June 15th and he took his seat in the House of Lords on July 23rd. The next entry in his engagement book reads: 'Leatherhead Church. 7 p.m. Preside: Church Rally.' The speech in the Lords for which he is best remembered is that he delivered when the Bretton Woods Agreement was before the United Kingdom Parliament in December, 1945; he was opposed to its provisions.

For him, the personal tragedy of the war came in 1944. His two nephews, the only sons of his brother Ronald and the only Bennetts of the succeeding generation, were killed in action in Normandy within a few days of each other. His pleasure in their presence in England had always been tempered by the fear that their purpose there was, in the end, to risk their lives, and now both those lives had gone. Ronald, the elder, serving with the Black Watch, the Royal Highland Regiment of Canada, with the rank of major, was killed on August 5th, and his younger brother, Harrison, a lieutenant with the Cameron Highlanders of Ottawa (M.G.) was killed nine days later. Both were then involved in the operations on the Caen-Falaise road, and both are buried in the Canadian Military Cemetery at Antheaux.

By 1944 Bennett knew that he had developed diabetes, and that he would now require constant injections of insulin, and with that knowledge came a slackening in his energies and interests. He spent the Christmas of 1946 at Juniper Hill, but immediately afterwards went to Sidmouth, Devon, once more to a hotel, and stayed there until March. His engagements were few on his return. In May, he paid a formal visit to Dr. Barnardo's Homes, attended the Annual General Meeting of the society known as The Men of the Trees, and gave the prizes at the prize-giving ceremony at the Surrey County Secondary School at Leatherhead. He attended the lunch given by the City of London on June 11th, 1947, when Her Royal Highness Princess Elizabeth was presented with the Freedom of the City. On the 17th, he responded for the guests at the Annual Dinner of the Institute of Brewing. Despite his early associations with Cross and the Calgary Brewing and Malting Company, it is ironic that his should have been the last public affair of its kind that he attended.

On June 25th, 1947, he spent the afternoon in London, at the

Dorchester Hotel, with E. J. Chambers, K.C., of Calgary, then in London on his first appearance before the Privy Council, where he was representing the Canadian Bankers' Association in an appeal to that tribunal on the constitutional validity of the Alberta Bill of Rights Act, passed by the Legislature of that province in the early days of the Social Credit Government. He invited Chambers to spend the following week-end with him at Juniper Hill. That evening Beaverbrook called, but Bennett did not seem too well and he made his stay a short one. In the early hours of the morning of June 26th, seven days before his seventy-seventh birthday, he died in his sleep at Juniper Hill.

I do not find it hard to understand why Bennett left Canada; he gave the primary reason in his own words: "because he believes that his activities of the past militate against his usefulness to Canada as a private citizen." There is the authentic touch of pride, almost of arrogance in those words: 'I have led my country: now that it no longer wants me, it will be easier for others if I am no longer there.' And it was a sound enough reason. He had made enemies as well as friends. His successor in leadership to the party would have been as embarrassed by those who said, 'I will give no help to the party that man man belonged to,' as by those who said, 'How much better things were handled in Mr. Bennett's day.' From the point of view of their successors, there is much to be said for party leaders who die in office.

Nor is it hard to understand why Bennett chose to settle in England; again he said so. He was a very proud and loyal citizen of that Empire and he wanted to be at the centre of world events. In 1938 England was to be at the centre of world events, beyond any doubt at all. Whether he had formally retired or not, he did not intend to surrender a position as close to the centre of the stage as he could manage to secure. Not for him Montego Bay or the Channel Islands, Bournemouth or Victoria, B.C. Twenty-five minutes by electric train from Waterloo Station—that was as far as he wished to be from the centre of things.

But I still do not comprehend what he expected to find in Britain, and whether he found it or not. Surely in 1938 he expected to find a war, for with his sources of information the imminence of that must have been quite obvious by then. But what kind of war did he expect to encounter, to have to endure? No one then, of course, could have foreseen exactly how the civilian population would fare, physically, and Bennett had courage enough to face the actual dangers as they came. But did he foresee that he would arrive just as the old way of life he had known would be ending, that easy and comfortable country-house life—servants, cars, petrol, travel, leisure, conversation—was about to vanish? Nothing is more pathetic than the stories of Bennett, in the later years of the war, wandering from cinema to cinema in London, since watching the movies had become for him the most effective way of killing time.

Did he believe that he would be called upon to play a greater part in the war than in fact he did? Did he overrate his remaining strength and capacity? Did he imagine that his friendships in England would open doors that in the event remained obstinately closed? Did he, in short, underestimate the closeness of the fabric that knits the Establishment together, and the strength of the resistance it offers to anyone attempting to force his way in from outside; entrance into the Establishment is strictly by invitation only. Did he think that what Beaverbrook and Bonar Law and Smuts had done he could do also? Did he ever estimate accurately how far inside even those men had finally managed to penetrate? Or was he content with the place he did win for himself, a participant in useful but subordinate activities? I hope he cherished no unrealized dreams, but, having moved in the reverse direction, having seen that in Canada anyone from outside may go as far as his abilities and his energies will take him, wherever he may come from, I wonder if he may not have deceived himself with his experience of his own country.

Sigmund Freud came to Britain at very much the same time as Bennett, from Vienna. He came as a famous man, but as a refugee. He was received with dignity and honour. He was desperately ill and he had no more than some fifteen months to live, but his perceptions were still acute. In *The Life of Sigmund*

Freud, published by the Hogarth Press, London, Ernest Jones writes this:

"He had written on February 20th [1939] to Arnold Zweig giving him an account of the uncertain progress of his condition, and on March 5th he wrote his last letter to him. In it he advised him to emigrate to America rather than England. 'England is in most respects better, but it is very hard to adapt oneself to it, and you would not have my presence near you for long. America seems to me an Anti-Paradise, but it has so much room and so many possibilities, and in the end one does come to belong to it.' "

Did Bennett feel in Britain that he had come to belong?

Perhaps to have fulfilled his earliest ambitions was enough. He had become Prime Minister of Canada. He had been granted a peerage of the United Kingdom and sat and spoken in the House of Lords within the Palace of Westminster. He had been an elected member of two Legislative Assemblies, those of the North West Territories and of Alberta, and the Canadian House of Commons. He had spoken for Canada at an Imperial Conference, in the League of Nations, at the World Economic Conference. He had served his King, his country and his Empire to the best of his abilities, and with a tenacity of purpose few men ever display. He had more than enough to give him contentment, if it was in his nature to find contentment in the end.

It would be an impertinence for me to guess at the answers to these questions. I would quote again one sentence from the words at the beginning of this book: "Perhaps that is the most a biographer can ever hope to do; to clear, in the icy crust of each man's incomprehension of other men, a little patch, through which a faint intermittent light may shine."

Chapter Seventeen

MONEY AND PARTY

I DO not intend to attempt anything approaching a final assessment of Bennett—either as a man or as a politician. It is too soon after his death, too soon after the events in which he took part, for that to be done. But I do not think anyone can make even a provisional estimate of his proper place in Canadian history unless they take into account two other aspects of him: his attitude to money and his value to his party.

There are two kinds of generous men. One is the man who does not attach too much importance to material possessions and who can with relative ease give away to others from what he has. The other is the man who has a strong attachment to what he owns, particularly if he has won it by his own efforts, and yet who believes that it is his duty to share these with others. Bennett was of the latter kind. He was never quixotic about money; it was not a thing to be quixotic about. It had far too great a capacity for good or evil. But he did believe that he had a duty to use his money, to put it to work for others as well as for himself, and throughout his life one of his constant preoccupations was how best to discharge this responsibility.

His private gifts were innumerable. He kept no complete record of them, and he told no one of them save those who had need to know. He was always concerned to help a friend, or someone who had helped him; the family of Lemuel Tweedie, of Chatham, New Brunswick, was one. Tweedie had given him his first start, by his encouragement, by his kindness when he had boarded with his family, by employment in his law office. Their ways had parted in 1897, but it was not until 1943 that Bennett finally discharged the last of the liabilities he had incurred to a bank under guarantees given on behalf of the Tweedies.

But it was not only a matter of meeting a direct obligation. He sought out those he felt might need help. One was Colonel D. G. L. Cunnington, of Calgary, who followed him as M.P. for Calgary West. Cunnington had a son at the Royal Military College and Bennett was concerned to see that conditions in Calgary during the depression did not break off the boy's education there. "Doug," he said to Cunnington one day in Ottawa, "if ever you feel you can't manage it, let me know. I'm looking after eighteen young people now, and some of them I don't even know." Cunnington did manage it without aid, but all over Canada there are men, and women, whose education was paid for by Bennett, in full or in part.

He never gave money as though it did not matter. He insisted that it should be properly used. He preferred to give aid by means of a guarantee to the bank that made the direct loan; then there was a more concrete obligation on the borrower to use the money carefully and work towards the discharge of the debt. Equally, he was never too busy to be reluctant to give time and advice as well as money. Just as he had spent evenings in his office at Calgary explaining to his students what the textbooks they were reading really meant, so a woman who was then a young typist in that office remembers him lending her Macaulay's *Essays* to read when she said she wanted to leave to finish her education.

The same combination of caution and concern, of prudence and generosity, went into all his public gifts. Some were of pious tribute to his family; the restoration of the church at Hopewell Cape and the gift to it of a bell, the stained-glass window in the church at Vancouver in memory of his sister, Evelyn Coates. There were the inevitable small gifts a wealthy politician is almost bound to make—it was said that any parents naming their child 'Richard Bedford', and being careful to notify his secretary that they had done so, could count on receiving a silver christening mug suitably inscribed—but these were matched by his spontaneous responses to some of the legion of appeals that descended upon him, as, for instance his gift of a radio set to a small girl who wrote to him from a remote island off the coast of Nova Scotia. But in general he used his money to advance those causes he thought should be supported.

One of his first educational foundations was set up in 1922, a fund to provide grants of from $50 to $150 to the best six students in Calgary High Schools each year. In 1942 he augmented that fund with a gift of $15,000 to establish the Viscount Bennett scholarships from Calgary to the University of Alberta. He gave land at Stag Hill to the Church of England for the new Cathedral at Guildford, Surrey, and in 1943 he made an anonymous gift of £10,000 to the building fund. In Ottawa he was a regular supporter, financially, of the Symphony Orchestra, the Ottawa Welfare Bureau, the Protestant Infants' Home and Hospital, and the Canadian Council on Child Welfare. Out of his income in those years he regularly gave $25,000 a year to support such institutions.

Education remained his main concern. When he settled in England he set up a number of scholarship funds, some in conjunction with Beaverbrook, but it was to the two Maritime universities, Dalhousie in Nova Scotia and Mount Allison in New Brunswick, that he gave most, particularly to Dalhousie, his own University.

He became a member of the Board of Governors of Dalhousie in 1920, when, as one of the executors of Jennie Eddy's will, he was concerned with the administration of the gifts she had made to the University, including the Shirreff Residence for Women. From then until he left Canada he was intimately involved in the University and its affairs. He was a member of the Library Committee for most of that time, and made yearly gifts to it of money and books. In 1925, he gave $25,000 to purchase a residence for the President, and he was active in the campaign to raise $100,000 to found a Dean Weldon Chair of Law; his own contribution to that was another $25,000.

In 1943 and 1944, he turned over the bulk of his remaining Canadian assets, some £230,000 in sterling, to these universities. At Mount Allison the money went to establish a Chair of History and five scholarships, named after his mother and his brothers and sisters. His gifts to Dalhousie totalled $762,000, of which $12,000 went to an endowment fund for the Law

Library and that at the Shirreff Hall, while the balance endowed three chairs, one in chemical research, one in epidemiology and the third in law, two being named after the Shirreff brother and sister and the third after himself.

To the end, he sought to maintain a proper balance between the claims of his own family and those of the public institutions he wished to support. When it came to his will (he left an English estate of £872,937 net) the public charities were subordinated to his family. After a great number of specific gifts of silver, books and furniture, the residue of the estate was divided between his two surviving nephews, Richard Coates, the son of his sister Evelyn, and William Herridge, Mildred's son.

In the public mind, Bennett and money were inextricably mixed; he was always the wealthy Conservative politician, and as a politician he would have been less harassed had he had less money. For him, money represented success, and he was able to manage success with a firm hand. Failure could bring out his weaknesses, his impatience, his quick temper and his equally quick regrets, and the hasty decisions that accompanied them both. Success did not distort his judgment on affairs, nor lead him to indecision or uncertainty.

But in the end money had very little to do with his value to his country. He used it to buy the freedom he thought he needed if he was to serve his country, but what use did he make of that freedom when he had won it? As a man, he was unlucky in the time at which he came to political power. Was Canada equally unfortunate that he was the man who did come to power at that time in her history?

In striking any balance sheet of Bennett in relation to Canada, his energy may well be left out of account. That may have been no more than a physical attribute, like an ability to throw a ball straight and hard. What he did contribute was an immense capacity for application, for sheer hard work, and that is a matter of character. It is not too difficult to learn to speak agreeably on any subject without an extensive knowledge of it, as Bennett could and on occasion did. But he displayed to a remarkable degree the capacity to acquire a working mastery of most of the subjects he encountered throughout his career—

law, banking and monetary theory, economics, business management and administration, the international commodity markets, the working of the whole machinery of government; he was not born with any knowledge of these.

Another quality he had and used was courage. It required courage at twenty, particularly in a young man to whom failure was the enemy, to leave the security of a post for which he had the qualifications, and challenge a new profession at Dalhousie. It required courage, later, to leave the province he knew, and the security of an established law practice in which he already had an interest, for the North West Territories as they were at the end of the last century. He knew that he would not be easily accepted in what must have sounded like a very new frontier community. Ambition, and the courage to give rein to his ambition, drove him westwards.

Bennett was ambitious, of course. What sane man would tolerate the life a politician must lead if he were not driven by that goad? But many ambitious men have been entirely successful by their own standards, and the good or harm they have done are, for them, the not very important by-products of their lives. Bennett's courage did not only flow from his ambition, and it was more than the recklessness of youth.

It required courage to set off eastwards again at the age of sixty-eight, into a rapidly gathering storm. As he himself said, there were other places to which he might have gone and in which he would have been welcomed, places other than the centre of world activity, likely to become so soon an activity of a personally dangerous kind. It required courage, too, of another order to deal with a crisis that came whilst he was in office, when Canada was on the brink of what would have been the worst financial disaster the country could have encountered at that time. It concerned a major life insurance company at the depth of the depression, and unless Bennett had acted as he did it might have been declared insolvent. Until the full story can be told, it is not worth while speculating on the details, but when the story is told it will show that Bennett risked a very great deal—friendship, political backing, even strict constitutional propriety—in order to fend off a collapse that would have brought ruin to many thousands.

His invincible sense of mission was of equal value to his country. A people moving from colony to nation is as incomplete as a nauplius before its carapace had hardened; that is the time to put out more flags. Some of his fellow-countrymen rejected his vision of service to the Crown, its symbolism and its history, but that rejection itself was no bad thing if it compelled them to ask themselves what it was they did believe in. The total of all the practical matters with which a politician must deal, from the founding of a Bank of Canada to a decision over a postmaster in his own riding, is always less than the whole. There must be some larger end he must serve.

Perhaps Bennett believed that Canada would grow to be her ultimate self more speedily and more securely within this romantic envelope of an Empire than she would if she were no more than a very sparsely populated half of the North American continent. Certainly he hoped that his Empire would become more than a romantic envelope, but he never thought of turning his back on it when it did not.

Another service he rendered his country—to my mind, as vital as any—was what he did to remind the Conservative Party in Canada that it had a radical tradition, and he did so with all the strength of his personality. He did not convince them; if he had, he would have been returned to office in 1935. But the programme he fought for and put on the Statute Book did ensure that the Conservative Party remained as one of the two major parties in the State.

The two-party system remains the solid rock on which parliamentary democracy rests. Unless there is a second party to which the electors can turn, one large and cohesive enough to be able to provide from within itself all the men needed to man a government, parliamentary democracy as we know it will die. It may be replaced by a featureless lump, dominated by a small group of men, the fate of the Liberal Party in Canada between 1935 and 1957, or by a shifting coalition of adroit politicians, of which France before the advent of Charles de Gaulle was a nauseating example. The people of Britain, over the period of a century and a half, have come to realize this essential fact. They have declined to kill off one party before they were satisfied that there was another second party in effective existence. A federal Constitution, giving the provincial governments some of the attributes of an opposition to Ottawa, have hampered Canadian appreciation of this truth.

Bennett was not a two-party man in the sense that he would have sacrificed the interests of his own party to help keep the Liberal Party alive, but he was determined that his party, the Conservatives, should be truly national, and therefore that it should be responsive to the needs of all the people in Canada. He compelled his party in the end to face the fact that if it became, or seemed to have become, a class party it was doomed, and that the cause of Conservatism was doomed as well. Sir Charles Petrie has written of the Conservative Party in Britain in the first quarter of this century:

> "In effect, the party lost the confidence of the people on the day when it laid itself open to the charge that it was engaged in a capitalist conspiracy and it did not regain that confidence until, many years later, it cleared itself of the aforesaid suspicion."

Bennett would have appreciated that comment perfectly.

To him, the reform of any society, the need for constant watch to see where reform had become necessary, were not the unfortunate tributes that had to be paid to an electorate as part of the price for their support once every five years. They were a condition of life itself. Capitalism was not ordained from on high as the natural order of society for intelligent and hard-working men. It was no more than one of several possible methods of producing and preserving wealth, and of distributing its increase, all of which had to be justified by results. 'By their fruits ye shall know them.'

Yet, in August, 1935, he seemed to have brought nothing but disaster upon his party. It had ended its five years in office with an open split between its two leading members. One of them had flung at the country a new programme, half-baked, some said, far too radical, in the opinion of others. The other had bolted his party and formed a new party of his own, capturing one-quarter of the votes the Conservatives had in their count. The Conservative Party in its turn had been soundly beaten by the Liberals again, and again at the hands of King; the blow inflicted had been more severe than that the party had suffered in 1926. The situation in which it found itself may fairly be called desperate. What would the consequences be for Canada?

One possibility was that the Conservative Party would disintegrate, and that no single party would emerge to replace it. The votes cast in the election show that could not be ruled out. Two million to the Liberals, rather over 1,250,000 to the Conservatives, and after that:

Reconstruction Party . . .	389,708
C.C.F.	386,484
Social Credit Party . . .	187,045

Not one of these three had a really decisive lead over the others. Each had every incentive to try to preserve its identity. Had the Conservatives sunk without trace, Canada might have been governed by a Liberal Party possessing size but no principle, surrounded by a group of splinter parties individually unable to offer an alternative government and collectively unable to make any lasting union amongst themselves.

It would have been an exceedingly dangerous situation. There were fascist ideas abroad in Canada, as well as in other parts of the world, in those years before the Second World War. Parliamentary democracy did survive, but the fact that it did is no proof that it was inevitable that it should. Its chances of doing so would certainly have been lessened had the opposition in Parliament consisted only of the C.C.F. and the Social Credit parties. It is the absence of a real opposition that permits the tyrant, whatever his label, to grow to man-eating size.

A second possibility was that one of these three parties competing for third place would pull ahead of the others and become the second party in the State. It is unlikely that the Reconstruction Party would have been the one to succeed. It was a party of a single protest, the vehicle for a clash between two personalities, and once the clash had taken place it had no further real function. It had no roots. But the C.C.F. and the Social Credit parties were different. They were parties of protest but each claimed to possess an alternative political and economic philosophy, different in kind from that held by both the Conservative and the Liberal Parties. In fact, the C.C.F. for a period, some ten years later, did look as though it was a serious contender for position as the opposition party, and it seemed possible that Canada might shift on its political axis, leaving the Liberals as the party of the right and the C.C.F. as the party of the left. That did not happen.

A third possibility was that the Conservative Party might allow itself to become no more than a fossilized party, a fate which the Republican Party in the United States did not entirely escape. The leader of that party did not see any need for anything resembling a New Deal. He was defeated by a man who did, and who took action accordingly, and although the Republican Party has endeavoured since to shake itself free from the influence of those who, as the saying is, have to be dragged screaming into the twentieth century, it has never wholly succeeded. In Canada the consequences of such a situation would have been even more divisive. There would have been no Northern Republicans to balance the Southern Democrats. There would in fact have been no more than a rump of a Conservative Party, standing fast behind its barricades in Bay Street, and the true Conservative spirit, which is as enduring as humanity itself, would have been without a vehicle for its expression. That, too, did not happen.

In the end, after a considerable journey through the wilderness, the Conservative Party did return, and return to power. Why? I think the explanation lies in the fact that Bennett left with it both a solid legacy of effort and partial achievement and some touch of his uncompleted vision, and that these two elements kept alive in sufficient people a belief that here was a party with an unfinished task.

Whatever the reasons that drove Bennett into the furious activity he displayed in the last ten months of his administration, whatever may have been the disadvantages that flowed from his earlier lack of real contact with and understanding by his colleagues over the issues on which he finally chose to fight, the fact remains that his 1935 policies and programme did give the party the vitality it needed to survive the long winter of its eclipse. No one else could have done it. If he had not attempted it, no one else would have tried, and without that attempt, without the fertilization that came from his programme,

Conservatism in Canada today would have been a sterile thing.

Bennett was a very great man, but wherein lies greatness? In success, in achievement, in wisdom? Not wholly, although each is an ingredient. It lies, too, in endeavour, still more in what is endeavoured. In public life—and the greater part of Bennett's life was public life, in this sense—Bennett gave all he had, his energy, his abilities, his experience and his fortune, to the service of his country and the betterment of its people. In the success he achieved in office he stands comparison with any contemporary leader in any other country. In his ideals, in his sense of duty, in his capacity for self-dedication to the fulfilment of his efforts, he is outranged by not one of his contemporaries.

Bennett performed no miracles. He did not save his country, particularly the west, from all the hardships of the depression he inherited. He could not bring down rain from the skies. But he did help to save for Canadians their confidence in themselves, and their belief in their future. Under his leadership they were not in danger of disintegration as a people, of falling into the despair that Roosevelt encountered in 1933, or into the nightmare that was Germany in that decade. His imprint remained. Until the outbreak of war, where the administration that followed him changed his policies, it found none better—often none at all —of its own.

Considering his circumstances and what they might have made of him, he became—by the Grace of God, he would have added—a very great man and a very great Canadian.

Calgary, Alberta.

THE BROADCASTS OF JANUARY 1935

IN using the radio to explain a programme and to launch a campaign, Bennett, of course, was following in the steps of Franklin Roosevelt, but he was breaking new ground in Canada. No Prime Minister before him had made use of the radio in that way.

He would seem to have had four very understandable objectives in mind. First, he intended to justify the actions of his Government over the preceding four years. Secondly, he took care to answer in advance the likely criticism that his proposals for the future were coming rather late in the day. This he did by arguing that the first duty of his government had been to overcome the worst of the emergency and that reform—reform of the kind he proposed—could only safely be pursued when the emergency measures had begun to produce their effects. As he said in the third address:

> "What I said was that, even though from the outset, ultimate reform of the magnitude I have indicated, was clearly necessary, it would have been the height of folly to attempt to introduce reform until the first fury of the depression had been brought under some sort of control. For reform on a comprehensive scale was impossible before we had succeeded in achieving some stabilization and improvement in conditions. That was an emergency task and we therefore applied emergency measures to accomplish it. Before repairing the ship it was our job to navigate it through the storm."

(In this he was a little ingenuous.)

Thirdly, he intended to challenge the Opposition to meet his proposals, to attempt the necessary if difficult task of pinning Mackenzie King down, if he could, on a battleground of his

own choosing. Finally, and this was, perhaps, the most important of all his objectives, he intended to confront his own party
with what he regarded as the challenge of the times, to demand
that they recast their thinking and the image they showed
before the electorate, or be swept aside as a thing unable to
adapt itself to the conditions of the day.

Looked at objectively, his positive proposals were not startling, nor were all of them new. Certainly they fell short of all
that President Roosevelt had planned to do to revive and recast
the economy of the United States. Bennett talked in his second
address on the inequality of incomes between the 'producer'
and the 'non-producer', or *rentier*, but he proposed for its
remedy no more than "some plan of taxation". He was more
definite on conditions of work. There should, he said in the
same address, "be a uniform wage and a uniform maximum
working week. There must be an end to child labour. There
must be an end to sweat-shop conditions. There must be an
end to the reckless exploitation of human resources and the
trafficking in the health and happiness of Canadian citizens.
There must be an end to the idea that a workman should be
held to his labour throughout the daylight hours of every day."
Those were reforms Conservatives in the United Kingdom had
accepted a generation before. Their practicality in Canada was
more a matter of overcoming the difficulties produced by the
division of powers between Federal and provincial governments
than in convincing the majority of employers that the nineteenth
century was now well behind them.

Unemployment insurance was another commitment, but one
not accepted without some qualifications. "However few or
many unemployed we normally have," he said, "no man must
be left to the circumstances of private charity or to the humiliation of Government gratuity. . . . As a member of our economic society he should have security, provided always that he is
willing to work. . . . Therefore, the worker, when unemployed,
must with the help of the State be provided with the means to
effect his own security against unemployment. This security
will be provided by means of unemployment insurance." He
was less specific over the need for health, accident and sickness
insurance.

For agriculture, he had three schemes to recommend, two of which were already on the Statute Book. The first, the Farmers' Creditors Arrangement Act, passed the preceding year, which gave the farmer an opportunity to seek relief from his liabilities, both in terms of how they should be paid and of how much they should be paid; his second, the Farm Loan Act: "In recognition of the national importance of agriculture in this country, the corporate strength of the State should be used to assist farmers to secure their operating capital at low interest rates." The third, again one carrying constitutional complications with it, was the Marketing Act, also passed in 1934. That had already met with a mixed reception, the commonest outcry against it being that it enabled a majority of producers to compel the minority to conform.

The rest of the programme he outlined can be described as one of orthodox reform. He defended his creation of the Bank of Canada, as a central bank "charged," he said, "with the responsibility of seeing that the volume of credit available in the country does not depend solely on the working of competitive business forces". He recalled his debt-conversion operations, which had refunded some $1,000,000,000 of national debt and cut the rates of interest on it from 5 per cent and $5\frac{1}{2}$ per cent to less than $2\frac{1}{2}$ per cent on short-term issues and to $3\frac{4}{5}$ per cent on long-term bonds. He promised a comprehensive reform of the Civil Service, and he made fair reference to the Price-spreads Commission:

"When the report of the Commission is received by the Government, Parliament will be invited to take action in accordance with the Commission's recommendations. I think that tonight I need only say this to you: should the Commission find that the primary producer has been denied his rightful profits or that the consumer has had to bear the excessive profits of a dominant industry; if as a consequence of this, the primary producer or the ultimate consumer, has had his standard of living adversely affected, action will be taken to put a stop to these iniquities. So long as I am head of the Government of this country, I will see fair play between industry and the public. I have no prejudices, I hope, and I play no favourites. But I could not better show my concern for industry than to rid it of those practices which unfairly affect the pocket-book of the great bulk of the people of this country and work a damning injury to industry itself.''

Twenty-five years after, no Conservative in Canada could describe the proposals Bennett outlined in January, 1935, as revolutionary. What startled and dismayed many of his supporters, both party members and in the wide ranks of the uncommitted, was the tone of his criticism, the rough treatment he seemed to be prepared to give capitalism as they knew it and as they operated it. Bennett talked of the need for 'reform', and it is significant that, when the five addresses were later published in book form by the party, the volume containing the last speech included a reprint of the first speech he had made in the Commons, in November, 1911. But to many who heard him, what he called 'reform' was something stronger; he talked as a radical talked. What could be accepted from a back-bencher in 1911 sounded very differently when it came, in 1935, from the Prime Minister himself.

I would venture no further comment; let the words speak for themselves.

In his first address:

"In the last five years, great changes have taken place in the world. The old order is gone. It will not return. We are living amidst conditions which are new and strange to us. Your prosperity demands corrections in the old system, so that, in these new conditions that old system may adequately serve you. The right time to bring about these changes has come. Further progress without them is improbable. To understand what changes and corrections should be made, you must first understand the facts of the present situation. To do that, you should have clearly in mind what has taken place in the past five years; the ways in which we have made progress, the ways in which we have not. To do that—to decide wisely—you must be in a position to judge those acts of Government which have palliated your hardships, which have preserved intact our industrial and financial structure, and which have prepared the way for the reforms which must now take place."

Five minutes later:

"If you are satisfied with conditions as they now are, if you think that there is not need for reform, if you feel that the Government is not required to do anything more—then I am not willing to continue in this office. For if you believe that things should be left as they are, you and I hold contrary and irreconcilable views. I am for reform.

"And, in my mind, reform means Government intervention. It means Government control and regulation. It means the end of *laissez faire*. Reform heralds certain recovery. There can be no permanent recovery without reform. Reform or no reform! I raise that issue squarely. I nail the flag of progress to the masthead. I summon the power of the State to its support."

More followed:

"Therefore, now that the time has come, I am determined to try with all my strength to correct the working of the system in Canada, so that present unemployment conditions may be put an end to. When I say I will correct the system, I mean that I will reform it. And when the system is reformed and in full operation again, there will be work for all. We then can do away with relief measures. We then can put behind us the danger of the dole. I am against the dole. It mocks our claim to progress. Canada on the dole is like a young and vigorous man in the poor-house. The dole is a condemnation, final and complete, of our economic system. If we cannot abolish the dole, we should abolish the system.

"Now, you will understand that by recovery measures I mean measures which work no change in the economic system. They are emergency measures designed to support the system during the depression, but do not interfere with its operation, and do not, of course, contemplate any modifications or correction in it. Recovery measures of the proper kind minimize the dangers and ameliorate the hardships incident to the depression. They also stimulate the

I

movement toward recovery. This kind of assistance is sometimes known as 'priming the pump'.

"Reform measures, on the other hand, are measures designed to effect a change in the existing system. They are measures to be taken when it has been decided that the existing system is faulty in some major or minor respect, and that this fault must be cured before the system can satisfactorily function again. These reforms may be, as you can imagine, of very many different types and of varying significance; but, whatever their importance or character, they are all refutations of the old idea that government should leave business alone.

"But it is now necessary that we give further, and the most careful, thought to our economic system, so that we may the better appreciate its capacity to serve us in the conditions in which we live today. Our best interest leaves us no alternative. We will examine the system without prejudice of any sort. We neither hate nor love it. It is here to do you service. That is its only purpose. If it has failed, then we must change it."

His second address continued the story:

"Behold the sad and idle multitudes throughout the world. If the system is functioning as it should, why are there so many unemployed? We are told that machine labour has replaced manual labour. In a sense there may be some truth in that statement. But certainly it does not begin to answer the question to my satisfaction. The real answer is that there is something wrong with the system and the real duty of the Government is to find out what the trouble is in Canada, and to correct it.

"Then as to the third group of producers—the farmer. His income depends upon the market—that is, his income depends upon the quantity of produce sold, multiplied by the difference between the selling price and the cost of production. The selling price, again, depends upon the demand. The demand, of course, depends primarily upon basic conditions of trade. But I am afraid that we must admit it is also sometimes unfairly influenced by unconscionable monopolistic purchasers or by certain types of middlemen and distributors, some of whose activities would properly include them within the classification of economic parasites."

He defended the Bank of Canada from the same standpoint:

"Why do I call it a reform measure? Because it is designed to be a powerful instrument of social justice; because it will be the means of insuring a greater measure of equity in the dealings of class with class; because it will aid in correcting disabilities in the old system; because it will be an independent source of advice and assistance in all matters relating to finance; because it begins a new chapter in the history of Canada's financial life."

He criticized, as he had so often before, the mechanics of company formations:

"Notwithstanding the legislation of recent years, the protection of the investor must be improved. It is still inadequate. There must be stricter government regulations of finance in this field so that improper practices may be detected in time and effectively dealt with. The ravages of the promoter who operated in the period of 1922 and 1930, cannot now be repaired. But we can at least see to it that he does not again operate in the same way. Our Dominion Companies Act will, therefore, have to be strengthened. There must be drastic simplification of capital structure so that the investor will be able to understand the nature of the stock or security he is purchasing. At the next session of Parliament, the Companies Act will be amended so as to abolish the right to issue shares of no par value. The searchlight of publicity must be focussed on every issue of securities offered to the public. Adequate machinery must be set up to inquire into and report on, corporate developments which tend towards consolidation and concentration. In other words, the door must be locked before, not after, the horse is stolen."

He claimed that reform could only be postponed at the risk of something worse:

"If this system is wrong, if under its present form, hardships increase, the system will most certainly be changed. Elemental economic and social forces will see to that. But the method of its change may be a destructive one. These basic forces are not permanently resistible. They can be ignored but not for long. And yet, at present, they are manageable. They can be directed. Their forward course can be made orderly and natural. That, as I see it, is the job of government."

He did not shrink from the charge that he might be a radical:

"Our task—simple in theory, difficult in performance—is to replace in the old system those elements which are worn out, broken down, obsolete, and without further utility, so that the system may work. Perhaps some would call that 'radicalism'. If it is, it is the sort of radicalism you will have a lot more to do with, so long as we live under a well-ordered system. That type of radicalism makes for continuity of reform. It is the only guarantee of peaceful change. It is the only hope of prosperity. Imperviousness to change, the hatred of things that are new, the unbending adherence to old customs, not because they are good or helpful, but simply because they are old; these things retard progress. They check the advance. They make it disorderly. They build the dam which breaks and submerges in a chaos of destruction, those whose folly and selfishness have set them to oppose the forward march of civilization."

And in his final address, his challenge to the Liberals to stand up and be counted, he was at his most positive:

"Upon those measures we have now embarked. You have seen some of them already in operation. I have told you that work upon the others has begun. Collectively, they will comprise a scheme of reform which, as I have said, will be more comprehensive, more far-reaching, than any scheme of reform which this country has ever known. It will mean a new relationship between business and government. In very truth, government will have a new function to perform in the economic system. It will be a permanent guide and regulator, with the right and power of correction, with the duty and

responsibility of maintaining hereafter in our whole industrial and capitalist system, a better and more equitable
distribution of its benefits; so that wealth may come more
readily to the rescue of poverty, so that our standard of
living may be raised and broadened, and so enjoyed by all
classes of the community. For, when capitalism is freed at
last from its harmful imperfections, when government
exercises the intended measure of regulation over capitalist
groups, capitalism will be in fact your servant and not
your master."

The Liberals were labelled the party of non-interference:

"My concern is with the Liberal Party in Canada since the
war. Ask its leaders wherein they have changed from what
they used to be. Ask them to show in what way they imposed
controls over capitalism. Ask them to tell you, and demand
an answer, what they did in the period ending in the crash,
when capitalism went wild and wrecked us by the thousands.
They kept on talking about the open market-place and free
competition and the virtues of the profit system and the
hideous iniquity of government attempting to interfere with
the operation of capitalism, regardless of what it might do
to us.

"It is agreed by unprejudiced people that there are now
many faults and injustices in the capitalist system. There
have been for a long time. We all know that. Make your own
list of them; child labour, sweat-shops, slave wages, crush-
ingly long hours, inequality of benefits, low prices to the
primary producer, high prices to the ultimate consumer.
These manifest the evils and imperfections in the system.

"In what conditions did they flourish and multiply? They
flourished and multiplied in conditions of unregulated
business, in the days of *laissez faire*, in the times when
capitalism ran itself, ran the people, almost ran the State.

"In some ways, though only in some ways, conditions
have improved since early times. Who made them better?
Why, the State. In the past, even Liberal governments, now
and then, in times of crises, had to swallow their economic
principles and come to the rescue of the people. *Laissez faire*

had worked such frightful hardships in the circumstances
that even the apostles of *laissez faire* had to take note of that.
But what a feeble, halting intervention. Now today, the
accumulated inequalities of capitalism demand independent
and courageous action by government. Is the party of
laissez faire ready to take it? The tragedy of these times has
put that question straight up to it. Why has it not answered?
I will tell you. Because it cannot say, 'Yes.' Because it dare
not say 'No!' That is why it is dumb. That is why it has sat
silently by and counted on hard times to defeat a government
which has given its heart's blood in your service, which has
fought to help you, fought adversity, fought the Liberal
Party, and will go on fighting both.

"Why is that? Why have they no constructive policy?
Why have they no policy of reform? Why have they not
come fairly out and said what caused the evils of this depression? Why have they not declared that the causes of
these evils are the faults and the inequalities in the capitalist
system? They must believe it. Why do they not say so? In
the good old days, Liberalism was quite willing to have
capitalism run itself. In these days, it may be that
Liberalism is quite willing to let capitalism run it? That
starts a line of thought. Pursue it, and you may learn the
reason for the mysterious silence of the Liberal Party. But
be careful in your judgment. For when capitalism controlled
the modern state, the result was Fascism. And there is no
place for Fascism in Canada.

"The issue is clearly defined. If you are satisfied with
conditions as they are, support Liberalism. If you want no
changes in the capitalist system, declare for that party. If
you are against reform, back Liberalism with all your might.
For Liberalism, as you see, has no intention of interfering
with big business. For Liberalism stands for *laissez faire* and
the unrestricted operation of the profit system and the
complete freedom of capitalism to do as it thinks right or to
do as it thinks wrong. So, if you desire a party which supports
reaction, back Liberalism.

"But if you believe in progress, if you believe in reform,
if you believe that the present situation cries aloud for

betterment, if you believe that it is the duty of government, by all right and fair means, to strive to secure betterment, if you believe that in big business, that in capitalism, there are abuses which work hardship upon the people of this country, if you believe that the faults of capitalism have brought about injustices in our social state, if you believe that these injustices manifest themselves in lower wages and too high costs of living and unemployment,—then support my Party. For my party has already undertaken and will pursue to the end, a programme of reform which will rid the system of these disabilities. It stands for the freedom of the individual and private initiative and sound business, but it stands with equal certainty for permanent and better relationship between the people and those instruments of commerce and finance which are set up to serve them. It stands not for traditions which are outworn or practices which belong to another age or for economic faiths which, if pursued now, mean economic hardships. My party stands simply for the greatest good of the greatest number of people. And it shapes and will continue to shape its policy of reform, to make that sure."

The words, and some of the ideas, belong to another day, but even twenty-five years later the throb of the immense vitality behind them comes through.

INDEX